T0197185

A JOURNEY
to a *Miracle*

Jessica Groom

BALBOA.
PRESS

A DIVISION OF HAY HOUSE

Balboa Press books may be ordered through booksellers or by contacting:

Balboa Press
A Division of Hay House
1663 Liberty Drive
Bloomington, IN 47403
www.balboapress.com
1 (877) 407-4847

Because of the dynamic nature of the Internet, any web addresses or links contained in this book may have changed since publication and may no longer be valid. The views expressed in this work are solely those of the author and do not necessarily reflect the views of the publisher, and the publisher hereby disclaims any responsibility for them.

The author of this book does not dispense medical advice or prescribe the use of any technique as a form of treatment for physical, emotional, or medical problems without the advice of a physician, either directly or indirectly. The intent of the author is only to offer information of a general nature to help you in your quest for emotional and spiritual well-being. In the event you use any of the information in this book for yourself, which is your constitutional right, the author and the publisher assume no responsibility for your actions.

Print information available on the last page.

ISBN: 978-1-5043-0108-4 (sc)
ISBN: 978-1-5043-0109-1 (e)

Balboa Press rev. date: 10/12/2016

CONTENTS

Some Big 'G' for my peeps (That's Gratitude)

I never saw myself writing a book and I have to say I was pretty proud to have completed it. I feel that I need to share my story, not because I want everyone to know who I am, but because I want people who share a similar story to me to know that they are not alone, that there is hope, and that since I got through it, so can you. I wrote this book to tell you about my travels, about what goes on in my head, and how I got to a place of such utter desperation, that I decided to end my life. People need to know that it's OK to talk about suicide, and that by talking about it, will actually help the wounds. So this is my story. I have never written a book before and got no help whatsoever with my writing, so please be patent, be kind and keep reading.

I dedicate this book to my ever loving, ever giving, supportive, rock solid family and friends. A very special mention needs to go to my brother Billy and his girlfriend Laura who never gave up on me. I can never thank them enough.

INTRODUCTION

Whatever your reason for reading this book, I am so happy that you are here. I am very excited to share with you my miracle journey, what I have learned over the past few months and how I have managed to completely change my life.

I have ways considered myself a pretty together person. I held down a good job, had lots of friends, partied hard, worked hard and lived a life many would be jealous of. I thought I was happy. I had bumps along the way, who doesn't these days? I was doing what I wanted, when I wanted, and had no one to answer to. I had the world at my fingertips, or so I thought. There was lots of travelling, I have lived in London, New York, Malaysia, Pakistan and Australia and have had many holidays abroad to assist in fulfilling my endless desire to see the world. I have a loving family who I care deeply about, and friends who mean the world to me. I should have been happy, I should have been content, but I wasn't. I was miserable and had no clue what happiness was. I was continually searching for happiness everywhere but inside of myself. I thought shopping and buying stuff; clothes, handbags, shoes, etc could help my happy levels. I thought travelling would hit my happy spot, I thought drinking excessively and taking recreational drugs was a fun thing to do. Little did I know that inside I was dying, because I now believe that if you are not growing, you are dying. I was anything but growing, and by growing I mean learning. I was headed towards a car crash, a devastating suicide attempt in a bid to end the madness. It was then my miracle journey began.

I was the envy of all of my friends when I told them I had quit my full-time job and was off to travel around Asia for up to six months. I had worked hard my whole life and I had finally given myself permission to follow a dream that I have had for years, I wanted to travel Asia and not in a 2 weeks away sort of way. I was so excited to finally not have to worry about work, I was excited to feel free, to live it up and to not have any regrets.

I was a workaholic, married to my role and I thought that my job defined who I was. I gave up everything to be recognised in work, and was more masculine than half the men I worked with. When I finally decided to pack it all in, it was ground breaking for me. I thought I was tuning a corner, that I was opening up to a brand new lease on life. Little did I know that all of my demons were waiting for me, waiting for that moment where I gave up my addiction to work where they could slip in and taunt me all day, every day!

As soon as I took off on my once in a lifetime trip they were on my back, those f**kin demons were there to make sure that I didn't have the fun that I wanted to have, and they were there to make sure that this was going to end badly. Badly for me that is, as well as for my family, my boyfriend and my friends.

I was never given the tools I needed to be happy, I never knew there was tools, and I'm sure 3 years ago if someone told me I could buy the tools I would have bought them... but would never have used them. This is typical of many people. They think they want to know how to be happy, although once they are given the tools, they do not follow through. The question you need to ask yourself is 'am I ready to be happy?' and 'can I commit to staying happy?' For some the answer might be that they are not ready, and that's ok. Your time will be your time, but no time will be your time if you don't take the time!

Being 'happy' is what we wake up every day and aspire to. I don't know many people who wake up in the morning and say 'hey, today I want to be miserable'. It is what we aspire to do, yet we find so difficult to do. Why is this? We have been trained to put ourselves down, to think we don't deserve happiness, and to think that we are just another match in the box! It has been so inbred into us that we don't know any different. In fact, on average 80% of our thoughts are negative! Our brains are actually negatively biased to order to protect us, but unfortunately this bias ends up hurting us. It makes us compare ourselves, hold onto hurtful comments for decades, and build up fears that should never exist. When we try to suppress our negative thoughts, we end up thinking these thoughts not less, but more. Which means that you can't make yourself happier and more positive just by pushing away, or blocking off your negative thoughts. It simply won't work. Instead, you must realise that your thoughts are not facts. (Write that one down!) Your thoughts are simply a combination of words, and words my darling cannot hurt you. Even though we let them, because we believe them.

Back in the good old days our brains were given this hard wired negative bias to prevent ourselves from harm. For example, 'that fire burnt my hand when I put it on the flame, therefore I should not do that again'. We are far more inclined to remember the bad stuff over the good stuff, thanks brain! What we need to do to overcome this is, firstly, acknowledge that we know this, and secondly begin to change the pattern. Neuroplasticity is how the brain can actually rewire itself. Yes, we are negatively biased, but we can change it.

Our unconscious mind is there to serve and protect; and in some cases we have actually programmed it to protect us from happiness. Our mind is an insanely powerful tool for our happiness and what you say to yourself creates the world in which you live in. As the saying goes, 'be careful what you think, as you thoughts become your feelings'. A negative thought can spiral out of control, just like it did with me, I lost my sunglasses and decided to end my life. Positive thoughts lead to a positive and happy life. And I am the perfect example of this also, every day may not be fabulous but I try to find the fabulous in every day! And the days when fabulous is hard to find, are the days that it is most rewarding when I do.

I have lived in countries across the globe, I have looked for happiness in many nooks and crannies. I would run from things as soon as they didn't go my way. I was spoilt, selfish, cruel and totally unaware of it. I thought I was being nice but I didn't know what nice meant! I only showed up when I wanted to, and I mean in every regard. I'm embarrassed to say this, but even when my sister chose me as her bridesmaid for her wedding, I organised her hens dinner but didn't go. I put drinking and drugs before relationships, I dated some horridly mean guys and I thought they loved me. I bailed on mates, never listened to 'advice' and had fierce social anxiety unless I was drinking. I may have been successful with work, but in my personal life I was a mess. And by successful I mean what society has labelled as successful.

We are told that if you are successful you will be happy, but I have met many people on my journey who have been extremely successful in their roles but are miserable in life. If you are passionate about something, and you are also driven to make your passion your business, then you will be happier than working a job you hate. I think people nowadays work too hard, have no time for friends or family, are continually stressed out and think that living this way is normal. We are led to believe that we must make a lot of money so we can buy things in order to make us happy. Of course, we all have bills to pay, and the world won't work if we all just quit our jobs and focused on just being happy. We have become so materialistic in our pursuit of happiness, but materials give us nothing. Happiness is an array of things, but what it is not, is a purchase or a partner. It's a combination of how satisfied you are with all areas of your life; therefore YOU control your happiness.

Before I share my miracle journey with you, I want you to commit to giving everything you've got to making yourself happy. Once you experience the REAL feeling of happiness, pure contentment, pure joy, peace, and love, you will want to keep it. You will be so happy when you make the decision to *be* happy! Each day, every moment I commit to a life of joy, I choose to live in happiness, and even though there may be times that I am pushed to my limits and I can feel depression setting in, I know that my decision and commitment will keep me forever on the journey of joy. Almost every day you can experience a miracle when you decide to. *A miracle is a shift in perception so please get ready to open your eyes to a new perspective.*

I want you to know, I am in no way perfect, or am I this crazy bundle of joy 24/7. I am human and I get frustrated, upset and sometimes react without thinking. Sometimes I forget I have made a commitment to a life of happiness, and I end up on a train to negative town, and sometimes I want to get there faster than the speed of light. But when I get stuck in this vicious cycle I pinch myself and bring myself back to reality where I am safe, and I can soon turn myself and my thoughts to a more positive, loving space. I have learnt that even though life can be a *bitch* at times, doesn't mean that all of life has to be that way. Those *Beep beep* moments can be few and far between, and you can get to enjoy life so much more, as soon as you are ready to.

Although this book may appear to be just another self-help book that repeats everything you have already heard about how to find happiness, please understand that it is much more than that. What you are reading is my true story – a true account of how I went from feeling so depressed that I felt I couldn't go on anymore, to a feeling of total happiness in every aspect of my life. My story starts with my adventure as I travel through South east Asia on what should have been a trip of a lifetime. But for me it turned out as my road to hell, and inevitably my suicide attempt. I'll share my story and you will notice how easy it was for me to appear normal on the outside, all while my inside was screaming and dying. It happened to me. It can happen to anyone. It can happen anywhere, anytime. I want you to know the warning signs. I want you to know you are not alone. And I want you to know that life can be so much better. I should have asked for someone to save me, but I didn't, until the last moment. That is why I'm writing this book, in a hope to be able to save someone from their own suicide attempt, or worse still, suicide.

You can escape the inner mean girl/boy and you can master life. Learn from me. Follow my transition. See the subtle changes in my thinking and notice what worked for me and what didn't work. If I did it, you have the power too. Are you ready? Come join me!

1

The cold hard truth

When I woke up from my suicide attempt I felt useless, stupid, afraid, vulnerable, exhausted, anxious, but most of all "depressed". I was over life, and I wanted out. I hated waking up, I hated that someone tried to save me, and I hated that I now have to talk to people and tell them why I did it. I was confused, worried and also eager to try it again. I knew now what didn't work, so it was going to be easier to find what did work.

When I was struggling with depression, I always thought it was just me who thought that life was way too hard, and I thought that I could never speak to anyone about my real feelings or they would think I was crazy! The negative voices that I had in my head were nonstop and I always thought only I had these voices. I thought, it's just me over analysing myself constantly; it's just me who has the hard life; no one understands; I'm so alone....

I walked around thinking everyone had an easier life compared to me. If people couldn't understand me, or called me out on my irrational behaviour, I would think, 'what do they know anyway? They have had such a simple, easy life compared to me.' I didn't see my outlook on life as pessimistic or negative, but it definitely wasn't positive either. I used to look at things from an analytical standpoint. I would do things based on not facing the consequences. For example, instead of wanting to go work, I would go because if I didn't I wouldn't have money. Some people may say that is a negative way to see things but to me it was just common sense, or so I thought... maybe it was how I was brought up, but my thinking made sense to me back then. I judged myself so harshly all of the time as I thought I needed the tough love approach, in hindsight it was the only approach I knew, having not had my parents around much when I was growing up.

It wasn't that I felt sorry for myself; I always look at things in relativity. I mean to someone their biggest life trauma could be that they didn't get a new car for their 16th birthday. Then you have others who have been through so many negative experiences by the time they were 16, like losing a parent or sibling, abuse, or disabilities. I think it's all relative to your world and what's happened. Some people might look at me and think; wow, you had such an amazing life, while others might look at me and feel sorry for me when they find out about what I have been through.

I have spent my life running away from anything that I didn't like. I have moved from country to country countless times. I was continually thinking about the next thing on my to-do list, rather than living in any given moment. I was continually chasing the future, or analysing the past. I never took note of the moment that I was in, and even though I had so many people try to teach me how to 'make every moment count' I just didn't understand… until I did!

My internal dialogue drove me to me grind my teeth, not only when awake but also in my sleep. A constant chatter of what was wrong or right with my life was playing in my head like a bad movie on repeat. I have suffered badly from depression to the point where I couldn't eat, sleep or work. Not only that, I have self-harmed. I have seen numerous counsellors, psychiatrists, have taken pills, been up, been down, and been all around. I have drunk heavily. I have taken recreational drugs. I have tried lots of things to dull the pain I felt on a daily basis. Many of the things I took worked for me, but it was always a temporary fix.

The drug taking was all social, or at least I thought it was. In hindsight, doing drugs or drinking excessively is not a good social behaviour and maybe the people I was hanging out with were in the same pain I was? I hadn't realised that the pain was present, as it was so normal for me. I went through life feeling miserable and having some serious issues from my childhood, that still to this day affect me. I never knew any better, so I continued on living the way I knew how to. I thought I was happy and I thought I was doing a good job at life.

I thought that life could be better but I was waiting for something to happen to make it so. I never realised that I had to make the choice to be happy, I always thought that happiness would come with prince charming, or maybe even winning the lottery, wouldn't that be nice?

I suffered from depression on numerous occasions throughout my life, so I know how easy it was to relapse. I would start therapy each time as per the doctor's orders, but as soon as I started to feel a little better, I thought, 'Great, I'm fixed! Cheers, I'm out of here!' The reality was that I was waiting for someone else to fix me, having no idea that I was the only person who could fix me. It was far easier to blame someone else for my craziness; I couldn't blame my parents as I barely knew them. I couldn't blame my brothers and sisters, they were my lifeline. I could however blame depression, and that was very convenient for me, I think I was actually relieved when I was told I had depression. It meant I could use it as an excuse. I loved excuses, anything to shift the blame off me.

I lived in Sydney for 5 years, and for those 5 years I have worked a minimum of 60 hours per week. 16 hour days were normal for me, and I loved being so freaking busy! I even wanted to start my own t-shirt slogan business with "I'm too busy!" I sacrificed everything for work, no one asked me to, I made the choice to do it, I was empty inside and work filled the void. In 5 years the furthest I travelled in Sydney was a 10 mile radius. If it wasn't close to work then I wasn't going.

While I absolutely loved my time running some very cool venues in Sydney, the stress and hours took their toll on my body. Furthermore, the hospitality industry has a hard core party scene. Add all of this together and I found myself in hospital after having a stroke at the ripe old age of 31!

This wasn't an immediate wake up call for me to slow down; when I finally checked out of the hospital I went straight back to work. I was far too tough on my body, I knew that I had to slow down and have a healthier lifestyle, but knowing and doing are two very different things.

Soon after the stroke I changed jobs and went to another venue, which actually turned out to be much more stressful. I moved to a much bigger venue, well actually I was now general manager of two venues. What was I thinking? I did try to cut back my hours but it didn't work, and before I knew it I was back in hospital being told something needed to change. My body was not coping with long hours and stress. I remember turning to one of my good friends and saying, "I don't know why the doctors keep telling me to stress less, I don't feel stressed out at all", to which she replied "that is because your whole life is so stressful you wouldn't know the difference". This struck home with me, I never looked at it like that. For so many years I could work like a Trojan and not feel a thing, it was perfectly normal to work crazy hours. What I may have thought was "normal" was in fact a ticking time bomb inside of my body. My mind and body had enough and was no longer going to let me get away with it.

The doctor told me that I needed a change of pace, I had to do something, otherwise I would keep ending up back in hospital. So I did what the doctor ordered; I quit my job and planned to go home to see my sister in Ireland for a bit. I wanted to take a rest, plus it was my sister's birthday at the time so I wanted to see her and celebrate with her. I needed a time out, and I knew that by going back home I could just be myself and no one would judge me. I was excited to see my sister, who is my absolute rock in life. I was going to surprise her but I couldn't hold the secret. I told her I was coming home to see her.

Before I even had my leaving party from my job, I was offered another one. It sounded easier, the pay was great, and one of my best friends was working there. They needed me to start straight away, and they promised me a free trip back to Ireland for Christmas! I figured Christmas was such a special time to go back home, so I cancelled my trip home for my sisters birthday, and had only one whole day off before starting the new role.

The new job started off well and I was really enjoying it. There was nothing I loved more than taking on a venue that needed help and turning it into a well-oiled machine. Before long I had a fabulous crew of managers, the place was full steam ahead and Christmas was well under way. I had been only been there four months and was already taking leave to go home. Getting to go back to see my family in Ireland for Christmas in my line of work was a real treat. I have always been the one who has worked through all the Christmas holidays; I used to be the one serving food and drinks while my friends were out socialising and enjoying themselves. When I was in love with my job it never bothered me, most of my good friends were in the same boat so I never wanted time off over Christmas, but as you get older things change... I started to envy people outside of hospitality. I wanted to be the one out enjoying myself and not the one making it happen. I knew my time in my hospitality was coming close to an end when this feeling came to town. The break couldn't have come at a better time; I was exhausted, and needed to see my sister.

After I got back from my Christmas break my thoughts were constantly drawn towards wanderlust – the irresistible desire to travel and experience the unknown. I initially kept thinking that I was too old to quit my job and go travelling. I brushed away any thoughts and feelings and I continued working away. I managed to really get my hours down, I was only working 50 hour weeks most weeks which helped me to get my life back.

Now that I was starting to have a better work/life balance I could start to see that I was so miserable in that job; ironic, but that's what happened. I not only saw that there was more to life, but I also wanted more from life. I had spent the last five years in Australia but had spent pretty much all of that time working, and any free time I had I spent thinking about work. Added to that was that my love for this particular venue was dying, fast!

Before I knew it I had written my resignation letter and handed it in to my boss, he was shocked, to say the least. I had also just gotten back with my on again/off again boyfriend and decided to leave him behind. I did ask him to come but he couldn't, he also respected my decision to leave. I would have loved if he could have come with me, but at the time it just wasn't viable. Anyway, I had to do this for myself, I felt a immense calling, it was strange as I had never allowed myself to feel anything like this before because I had filled my life with work. I knew I had made the right choice and was so freaking excited to get going. Freedom was calling me and I was excited to meet it! I had never planned such an extensive trip without any work, mainly because I could have never afforded it until now. No more waking up at 4.30am for work, I could sleep in, wander, get lost and soak up sunshine every single day! Oh yeah baby.

Where to from here

My notice period was six weeks – six long weeks! I just put my head down and kept on working hard like any other day. I had a fire of excitement in my belly, and even though I had a long notice period, I had so much to look forward to and the time flew by.

Having already been to many places around the globe but never to Vietnam, Cambodia or Laos I wanted to see for myself why so many people take this journey. Thoughts about seeing Japan kept springing to mind, mainly because I was fascinated with the photos that used to fill my Facebook stream from 'the most amazing places' and pictures of the most magnificent gardens filled with cherry blossoms, which I fell in love with. I was thinking Japan would be a fabulous place to visit but it could be difficult to get around by myself, so decided to look into tour groups. They were all so expensive and I needed to make my money last so I looked into China as another option. I have also always wanted to see the Great Wall. When I started doing more research I feel in love with China before even getting there. There was so much to see and do, and so many choices when it came to guided tours, plus prices were far more economical then Japan.

So China it was... I booked my tour and planned to see as much of China as I could. The trip finished in Hong Kong where I had friends to visit – perfect! I booked a flight to Hanoi – Northern Vietnam from Hong Kong so I could make my way down through Vietnam and into Cambodia and Laos.

The trip was all planned in about week, typical me style, I was organised way too soon, so I was left with lots of spare time. Luckily my boyfriend wasn't working at the time so we could hang out and have fun. I also had plenty of friends who worked in hospitality; therefore they were free during the day to have wine with. And then the ones who didn't work in hospitality I could meet in the evenings for more wine. So many goodbyes were had, so much wine was drunk, and I loving the unemployment thing. I never imagined myself being content with no job, but I was so happy and I was imaging myself off work for up to 6 months while travelling around Asia. I was ready for the biggest, most awesome break I have ever had and I felt so lucky to be able to have this opportunity. I had no kids, no responsibilities and I was free and ready for fun!

> *When one's mind is busy, it never sees, it is clouded with mindless tasks. Take your mind overseas, open it, stretch it, and let it breathe. You won't believe what's underneath – a whole new you with so much more to explore. Life begins at the end of our comfort zone!*

My best friend from back home in Ireland had agreed to come and meet me in Vietnam and travel down for two and a half weeks with me – awesomeness! I had also told my 16 year old niece that if she got a job for the summer I would pay for her ticket to fly over and meet me. I wanted her to save and be rewarded at the end with this trip, I wanted her to see the world. Being lucky myself and having seen so much more than the average 16 year old, I wanted her to see that there was so much more to life than Ireland, and of course the usual holidays in New York or the south of France. I had lived in Pakistan and Malaysia before I was 15 and got to travel a lot at this time. I had seen more than the average 16 year old form Dublin and it has really broadened my lens. I was so super excited to see my niece and my best friend, it was a trip of a lifetime and I was about to get going.

Take Off!

The day finally arrived for me to leave Sydney. I had to say goodbye to my boyfriend Jason. The heart wrenching feeling of saying goodbye to a loved one was familiar to me, I have said goodbye to my family many times in the past, it all started when I was 12 years old and I moved away with my mother and two brothers to Lahore, Pakistan. Over the years I have lived in many countries before settling in Australia, so I have had my fair share of saying goodbye. It really never gets easier, in fact, I think it gets harder as you get older because you appreciate so much more when you are older.

Having tried, and failed to give up smoking on many occasions over the years, I decided that I this time I was going to stop smoking as soon as I walked through the gate in the airport. Of course I had help in a tablet form, some sort of non-smoking pill (oh how I love modern times) so I popped one of the pills as I said goodbye to Jason. I was balling. The tears were like rivers flowing down my face. Lucky I didn't wear any make-up, being a professional goodbye say'er I knew what not to do. After getting through customs they started to dry up, thankfully. Off I wandered through duty free – not buying cigarettes as I was now a non smoker. I wanted a cigarette terribly, but luckily there was nowhere to smoke in the airport.

I boarded the plane and settled in. I knew that China eastern didn't have individual TVs like I was used to on all other flights that I have been on so I had a good book to read as well as numerous trashy magazines. Just as we are about to take off a passenger sitting on the opposite side of the wing to where I was sitting started shouting 'don't let this plane take off'. I thought he was drunk or on drugs, but he kept on saying it. An air stewardess came over and with very little English was trying to calm him down, he had seen some liquid leaking from the wing and insisted the stewardess call the pilot, which she did.

My mind kept going back to the movie 'final destination' I mean, was this really happening? The gent who was sitting beside me found it all hilarious and lucky he did as he calmed me down. The pilot came back and inspected the supposed leaking fluid and decided that we needed to go back to the airport and have it checked, this of course did not help my anxiety, I just wanted to get off that plane and have a cigarette! We were not allowed to get off the plane while they investigated what was happening, but it wasn't long before they turned around and said, "all was good". We headed back to the runway for round two of take-off. I think half of the plane was relieved to get going, where the other half – which included ME, was terrified that we were going to die. Goes to show how I always think the worst in every situation. I used to think it was me being practical, but now I know that I had trained my brain to think this way. Negatively.

Round 2 was successful. We made it, we were up and flying, thank goodness. As soon as we took off again I grabbed all my hand luggage and headed for one of the many empty rows where I could stretch out and get some sleep. I loved getting four seats to myself, it rarely happens so I was delighted and fell fast asleep. I was woken for food, of course, a girl has got to eat! I had another little nap, read some magazines, then the boredom started to set in... After four hours sleep, two magazines-back to back, two meals, two pretend sleeps and an hour and a half of iphone games – still not in China. It felt like an eternity before we landed in Beijing.

2

China

I was exhausted on arrival, I literally went straight to bed. I had the most amazing sleep and almost didn't want to get out of bed, until I realised that I was in CHINA!!! I had to get up and hit the streets. I didn't notice the tiny door frames in the hotel as I banged my head pretty hard when I walked into the bathroom (I am very tall, 6'2). I quickly get ready as I was so excited to get outside and explore.

Wow, it's hot, and magnificent. My hotel was literally a five minute walk from Tiananmen Square. It's packed with so many tourists, mainly Chinese. I couldn't help but giggle at the umbrella hats they were wearing. I mean seriously, were they joking?

The immense size of it all was seriously awesome. Everything feels so big, while I feel so small. Smack dab in the middle of Beijing, this huge city square was named after the Tiananmen Gate (Gate of Heavenly Peace) which leads to the Forbidden City. Did you know that Tiananmen Square is the third largest city square in the world (440,000 m^2 – 880×500 m or 109 acres – 960×550 yd). To the Chinese this square is super significant as so many historical events have taken place there, it's a tourist hot spot for the natives as well as for us foreigners. It really is the heart of China.

When in China you can't look up the Tiananmen Square massacre on the internet; this is all blocked to the nation so no one really knows the truth of what happened. We will never really know the whole truth as China likes to keep it all very quiet. I thought for a moment what it would have been like to be at the massacre, I vaguely remember the news and images, I was only 9 years old when it happened. I took a moment of silence to remember all those who were killed so sadly.

After making my way around the gigantic square, most of the time with my mouth down around my ankles, I wandered down a cute little laneway and ended up on a beautiful shopping street, where I almost got run over by a tram, I wasn't expecting that! It wasn't long before my stomach started rumbling. There was no breakfast included in my hotel, so of course I do what most foreigners do in a new country they were visiting – headed straight to McDonald's! I knew I shouldn't but it was right there in front of me and I was excited for a hash brown. Ah, the coffee and sausage and egg mc muffin tasted like home, even though Mc Donald's for breakfast back in Sydney was a once a year thing for me.

Once my tummy was filled I was ready to go back and explore that street with all the shopping. They had all the usual high street shops such as Zara, H&M, just like any other city. I wasn't interested in shopping, I didn't fly to Asia to shop in high street stores. I started to wander a bit off the beaten track. I tried to go and find somewhere that I could buy a sim card for my phone so I could call home and let them know I was safe. I went into a few stalls checking out what the price should be, but as soon as they saw I was a foreigner, they doubled or tripled the price; luckily I was clued in and asked around before making a decision to buy.

After all of the excitement, and heat, I was exhausted and headed back to the hotel for a rest and to make some calls. To my dismay, Facebook was banned in China, someone did mention that to me before the trip but I thought I would still be able to use it on my phone for some reason: nope, I was wrong. So I sat there wondering what will I do without Facebook for 21 days? Oh the times we live in! I kept my cool, after all was I really that addicted? Really? I figured out that I can still access Instagram and upload pictures there for all to see and follow my adventure; a picture a day will say a thousand words.

First post – me trying to get through the doorway. You can barely see my head....

The time had come to meet the tour group - we had to meet in the lobby at 6pm. Our trip notes say there can be up to 16 people a time travelling together so I was excited to meet so many new people and hopefully make some good friends. Maybe I could even meet someone who is doing similar to me and we can travel together through South East Asia? I was the first to arrive in the lobby and I sat there patiently waiting. Three guys walked up looking kind of shy so I went over and asked them if they were here with the group I was in - they said yes and we started chatting. There were three English guys but one of them lived in New Zealand. All very lovely, friendly and chatty so I figured this was a great start. I was excited to meet the rest of the group.

Our tour leader was so lovely, a Chinese girl, who was of course so friendly. She came along and said that we were waiting on two more guys. Suddenly it dawned on me, our group was far smaller than 16, and they were all guys! There were six in our group and I was the only girl. No girls to talk girlie to, no one to swap clothes with, no one to get my nails done with. But on the bright side, at least I have my own room, all the boys have to share with each other.

It wasn't long before we headed off for dinner, we were still missing one more guy from the group but decided to get moving as we were all starving. Our tour guide was leading the way – we ended up in some dingy little place where you honestly wouldn't even know was a restaurant if we hadn't been guided there.. We went up the back stairs and into a private room. It was a bit awkward to start and no one was talking, all of a sudden people were shy, very different to 5 minutes ago in the lobby. Our tour guide offers to order, and as we had no idea where we were, or what was good, we thought that was a great idea. She ordered an array of traditional Chinese dishes, some I have seen before and others I was keen to try out. She spoke about the tour and how/where we were going to travel, along with some guidelines, rules, etc. We all went around the table and introduced ourselves, as we had already done the brief intros, we gave a little more background as to why we were here and what we were most excited to see. Most people, like myself, were excited to The Great Wall.

By the end of dinner we were all chatting away and excited for the next day when we could join forces and go explore. We headed back to the hotel to see if we could find our missing member, and we did. He was a lovely guy who had been busy exploring the city and wasn't paying attention to the time, hence he missed dinner. We left him to go through the rules with our tour guide again, and we went for a walk around the area. As I had spent all day walking around I knew where to go and showed the boys a few spots before ending up in McDonalds again for an ice cream sundae before bed, ha! I really wanted a ciggie to end the day but thought, don't go back there, you can do it! I went to bed to avoid the cravings. Going to bed alone was still a novelty, Jason was a big snorer so I was so happy to be able to sleep the night through in silence.

I woke up early the next morning as I wanted to go for a run – I had only started running back in Sydney a few months back but wanted to keep up the work, so I got dressed, walked outside and the smog hit me like a tonne of bricks, you could barely see in front of you. I was hesitant but insisted I give it a go. I started to run and after two minutes had to turn around and go back. I have never seen anything like the smog in Beijing – it truly does make it tough to breathe. Even though the city is so incredibly beautiful and vibrant, the smog makes it seem so grey and dull at times.

We met with our tour guide early that morning and she took us through the Hutong of Beijing (the back streets). We had some traditional dumplings for breakfast and some hot soy milk; apparently this was common practice in Beijing. They were big into their soy milk, but you will never find a soy latté anywhere.

The Hutong were fascinating – there were lots of traditional Chinese shops selling all sorts of breakfast offerings, nothing like we were used to seeing back in Sydney or the UK. Lots of dumplings, with all kinds of fillings, lots of really sweet bread and no coffee. I thought if I ate like this for the next 21 days I would for sure gain a few pounds, I had to find some fruit for breakfast.

We were brought into some of the family homes in the Hutong. The houses were so tiny, rooms what we would call a small bedroom, were housing entire families. There were literally up to six or seven people living in just one room. We were told that these people were very rich, and that the property was in fact worth millions as it was so central. When we walked around the corner we saw a lots of fancy cars: Porsches, Ferraris' etc... Apparently they all belong to families in the

Hutong – hilarious. I would much rather have a big house than a nice car, but then again I was a girl and have no interest in cars. To them though it is very common to live in such small spaces, after all we are in China, where the population is 1.357BILLION!!

Once we finished the Hutong tour and were stuffed full of pork dumplings, our leader went back to the hotel and we all jump on the subway to the 2008 Olympic park. The subway was so super easy to use, you literally cannot get lost, and no matter where you go a ticket cost the same cheap price ¥2, about $0.43 – it's for nothing! So off we went to the Olympic park, I was excited to see the place, I had only ever seen it on the TV. Once we got there though, the smog again was blocking the view. We could barely see things in the distance, we had to get very close to make out what we were looking at.

Everything looked so old, it has only been five years but it looks like at least 15. We walked over to the 'cube' (the water sports arena) and I took some pictures – it's hard to make it out through the smog. Then we walked over to the stadium. The boys want to go inside the stadium but I really couldn't be bothered, I know I should have, but I decided to hang out with Matt, he had been the previous day and didn't fancy paying again to see the inside, so we went to get some food in the food hall nearby.

I bought some soft shell crab which I usually love, but as I eat all of the shell I realise it's not like back home in Sydney, there were definitely bits that were not to be eaten but too late I was already choking! I manage to cough it up – nice, and get myself together, dump the rest and grab a drink. Meanwhile Matt sees some interesting food choices, tarantulas, scorpions and maggots. He decided to try them all. I almost throw up but have to laugh and take pictures while I was gagging. We sat outside and waited for the rest of the group to come find us after their tour of the stadium.

After the Olympic park we jump back on the subway again and head for the Summer Palace. It's so incredibly huge! There was so much to see and so much area to cover. We were all starting to fade with the heat and smog but we continued on as we didn't want to waste a second. The Summer Palace is a vast ensemble of lakes, gardens and palatial buildings. You can easily get lost, and we did! It covers almost

720 acres, three-quarters of which are water. To get to the top of the palace you have to climb so many steep steps, we were fading like crazy but we had to keep going. There were elderly Chinese locals making us look like wimps as they climbed to the top with ease. I was glad I had stopped smoking, it would have been very embarrassing as I coughed my way to the top.

We were getting tired and cranky and couldn't find the way out; we weren't sure if we had to walk all the way back, or just keep going. We decided that we would just keep on going until we found a gate. And soon enough we did, thank you lord!! I had no water, was starving, sweaty and almost ready to kill someone. The guys had no idea what would happen to me if I didn't get food ASAP!! The gate we finally got out of the palace through was nowhere near the gate we came through at the start, so we were lost again. Where was the subway? Outside of the gate there were so many people asking if we wanted to tuktuk back to the train station, as we had no idea where we were, and we wanted to have a go in a tuktuk we all agreed to the ride. Luckily we did, as it ended up we were about a 10 minute ride in a tuktuk to the station!

We go to the station and saw pizza hut, hells to the yeah, I had to have pizza NOW. My diet was seriously crap since I arrived I China, but I figured I was on holidays so it was OK. Once had some food in my belly, I felt human again and ready for the subway during rush hour. If you have never experienced this, just go to YouTube for some inspiration. It is one hell of an adventure, but not for the faint of heart.

Tonight we were headed to a kung fu show. I had really no idea what to expect, how often do you hear about king fu shows? To my surprise, it was a really great show – lots of dancing, amazing skills, very artsy, I was so impressed.

After the show one of the guys from the group tells us of how he got scammed on his first day in Beijing, he was wandering around taking in the sights when a lovely student came over wanting to practice her English. He of course said yes he would love to help and started having a conversation with her. She then offered to go and have a drink with him and some of her friends. They went into a restaurant and she ordered some wine, and when the time came to pay the bill she insisted that in China its tradition for foreigners to pay the bill. As they had one bottle of wine he agreed to pay the bill but once he was presented with the bill the bottle of wine apparently cost $250! If you are ever in China beware of such scams!

That night I was exhausted, I felt lonely and I just wanted my boyfriend. It wasn't long before the tears were streaming down my face. My legs were in agony – I was not used to all this walking around. I wasn't enjoying not having someone to share all my stories with. The boys were great, but I had no connection with them. I left my room sobbing like a baby and went straight down to the hotel lobby and bought some cigarettes. I hope that they would make me feel better, yes, I was lying to myself, but it felt good to have a cigarette. Once I did it, I felt remorse but there was no turning back. I headed back upstairs to bed and slept. Boy did I sleep... I was exhausted, frustrated, and being tough on myself because I should not be feeling any of these feelings.

The next morning I had canned coffee and a dove chocolate bar for breakfast, clearly my health was a priority. I had no idea that eating all of this unhealthy stuff was going to have such a huge impact on my mind. This morning's adventure was the Temple of Heaven (aka the Altar of Heaven). The temple is a complex of religious buildings for annual ceremonies of prayer to Heaven for good harvest. As we walked through the gates you can see hundreds of people, all dancing, singing and exercising, as well as entertaining – it's amazing! There were groups of people doing acrobatics, groups doing some weird body folding routines. Then there was lots of dancing, huge groups of people all following a routine, some were not, then there were the tourists who were just joining in for fun. It was fascinating. Everywhere you turned something more interesting and equally strange was happening.

Most of the people were elderly, but they were very mobile people. We saw some old guy literally get bent in half – weird. The exercise area was like a giant outdoor gym. I was literally gob smacked, it was nothing like you could imagine. I had to take some video footage as a photograph could not tell what was happening here. Hundreds of elderly Chinese come together here every morning to work out. The machines they were using looked like a cross between children's playground and gym, I had never seen anything like it before. There was lots of talking, so many voices all trying to outdo the other, it was hilarious...

All of a sudden the rain came pouring down and we were forced to run for shelter. We found a small smelly cafe and went inside to see if they sold coffee. I should have known not to expect coffee as Chinese people don't traditionally drink coffee; they are big tea drinkers, but you can always get an iced coffee in most places, a terrible one, but you can taste coffee. The rain kept on pouring so we had to head back to the hotel and change into dry clothes and get umbrellas. I was a bit upset as I wasn't ready to leave the place, it was so interesting. We only had a few days in Beijing and there was so much to see so we had to keep moving. Next on the list for today was We the Forbidden City.

The Forbidden City was the imperial palace for twenty-four emperors during the Ming and Qing dynasties. It took 14 years to build, and was forbidden to enter without special permission of the emperor, hence its name "The Forbidden City." Its entrance is at the top of Tiananmen Square, which I mentioned earlier. It's the largest walled in space in a city, the world's largest palace. Surrounded by a 52-meter-wide moat and a 10-meter-high wall, it hosts more than 8,700 rooms. The distance between the two gates, entry and exit, is 960 meters. Needless to say we walked our legs off before coming to the other side of the city and not having a clue where we were, or how to get back to the hotel. We walked around in circles for about half an hour before we jumped on a bus that everyone else was jumping on. We figured it would take us to somewhere we would recognise.

It wasn't long before one of the guys from our group sees a familiar shopping district, so we got off the bus and stumbled across another huge shopping mall. I was amazed by the size of the malls here, but I guess when you have so many people living here you need gigantic malls – there were roughly 20 million people living in Beijing alone which was about the same population as the whole of Australia! We went down a side street that was filled with traditional, as well as not so traditional Chinese food and drinks. Matt tried some snake this time and apparently it was very greasy. Yuk!

That evening we wanted to try some local food, in Beijing, Peking duck is the speciality. This was definitely something I wanted to try, unlike the snakes and scorpions. We walked down to a local restaurant that was highly recommended, but they had no tables. So we continued wandering trying to find somewhere else, after all, we were in Beijing and surely many restaurants would be famous for this dish. Once you start looking at menus on a busy street and someone spots you doing this you can guarantee you will be harassed by restaurateurs' until you decide to come in.

We stumbled across a place that looked very quiet but we decided to give it a go. The duck was to die for! We ordered three ducks between five of us. That's a lot of duck, but we were hungry and it didn't last very long. Full belly, sore legs, full pack of cigarettes, and I gave in and started smoking again. At least I wasn't crying this time. Tomorrow was a big day, The Great Wall, what we had all been waiting for, so we needed rest. The excitement wanted me to stay awake, but the exhaustion took over, thankfully, and I feel asleep when my head hit the pillow.

The Great Wall

It was time to leave Beijing, for now anyway, so we packed up and headed for the train station. There was no subway this time; it's a speed train to Shanhaiguan, woo-hoo! We left our main luggage at the hotel in Beijing, and hit the rush hour Monday madness. Holy big smokes, there are so many people all crammed into such small space. The trains run regularly and are super fast. Watching the way people line up to get into the train cabin is just fascinating. I wanted to just sit in a high tower and watch it all, but we had to move. If I had stopped I would have held up half of Beijing. You just have to keep moving.

Three hours later and we were where we needed to be. We got on our adventure boots to go to where The Great Wall of China begins. I was so excited, but then as soon as we got there I was blown away by how it didn't look anything like what I had in my head. It was all far too new looking. The Wall is over 2000 years old, so how can it possibly look new? There were mazes, temples, and lots of people trying to scam you; it was kind of eerie. I didn't realise that this was the very start of the wall, it had been kept highly maintained for tourists and that is why there were lots of shops and scammers, etc... The best of The Wall was yet to come.

As we walked back through the town, we went through the old city. It was creepy, it felt like a deserted thriller movie set. There were no people around, lots of empty buildings, and even an empty ghost train house, seriously! The one place that looked even remotely busy was the oldest brothel in town, which was not a brothel anymore, but a tourist attraction!

On the walk back to the hotel I noticed a woman carrying a baby that had a very obvious and intentional hole in its pants. I had seen this a few times now for it to be a coincidence, so I asked our tour guide "Don't babies use nappies?" She said no, and that nappies can not be bought in China. Babies have a hole in their pants so they can go to the toilet freely whenever and wherever they need to go. Even our tour guide thinks it's interesting and has asked her own mother how it all works, her mother's reply was, 'mothers always know when'.

The next morning we had an early rise for another move to Dongjiakou. This was where we were going to see the Great Wall in all of its glory! We got to the village and the home stay where we would be staying for the night and dropped off our bags. They were kindly skinning a lamb to throw on the BBQ for us later that day. The blood was dripping down the road, and the carcass was covered in flies. I was pretty grossed out, but I kept focusing on the Wall and how excited I was to finally getting to see it.

As we were getting ready for the hike, one of the guys asked where the toilet was and he was pointed to across the road. All of us had to go and check out the toilets, we wanted to see what was in store for us should we need to go. All we saw was a small wall and our travel companion's whole top body, the wall for the "toilet" was about 3 foot high. Not ideal, even for the sitting affairs.

The "toilet" was just a whole in the ground, and my goodness the smell was confronting! I thought to myself, I am not going to drink any water and try to hold off using the toilet for the next 24 hours! To top it all off, there were no showers - nowhere that you could do any sort of bathing. So after our trek up The Great Wall, we have no way of having a shower. Awesome, I definitely did not expect this type of accommodation along the tour.

I put those images behind me as we begun the trek up to The Great Wall. We had no idea what to expect as this was the first time even our guide has done this part of the Wall. It was very isolated, which was fantastic as you really get to enjoy the experience more when you were not sharing it with thousands of other tourists. We were all excited, even though it was very warm and we were about to trek up a mountain. The first few minutes were easy, but it wasn't long before the trek started to get pretty hard core, the mountain was very steep, and there was no 'tourist' way up there. We had to climb a few hundred steps with no proper trail and in some serious heat, we were all sweating up a stream within no time. This was how they carried the millions of pieces of stone to build the wall. I can barely carry my tiny rucksack filled with a bottle of water and some crackers!

It took us almost two hours to get to the top and once we did I completely forget about the sweaty trek we just did. It was absolutely stunning, just as I had imagined, but even better. You could see The Wall for miles and miles and the country side was so green and luscious; the view was simply breath-taking! It took a while before we caught our breath after the climb, and we all just sat in silence and soaked in the awesomeness of it all.

To get across The Wall you need to make your way up and down more steep steps and walkways. We took our time and of course we took lots of photos. Some of our group wanted to keep going at a steady pace, while others wanted to walk very slowly, after all it was quite a steep and slippery trek, so safety first.

I wanted to see as much as I could as fast as I could so I ended up being far ahead of our leader and group. I got to spend some alone time on The Great Wall of China - I had to get in the selfies after all. It was also so insanely hot that I rushed from one fort to the next one for shelter from the sun.

It took us about four hours to walk the part of the wall where we were. We got to a spot where there was no just way of getting through, but we luckily saw a walkway down the mountain at this point, so decided to take it. We would have loved to stay longer but we knew darkness would set in soon, and we only had about an hour and a half to get back down. Of course the trek down was so much easier. We were all out of water and dying of thirst, and as usual in Asia, a random little man appears from nowhere and offers us bottled water for a premium price; but at thirsty as we all were, we would have paid anything.

Once we got back to the bottom and were walking towards our home stay I turned and asked our guide "is there ANY way we can get out of staying here?" She laughed and said if the rest of the group wanted to go she would make some calls. I turned to the group and asked them what they thought, surprisingly they ALL said "Yes! Get us out of here!" Oh the relief of it all! None of us were keen to eat the skinned lamb that we saw when we arrived or sleep in the beds made out of bricks. We were terrified to use the toilet and couldn't face sleeping next to ourselves, let alone anyone else after the sweat we had built up and had no where to shower.

Our leader went and made some calls to find out if we could get out, we went and sat in the one room that was ready for us. The bed was made from red bricks absorbed the heat like a barbeque. It was so hot, and obviously rock hard. I really wanted a drink but didn't want to drink anymore in case I would have to use the disgusting toilet, so I just held my thirst. Our tour guide came back and told us that the call had been successful. We all had to pay some cash, but that was fine. The bus was coming back to pick us up and we could go back to the hotel we stayed in the night previously. Thank the Lord! I didn't fancy staying on a BBQ bed and being cooked myself, although I did feel bad about leaving our hosts. I mean it wasn't their fault, we were just used to our creature comforts. I'm sure they were happy they got to keep the whole animal for their own dinner.

When we got back to the hotel again I was so relived and happy to have the most amazing shower. Once I sat on the bed I started to feel angry. It was strange, but I couldn't control it. I was angry at myself for not staying in the home stay, even though I would never have lasted, my mind was beating me up about leaving. I skipped dinner with the group and headed out to buy more cigarettes and chocolate and chips for dinner. I sat in my room by myself playing games on my iphone and crying. I even smoked in the room! This was acceptable in China but not many other places. I was feeling frustrated that I was alone, even though I wasn't alone, that is how I felt. I felt isolated. It was weird, I didn't want to speak to anyone back home, I guess I didn't want them to think I wasn't enjoying myself. I was for the most part of it, but at night I would feel very sad and lonely.

Continuing on...

Back to Beijing the next day and we had a few hours to kill before we took the overnight train to Xian (train was approx. 14 hours). I was expecting booths and doors on the train, maybe four beds per cabin, and a food cabin perhaps? When we got on the train, none of the above was visible. There were six beds, like bunk beds and no 'cabins' as such; there were no doors to separate a person from the walkway.

The top bunk was about a 3 foot from the ceiling so you couldn't sit up on the bed. The bottom bunks were where everyone sat and chatted before heading to bed. The lights get turned off about 9.30pm so you don't have much time once you get on the train before the lights were turned off. The toilets were literally a hole in the train that you could see the tracks through, and of course as we were in China you can smoke beside the toilets, so when in China...

We were told by our tour guide to bring our own food and we had all bought the same without knowing what the other had bought: packet noodles. It appeared that everyone on the train has the same idea as boiling water was supplied in order to make the noodles, hilarious! Pretty much the entire train eats noodles for dinner and then goes to sleep.

It's actually easy to sleep on a train because they have that soothing swaying motion. I was starting to get used to the fact that I would not find a bed long enough for my 6'2 body in China, so I slept with my legs pulled up against my chest and of course my handbag beside me. There was nowhere to safely leave your valuables, so you need to keep them with you while you sleep. Even though we went to sleep early, I wasn't expecting the five am hustle and bustle...There were so many people up very early and once you hear people up walking around and talking, you can't stay asleep. When I say talking, I actually mean yelling.

Breakfast was the usual can of Nescafe, and just to mix things up I had a packet of Oreos and an apple. A bit of advice, always keep the fruit until the end of the journey as you don't want it to go through you and have to use the train toilets for a number 2! Of course, there were no showers on the train so wipes were an essential part of your morning freshen-up. I just really wanted a shower and some clean clothes but it wasn't long until we got to the hostel in Xian and so I could have a well-deserved shower and proper food.

Xian was home to the Terracotta warriors which was a collection of terracotta sculptures from the armies of Qin Shi Huang, the first Emperor of China. It was basically part of his huge tomb which was buried with the emperor in 210–209 BC and whose purpose was to protect the emperor in his afterlife. The figures were discovered in 1974 by a local farmer in Lintong District, Xi'an, and Shaanxi province. He was actually there signing books when we went to see the warriors.

The figures vary in height according to their roles, with the tallest being the generals. The figures included warriors, chariots and horses. Current estimates were that in the three pits containing the Terracotta Army, there were over 8,000 soldiers, 130 chariots with 520 horses and 150 cavalry horses, the majority of which were still buried in the pits near Qin Shi Huang's mausoleum. If anyone asks if you want to go visit the mausoleum say, don't bother - it's just a small mound and really looks like nothing at all. The warriors were what you need to see!

Other things to see in Xian were the Muslim quarter where there were even more delicious food offerings to try, some fantastic markets and a Great Mosque. We didn't get to see the warriors the day we arrived. It's quite a drive away from the city so we stuck to the Muslim quarter and of course when in China one MUST do karaoke! Our guide booked us a private room - that's how it's done here, and we grabbed some cold beers before heading in. We all started off very shy. I was on the song choices so picked some classics that I thought everyone would know, first up 'lemon tree' but no one knew it? I couldn't believe it, so on we went to the usual karaoke suspects, Aerosmith, Brittany Spears etc. Before you know it we all think we were pro's and you can't take the microphone off of us.

Even though I was having fun at karaoke I left early. When the guys didn't know the songs that I had chosen, I felt that they were judging me and I kind of freaked out a bit. Added to that, they kept buying rounds of beer for each other but excluded me. I felt uncomfortable and was it was getting to that time of night where I would sit in my room and cry. I headed off into the busy streets hoping that I would find my way home. I was terrified, this time I had to call Jason, I was balling and he managed to cheer me up and stay talking to me until I found the hostel. I got back to my room and cried myself to sleep.

I woke up the next day feeling fine and ready for some excitement. I wasn't going to let the boys ruin my experience so I met them that morning and was very polite. We were going to see the warriors. A couple of the guys and I decided to do it through our hostel as it was much cheaper than booking through our guide. We were warned about the 'shopping' stop offs and the time wasted but we were happy to see for ourselves. There were a few stop offs in these huge factories that sell fake warriors and other souvenirs to foreigners. You have to get off the bus and have a wander and man do they try and sell to you. They were persistent, that's for sure.

Once at the warriors we broke away from the hostel group as that particular tour guide was the most annoying guide EVER! Anytime someone even bought a drink she would insist that she get commission from the vendor for it, her tone of voice cut through you. We thought that we would just read the signs and figure it out for ourselves. It was such a fascinating thing to see, it's so incredibly old and was only discovered in 1974. It lay buried underground for all of that time – amazing!

That night we were booked in for a famous dumpling banquet – I thought to would take a lot of dumpling to fill me and the five guys, but I wanted to see what it's all about. Each dumpling was made in the shape of what filling was inside, so if there was a fish dumpling it's made in the shape of a fish, sweet potato, prawn, etc, etc. There were 18 different types and by the end of it you were very stuffed, so it's money well spent. After the banquet our tour guide and I wanted to go and check out the girlie markets. The boys decided that they also wanted to check them and followed us.

The markets were a girls dream come true, thousands upon thousands of bags, shoes, make up choices, clothes, underwear, toiletries, sunglasses, belts, jewellery - you name it. It's not easy to shop these markets with five guys following you around so I quickly suggested we got out of there. I planned to go back the next day alone and soak it all up.

On our last day in Xian we hired bikes and cycled around the city wall. Definitely a highlight. Such great views of the city. If you do go, make sure to get down early as when it gets hot it's 10 times harder to cycle.

After our cycle it's time for me to return to my idea of heaven! The girlie markets, oh I wish I had more room in my luggage as I just want everything. In the end I had to talk myself out of so many buys, and only came home with a new belt, sunglasses and some souvenirs.

My tour guide had organised for us both to go and get our hair cut in a nearby hairdresser - my hair needed a cut and I wanted to experience it. Once I got it done I wished I hadn't. The hairdresser seemed perplexed as to what to do with my hair, I assumed he didn't cut many 'foreigners' hair; he just kept cutting it until it was way too short. I didn't get upset though as I was just going to be tying it back for the next few months in this heat.

Our next overnight train was to Shanghai - 17 hours this time so lots more noodles were needed. The train stations were so incredibly busy, so many people pushing and shoving. In western society this would be considered very rude but not in China. This was normal - some people just need to get through and this was how they go about it. I was not bothered by the pushing but what does get to me was the staring. People literally stare at you for ages and they have no qualms about it. Again, we would consider this rude, but not in China.

With the longer train journeys you must board the train earlier in the day so we have much more time this time before lights go out. To pass the time we were given a Chinese lesson. Our guide also gave us Chinese names – mine was Guo Ying Jie, which means pretty, confident girl. I'll take that.

We all ate lots of noodles and plenty more junk food before lights were out. This time I took a sleeping pill and was off to sleepy land in no time. I had the middle bunk again, score! The bottom bunk is annoying as everyone sits there, the top is ridiculous as you have no head room. The middle is perfect because you have your on space, it is easy to get up and down, and you can sit up or lay down.

Shanghai

Shanghai is very cosmopolitan and I made sure to leave my backpacker look clothes at the hostel. The first stop was the Jing Mao Tower - 88 stories of offices and a hotel which you could see through the middle of the building. Of course as soon as we got to the top it starts pouring down with rain and we couldn't see a thing. It feels like a wasted trip as the photos of the skyline just look grey. Feeling a bit deflated we went to see 'the bund' but with heavy rain and smog, again it's difficult to see anything. The bund is along the waterfront in Shanghai and you (on a good day) could see all of the Shanghai towers light up.

Another must do when in Shanghai was go to eat at 'Grandma's kitchen'. This place has the most awesome BBQ pork dish that I have EVER tasted. You have got to go there - EAT IT!

The next day we were headed to one of the famous Shanghai water towns. After a super early rise and three hour drive, we got to the water town. It's very cute, picturesque, it's kind of like Chinese Venice. We walked around for about an hour and then realised we had covered the whole thing. Some of the group just wanted to get back to Shanghai and go drinking instead of spending the afternoon there, I wasn't fussed either way. We called for the bus to pick us up five hours earlier than planned and headed on our three hour bus ride back to Shanghai.

When we got back to Shanghai we went and spent the afternoon in the French concession. It was a foreign concession from 1849 until 1946, and it was expanded in the late 19th and early 20th centuries. The concession came to an end in practice in 1943 when the Vichy French government signed it over to the pro-Japanese puppet government in Nanking. It has had much development over the years and now stands as a cute concession holding some beautiful designer shops along with plenty of small bars and restaurants. It was like being in Europe, the shops that you saw along with the designers made you feel that you were very far from the hustle and bustle of Shanghai.

After this we went to Nanjing road which was the largest pedestrian street in China, a big change from where we have just come from. The super stores were like Beijing - HUGE! I wasn't interested in sopping but our tour guide was, so I went with her to check out some of the high street stores. As suspected, the clothes in China are made for Chinese people, so being my height and size I was never going to find something to buy. We caught up with the boys again and went to a restaurant for dinner. I didn't eat, I had no appetite, I wasn't sure what was wrong with me but I had an inkling that I was depressed. All the crying at night and paranoia was a giveaway. Everyone wanted to go out drinking after dinner so I went home by myself, again. I was keeping a journal for my trip but noticed that the last few entries were nothing about the trip and all about how sad I was. I should have done something then but I figured I would be OK soon so I ignored the warning signs.

The next day we were headed for our biggest train journey ever – 22 hours! This means a big food shop consisting of three packets of oreos, five chocolate bars, three cans of Nescafe coffee, and three packs of noodles. Sounds like a lot, but 22 hours sounds like a lot too!

Guilin

Guilin was the next spot, although as soon as we got there we had to get another bus for two hours to Yangshou. A place made famous by backpackers, obviously the Chinese knew all about it and kept it a secret, but it was now flooded with tourists. It's the most un-Chinese place I have seen since I arrived in China. The restaurants were all based on European cuisines, the bars were so tacky and all trying to sell you the cheapest drink. It feels like a cheesy teenage resort. The backdrop was so beautiful though - the mountains which look like giant rocks go on forever, and there is so much greenery. I imagined Vietnam to be like this, and was definitely not expecting it here in China.

Amidst the scenery there was a giant golden 'M', yes, it was McDonalds. The little streets were all pebble stone and lined with handcrafted gifts - it feels like everything was aimed at foreigners. We decided to try and find somewhere traditional for lunch, but it wasn't easy. We ended up in 'Lucys place' which offered both traditional Chinese food and apparently the 'best shepherd's pie' in Yangshou. I didn't try it. The boys did and loved it. They ended up going back numerous times over the next few days so it must have been pretty good!

My homesickness kicked in big time when in Yangshao, mainly because we have so much free time to think. There were plenty of optional activities but I only chose a few and was left with plenty of my own space while the rest of them were off doing cooking lessons, calligraphy classes, bamboo rafting, etc. I just decided on 2 activities, the biking tour and the famous Yangshou light show. I didn't want to waste my money on calligraphy lessons or cooking classes. I thought I would enjoy some time alone to explore.

The bicycle ride was fantastic! The country side was about a five minute bike ride from the town, once you got to the country side you were surrounded by rice paddies, lotus ponds, mountains and water, with not a McDonalds in sight. It was super-hot but I didn't care. I was in my element, bike riding through the most spectacular country side.

We had such a great guide for the tour, Peter was his name, his English was perfect and he definitely knew his way around, and was also super quick on the bike. We went to 'moon hill' for lunch, named after a wide, semi-circular hole through the hill. All that remains of what was once a limestone cave formed in the phreatic zone. It takes roughly 20 minutes to climb (about 800 steps) but as I had no idea we were going to be hiking I was in entirely the wrong footwear. I was wearing thongs (flip flops) so I had to stay at the bottom while the group hiked up. Again, this made me feel so left out. I was furious I couldn't go up to the top and even more furious I wasn't told to wear better footwear. I sat at the bottom of the mountain for an hour and half waiting, and stewing.

It had been raining the night before so the steps were very slippery and it was unsafe for me to climb. Although in saying that, there was a group of older women, probably in their 60-70's who insisted on climbing the hill with foreigners so they can sell them water at the top of the hill – very clever, the foreigners always need a drink and also feel sorry for the ladies who have just climbed the hill. I was amazed how they walked up that wet, steep 800 stepped climb with ease, and all in thongs! Once they came back down we all had lunch in this seriously daggy looking cafe at the bottom of 'moon hill.' The food was not exactly inspiring but was included in the trip price so at least that was something. It was a 22 kilometre ride once completed but it felt very easy.

Once we got back the boys then headed off for their bamboo rafting, I decided to go and have a manicure / pedicure instead. I thought I would find somewhere to get it done, after all I was in Chinese tourist-ville! So I walked and wondered and asked in about 50 different shops which included hairdressers, massage parlours, chemists, and even a post office but no one had any idea what I was talking about. Funnily enough as I was walking around looking for a mani/pedi an Australian lady came over to me and asked me if I knew where she could get a mani/pedi. We spoke for about 10 minutes on how funny we thought it was neither of us could find a place and she went one way, and I went another. Roughly 20 seconds later I walked down a small alleyway and found exactly what I was looking for. I went in to ask how much was a mani/pedi and I was told Yuan 180, which was about $40, which was what I pay in Sydney! Clearly I was being ripped off. I had no other choice as I wanted to get my nails done and they clearly had the monopoly in Yangshou. Almost three hours later I emerged from the 'salon' with a mani/pedi and headed back to my hotel for a shower. We had the Liu San Jie light show that night, it was the one show our guide our tour guide had recommended the most out of the whole trip – she said it is the best by far! Yimou Zang produced this show and he was also the one who produced the opening ceremony for the Beijing Olympics in 2008.

We got picked up from the hotel nice and early as apparently the traffic can get pretty hectic because of the show. It was about a half hour drive from our hotel and as soon as we got to the entrance gates we were given. I was hoping it wouldn't rain. The place was packed! It was the biggest natural backdrop show in the world, and boy oh boy was it one amazing back drop. You were literally looking onto the water and the tall rock mountains were a stunning background.

The show focuses on the lives of the people living around the Lijiang River and projects their culture, music and dresses. 600 actors perform in this show to a huge audience, we all sat in awe for 70 minutes. Liu Sanjie was a love story about a woman named Liu Sanjie, born in Liuzhou who had two sisters. The legend was that a warlord fell in love with Sanjie, but she was already in love with a man from her village. The warlord out of jealousy kidnaps her, but Liu's lover and allies find a way out and they both escape the trap of the warlord and lives happily ever after.

Someone did try to explain this story to us before the show started but no one in my group could understand a word he said. I have since looked this explanation up, although knowing this doesn't make it better, the show itself was breathtaking! I was smiling so hard my face began hurting. I wanted to take photos and video the whole thing but any photos or video I took did it absolutely no justice. If you look it up on the internet you could see some great footage. As soon as I left I sent messages to my friends and family telling them to look up the footage and see what I had just experienced first-hand. I was on such a high.

When I got back to the hotel I got a call from Rebecca, she had just gone to buy her ticket to Vietnam and realised that she didn't have a visa. There was not enough time for her to get one, so the original plan of her coming to meet me in Hanoi was out. As I had already bought my ticket from Hong Kong to Hanoi and had multiple trips booked once I arrived in Hanoi, I still had to do this journey. I was devastated, I thought that Rebecca couldn't come and that I had to do Vietnam by myself. In the state of mind that I wasn't I really didn't want to go it alone. I was worried about was the fact that I only had a single entry visa for Vietnam from the date that I arrived, so if I left I would have to try and get another visa somehow. Vietnam was the main reason for this trip. I wanted to see it all. I wanted to really take my time and travel down from the North to South. Efriends who had travelled to Vietnam said that they wished they had more time, and that I should give Vietnam at least four weeks, which I was happy to do. Now faced with this decision, I felt that I had to decide between Vietnam and my best friend.

In reality it was an easy decision, but I made it a difficult one. I honestly stressed myself out so much over something so trivial. At the end of the day, it was far more important that I got to see and spend time with my friend. I literally spent hours trying to decide what to do. Crying, stressing, making a million phone calls, I was back and forth on my decision so many times. I just couldn't stand the thought of making any decisions. For some strange reason this small decision felt like an absolute life changer for me. I was overwhelmed. I guess it wasn't just about the trip, it was about my life. I was at a turning point now. I did have a job to go back to if I wanted it, but I felt that there was more to life than running a restaurant or bar. I wanted more from life. The industry that I had loved so dearly was now my nemesis. It was killing me. I wanted to get out but had no idea how to. I had to make a decision to make changes but I couldn't make a decision what to have for dinner. I was a mess.

My poor friend Rebecca hadn't expected the reaction that I laid on her when she called. I was of course making the whole trip about me. Something I have always done throughout my life. I have always put myself first. Not intentionally, but I have done so because I have been hurt so many times in my past. My own parents abandoned me. I was a tough mudder based on the upbringing that I had. While I shared my life with my brothers and sisters I learned to look after myself first and foremost. This could be seen as a positive quality, but not this time. This time I was not thinking about my friend whose trip also had to change, I was simply thinking about me and how it effected what I wanted to do.

I asked my iphone tarot card for some advice and it pulled the 'world' card which stated I needed to open myself up to destiny. Perfect! It's destiny that I changed my trip route. After all, this journey was one to be made along the way. I finally decided it's much better that I get to see and hang out with Rebecca, then I get to see all of Vietnam. I can always go back again another time. Plans, routine and schedule were not allowed anywhere near me. The control freak in me was terrified to let go but at this stage I had no other choice. It was good for me. Or so I thought...

I called Rebecca and asked her if she would meet me in Laos. That way I could still do my planned trips in Hanoi and then I would fly to meet her in Luang Prabang and we could travel through Laos into Thailand together. She was more than happy to do that and off she went to buy her ticket. Secretly I was panicking a little, I had spent some time researching what to do and where to go in Vietnam and was relying on meeting people n the journey for Cambodia and Laos routes, but I must have faith. And after hanging with six guys for this entire China trip I was super happy to not only have a girl to talk to, but my best friend since I was four years old! The rest of the night and all of the next morning were spent recalculating the trip, organising the few days that I now have in Hanoi to make the most of them, and booking my plane trip from Hanoi to Luang Prabang which was where Rebecca was now flying into.

And the next day we are on the move again, two hours on a bus back to Guilin, we had left our big bags at the train station and then went to get another teeny tiny bus which was going to bring us to Dazhai. We were squished onto this bus, it really was not made for tall people. I was sitting window side on the back seat and with every turn I was pushed more and more into the back corner of the bus.

The roads were windy and bumpy and looked like they were seldom used, but then you see big coaches full of people coming towards you and then realise that this road was very much a used road. As I was at the window I could see the steep drop down the mountain and it was making me feel very nervous. The bus driver may be a pro but he was driving far too fast for these kinds of roads, and it's not only me who thinks this. We had to at one stage stop as people on the bus started to get claustrophobic and very anxious on the journey.

Once I got over the scare factor I could take in the beauty of the surroundings, it's stunning! One side of the road is all rock, and you could see falling rocks as you drive through, the other side was a long drop down to a river with so many little waterfalls, luscious green rice paddocks, cute manmade bridges which I wouldn't be crossing myself, but I was sure they were used frequently.

When we finally got to our destination, I saw some cable cars, and what looks to be a beautiful hotel in the distance (at the end of the cable cars) and I think- amazing! We were going to step it up and enjoy some luxury finally. Haha! No chance. We were told to start walking. Where we were going the cable cars don't lead to, so we started walking and within seconds I was dripping with sweat.

There were old ladies who offered to carry our bags for us, they would have been at least in their 70's, I only had a small backpack as our big bags were left at the train station. I thought it would be pretty bad if I didn't carry my own bag, and I walked ahead of the group while the boys all pondered about handing over their bags to the elderly ladies. The first five minutes was easy, flat twisty road but besides the heat it was completely doable. After those five minutes we started on the slippery, steep steps that twist and turn, and man they get tougher and tougher!

Only 15 minutes in and I wished I had asked one of those old ladies to carry my bag for me, we had to climb these steps for over two hours, everyone was so hot and exhausted that we didn't even pay attention to our surroundings and how magnificent they were, we just wanted to get to the guesthouse - any place that looked remotely liveable we asked "is this it?" When we finally got to our guesthouse, we all get water before collapsing into the chairs.

The place was cute, very basic, but homely. It was like a giant wooden cabin. The rooms were small, all the walls were wooden panels and the bed sheets were tartan which suited the decor. The shower was tiny and the walls so thin I could hear everything from my neighbours. I couldn't wait to get into the shower even though they told us there was no warm water, I didn't care – I wanted to get out of my smelly, sweat soaked clothes, and a cold shower was actually the perfect solution. After showering and feeling fresh, I headed downstairs and caught the view before it got dark.

I sat staring at the landscape and cried, it was just so beautiful. I hadn't paid much attention earlier because I was so uncomfortable, but I was shocked by the beauty, blown away in fact. I had never even heard of Dazhai or the Longji rice terraces and here I was sitting in one of the most stunning surroundings I have ever seen! Again, check it out on Google images. The rolling hills were luscious green like I had never seen before. The rice paddies were in small dots across the cascading landscape. It was hard to think of how the farmers would even get to their piece of land to look after it.

The Longji rice terraces were also known as the dragons back bone rice terraces. They stretch layer upon layer of rice paddies, coiling around from the base of Longji Mountain to its summit. I believe they date back to the Yuan Dynasty (1271-1368), and construction was carried into the early Qing Dynasty (1644-1911). The Dragon's Backbone Rice Terraces covers an area of 66 square kilometres and spans an altitude between 300 meters and 1100 meters - it was truly a magnificent sight. A Chinese saying 'Where there was soil, there was a terrace,' be it in the valley, with swift flowing rivers to the mountains summit with its swirling cloud cover, or from bordering verdant forest to the cliff walls, the planting looks precision like. It was made up of numerous patches no more than onemu (it was a traditional unit of area in China, currently call shimu) (about 0.16 acres) and each family or farmer ensures that they receive maximum benefits from this tiny plot of land. They do everything for that piece of land and treat it like a child as it is their main source of food and sometimes, income.

I was so thankful that I had made the trek, that I had picked this trip and that I got to see this. Even the photos on my iphone make it look fantastic, where as usually they don't do it justice. We were literally staying in the middle of nowhere. I was surprised I even had phone reception and even more surprised when I saw I had Wi-Fi. Once the sun went down it was pitch dark and I could see nothing, so I headed back inside.

After dinner we learned how to play mah-jong, a traditional Chinese game - Similar to the card game rummy. Our guide had printed off cheat sheets for us so we could understand all of the symbols and learn how to play, there are 144 tiles based on Chinese characters and symbols so we definitely needed some help to get us going. In most variations, each player begins by receiving thirteen tiles and the aim is to get a series of symbols or characters to win. If you asked me to play a game with you now I would probably totally forget everything I learnt that night, but it was fun.

The next day we were on the move again and this time the trek was five hours, we were all more than happy to hand over money to anyone who offered to carry our bags, we were far wiser and not willing to go it alone. The trek was tough, but not having your bag made such a difference. I found it hilarious that we were just told by our guide that intrepid, our tour company, were no longer booking water sport activities for their guests due to health and safety issues, yet they will allow us to do this trek, where one slip could easily seriously injure you. It was a rugged, slippery trek. When I asked our guide what would happen if someone hurt themselves, she said it had happened before and they had to wait for hours for a helicopter to come and rescue them. That was enough for me to shit myself, I was already scared, but that story just topped it. I was going to take my sweet time and I didn't care if people had to wait for me.

Our tour guide also told us that many people have broken down into tears by the intensity of it. If I didn't have someone carrying my bag, I probably would have been that person today. I wasn't being brave at all, in fact I was being a wuss, all in my own head mind you. I never let on to any of the boys that I was freaking out inside, although I think half of them were too. One of the guys was pretty unfit and he struggled on all of the treks. We even lost two from our group for about 10 minutes as they took a wrong turn in one of the villages. It was a pretty full on trek, but the beauty that surrounded you, when you could actually take your eyes off the ground, was breathtaking.

At least this trek there was a good mix of both up and down, yesterday's shorter trek was all uphill. Luckily I make it through in one piece, when we got to our next hotel I was the happiest woman in

Ping'an village. The hotel was again, very basic, but very comfortable, clean and best of all you could smoke inside! They were cooking some home-made tofu on the side of the street and our guide said it was a must try, I ordered it along with bamboo rice, rice that was literally cooked in a piece of bamboo on a barbeque, and boy they were both really scrumptious. The tofu literally melt in my mouth, I had never experienced that texture before with tofu. The bamboo rice had an incredible flavour though it, it tastes like Japanese sushi rice with a hint of green tea or leafy flavour, if you ever walk past a street stall selling bamboo rice, you must try it out.

After our freshen up and feed we were all happy and ready to go exploring again. Our tour guide took us across the village, which literally means walking around in circles on steps and then across waterfalls, down by some gigantic black pigs, some crazy roosters and to another hostel that has a view that was simply to die for. I wish I could show you a photo of what I am trying to describe, it was like something out of Lord of the Rings. Twirls, mossy, beaten up, but divine steps going up and down, and around. What should take you 2 minutes to cross, in this village, takes you 10.

When we got to the hostel we walked out to the balcony and all stopped in awe of the view, holy moly cats, the place is freaking amazing! You could see for miles and miles, rolling hills of rice paddies, luscious green, funny shaped rooftops and blue skies. I just never imagined that China could be so beautiful, that it could have such variety in land. We were shown some other treks that were suggested we do the next morning; I was keen to pack in my trekking shoes in after today's hike, so I passed when the guys were asking who was interested in a morning hike. The village was unreal. All of the houses were built on stilts that look like they could break at any given moment, even the new ones! It honestly felt fairy tale like, and so peaceful. The locals around were all so friendly and gentle. This was the place to experience Chinas ethnic minorities' culture. The Zhuang and the Yao nationalities live here, though mainly it was the Zhuang people.

These women dress in unique costumes and their hair is never cut, so they have this long and shiny, beautiful dark hair. They will happily pull out their locks to show them off and even show you how they wash it, an interesting sight. The traditional clothing is mainly black, but all of the clothing have very colourful borders. You can buy bags made from these fantastic colours and patterns – I wanted a bag, an outfit and the hair, although I am sure I would get sick of it pretty quick. The washing process is not conducive to backpacking...

I left the group early again that night as I felt that I needed some alone time. I don't know why I felt that I needed it. Maybe I was feeling homesick? Maybe I wanted a rest? I went back to sit in my room alone and started to cry. Why was wrong with me? I was in the most beautiful place I have ever seen and all I wanted to do was sit in my room and play silly games on my phone. I was feeling confused, alone and sad. I couldn't get out of my own head and I was wasting some precious time. I blamed not wanting to be around the others, but it wasn't them, it was me... I had a problem that was sneaking in but I didn't want to admit it.

I was convinced that the guys in the group hated me. I have suffered from social anxiety in the past and it was creeping back up on me. In fact, it is an anxiety that has followed me for years and years. I have never been able to get rid of it. I never enjoy meeting new people, I always think that people are judging me. Whether it was about the fact that I am so tall, or that fact that I have nothing to say, I become seriously shy around new people. Some people look at me and think I am confident because I hold myself well, as in, I walk tall. This comes from my mother always poking me in the back if I didn't stand up straight. The guys that I was traveling with probably though I was just rude, all of them seemed to be having great fun together but I just didn't enjoy hanging out with them. It wasn't so much them I was not wanting to spend time with, it was more me thinking that they did not want to spend time with me. I was timid, quiet, shy and only came out of my shell when I was drinking... This is why I used to drink so much. But this time I was too scared to let them see crazy Jess, the girl who drank too much and partied too hard. I knew she had to take a break. I just didn't know who else to be when I couldn't bring her out. I didn't know how to behave in a social scene without drinking. I wasn't ready for a pity party, so I took a sleeping pill and tried to get some sleep.

The next day we headed back to Guilin, we had five hours to wait before we got our last overnight train, so we headed into the city to check it out. It was a very big city, about five million people, which I suppose in Chinese terms means small, but it is the main city and train station for Yuangshou and the Longji rice terraces so was a very popular tourist destination, even though I have never heard of it before.

As always I couldn't shop because:

1. The clothes were far too small for me
2. I had no room in my luggage
3. Their t-shirts all had writing on them (in English) that made no sense, while I did find this amusing I wasn't going to wear one myself. An example: 'I will do my best, carnival is my best. Everybody likes freedom'

We wandered around for a few hours and stocked up on more overnight train noodles, before heading back to the station to get our bags and boarded our final Chinese sleeper train. Guilin train station was small, smelly, dirty, and by far my least favourite of the trip. I was hoping to not have to use the toilets but when nature calls, it calls.... the toilets were basically troughs, one must climb onto a step, pull down your pants and then squat in front of any other person doing the same thing. There were no doors, there were small walls at either side of the trough, but you could see everyone's waste travel down while you were squatting, an experience I would hope never to go through again.

While we were sitting around waiting for our train, a group of girls came over and asked if they could take my picture. People were just fascinated by my height! It's such a novelty for them. In fairness, even in Sydney people stare at me because of my height, so it's no surprise the Chinese were interested in taking photos. It's not the first time this has happened - a lot of the time people will try to take a sneaky picture. It's so funny - they think they were being subtle, but I am not blind and could totally see them pointing the camera at me while also calling their friends over to say "look!"

This time the journey was only 13 hours, sounds easy, pop a zanex, out cold and happy days. Hello Hong Kong – and a very easy border crossing. Leave China, enter Hong Kong, no visa required and you were in.

China | What was going through my head

As with any journey I learned a little from this part of the trip. I learned that one should open their mind to this wonderful world's abundance. When I said that I was going to China to start off my trip, so many people were shocked by my decision. People still think of China as backwards or dirty. Yes, the smog can be pretty bad in the cities, but they were also so full of life and culture, history, and beauty. I was blown away by the things that I saw, and the beauty. I was amazed by the people and how wonderful they were. I was dumb founded by the history and the detail to which all Chinese people know about their history.

The Chinese, especially the Chinese tourists in Sydney get such a bad rap regarding their manners. We may think it's rude, but in China it's actually their custom. I don't mean being rude is their custom, I mean what we may think is rude, is actually normal. Why should they change their values and beliefs when they are a tourist? I went to experience what they had to offer, and I did. I was welcomed and lucky to have seen and experienced what I did. We need to learn more, we need to see things form others peoples perspective more. We need to understand that we don't know everything and that when we are open to receiving information, culture and a new point of view it can change our world.

So many people these days walk around in their own little world, like a bubble. They get caught up in what is happening in their world, and make their world number one priority. I used to be this person, I used to never see what was right in front of me. I used to never hear what was being said to me. I used to wander around in my own bubble and miss what was happening around me. I would miss the beauty, I would never be grateful for what I had. I always wanted more, and not in a good way. I wanted more and more and never said thank you for what I had. I mean, I was getting a once in lifetime opportunity, I was being spoilt by beauty and I was so stuck in my own world that I didn't appreciate it.

I knew what gratitude was, everyone knows what it is. Its about being kind and saying thanks for a gift, sending thank you cards, stuff like that. I had no idea that gratitude is in fact an attitude that one must have, I was never taught that I should be grateful for the life that I have been given. I was never grateful as I was always in search of what more life had to offer. I was never grateful because I thought that life had given me a raw deal. I would never stop and truly appreciate a magical moment or a wonderful experience. The trip that I was on was great. I was enjoying it most of the time, but there was also so much pain that I was experiencing. It was like life, up and down, mostly down. And just like my life, it was so much easier to focus on the negative stuff. I was programmed this way. My default is to see the bad, to look for it. I am programmed to not put my hand in the fire, to stay away from strangers, to avoid love because it can hurt me. I have spent my life running away from everything, because it is so much easier to do this. I have never been grateful for the experience that life has given me, I have always been resentful for it. I never thought that I was a good person, I never thought that I was bad either, but how could I appreciate or be grateful for who I am if I do not think that I am special. I had to learn how to be grateful, I had to learn that my wounds were in fact my wisdom. I had to learn that I was in fact so incredibly grateful for every single heartache, for all the pain, for all of the madness that I have been shown. For all of this makes me stronger, it makes me ME and I am special. I am one in a billion!! I have so much to give, to offer. I have yet to reach the point on my trip where I fall so far that I decide that I can no longer go on. I have yet to decide to end my own life. I have yet to learn that this will in fact be the best thing that ever happened to me.

I am one of those people who moves at a million miles per hour. I am always doing something, and find it hard to sit still. I walk fast, to the point that people have to run to keep up with me. I talk fast, eat fast, work fast and even sleep fast. When morning comes around I literally jump out of bed and into the shower, I never snooze, ever!! I don't enjoy a lie-in, because when I wake up, I think about what I have to do and I can't relax until I get moving.

I actually thought that being the fastest is the best and sacrificed getting things done right for speed. At work I would send out emails and documents with multiple spelling errors all of the time because I think that if I slow down to read the email before I send it I am not working smartly! Sounds silly, and in reality it is. I wasn't get bothered by making mistakes; I was bothered by being slow… I would constantly walk around with a sense that there's something I forgot to do. I felt guilty when I actually took time to do nothing, like I have been doing on this trip. I have been doing so much, but nothing at the same time. I have been beating myself up for doing nothing, even though I am doing so much. I always do that. Beat myself up. I let the negative voices in my head take over and run the show. They kept telling me to do more, meet more people, have more fun, but my head was also telling me that no one wanted to be my friend, that I couldn't be fun without drinking and that I was wasting my trip. I knew I was, but I couldn't help myself.

My monkey mind was on overdrive. My mind is just the same as me, of course, its my mind. I t moves at a million miles per hour. It never stops, it will overanalyse everything, overthink things, and make up things that are not even there, I can make jobs for me to do like no one else. The staff who used to work for me were always amazed at how I could conjure up something for them to do in an instant all while they thought that everything was done. I had a habit of doing this. Making mountains out of molehills, making drama where there was none and making my mind a mess. I just didn't know how to slow down, I thought that slowing down was for the weak, for hippies, I was no hippie. I had to keep going forward at a fast pace, because if I slowed down I might start to feel the pain, to notice that my life was fucked, I might start to see that I could never let anyone get close to me, I might start to notice that I was in fact a complete bitch!!

My favourite saying 'make every moment count' was starting to make me laugh, but not in a good way. I was making every moment miserable, not memorable. I had never learnt to appreciate moments, I had no idea how to be in a moment, I barely recall my childhood because I was always trying to get away from it. It literally is so much of a blur to me because I try so desperately to hide from it. I should learn to embrace it, but I have pushed down the hurt so far down, that I can no longer access it. I can no longer learn what I needed to learn from my past. I have removed it from my consciousness. Here I am on a trip I have dreamt about for years but I was hating it because I couldn't learn to be in the moment. I spent the whole time 'in my head' and missed out on what was right in front of me.

I had learnt to open my eyes to new cultures, that is what travelling is about. No big surprise there… I was opening my eyes to new people, but yet to learn to open my eyes to myself. I was relying on other people to make my trip exciting. I wasn't going out there and making it exciting myself. I would spend my time on telephone to Jason arguing over the silliest things and blamed him so many times for putting me in a bad mood, all when I should have been out enjoying myself. I again hadn't realised that it was only I that had the power to make this trip into an amazing one!

I was so worried about spending money, even though I was nowhere near reaching my budget. I was worried about giving up my job back in Sydney and how this would affect my future career. I was worrying if I was making the right decision leaving Jason back in Sydney, I was worrying if I should have even got back with him in the first place. We had spent so long going back and forth with our relationship and now I have left it again.

When Rebecca told me that she couldn't come and travel according my plans I completely freaked out! I was used to laying down the law; running things how I wanted to run and having people do what I asked them to do. I was a control freak. I felt unprepared to make the big change to my trip and didn't want to take on the responsibility of figuring out what to do and where to go, I wanted someone else to make my decisions, sounds silly but that was where I was at. Seems like a contradiction to my controlling self but maybe my mind needed a break, but just couldn't exactly figure out how to get it. The fear of choice was crippling me, why? What was it about choice that was so scary? I had made through so many years of my life and made some good and some bad choices but I had made them. Why now did choices seem so crippling?

I was afraid of change, I know for sure that I am a creature of habit. I know this because when I was younger we never had stability, and I now craved it. I would get upset when plans would change, and I would generally back out if I could. This time it was not an option, because I had to save face, I couldn't go back to Sydney as I couldn't decide where to go, or because I was too scared of trying something new. This was the whole reason I was challenging myself with this trip!

China was fantastic, but my head was starting to go mushy. I thought that a change of country would be great! On to Honkers!!

3

Hong Kong

Now that we were in Hong Kong we have access to Facebook again, thank goodness! And of course that will take at least half an hour to go through but I must make it fast as we were finally in Bonkers Honkers and there was so much to see and do, and I was also about to get to see my friends who live here. I was starting to get excited about not having to hang out with these guys anymore, not because I don't like them, but more because I just need some fresh new energy.

After a quick shower, we headed on foot towards the ferry to Hong Kong Island as we were on the mainland. It's just as I imagined it. It was so busy, with so many people, it feels a little Chinese, but also very Western. There was such a mix of people - so much advertising, so many sky scrapers, far more than you can ever imagine. The skyline is completely packed full of skyscrapers, I can't even fathom how many people live in this place with this many skyscrapers. It is just mind blowing.

Once we got to the ferry and we could see the island from the water, we got to see how built up it was. Every building was an amazing multi-story architectural phenomenon. As soon as we got to the island we headed to the main shopping street and left the boys behind so we would go spend some money on fashion. I had already decided that I will shop till I drop and post all my findings back to Sydney for my return. Once I started hitting shops like H&M (which we don't have in Sydney) and then Zara etc., I thought, Jessica, what were you doing? You did not come to Hong Kong to shop - get out there and see the place!

So I left my guide and ventured down the road alone trying to find my way back to the hotel to drop off what I have bought. On my way back, I of course got lost - it's pretty easy to do, with no map. Luckily I got lost in a good spot though as I stumbled across the Temple Street night markets, sweet! I wandered through and fell in love with a cool pair of sunglasses. They don't take up too much room and were a necessity on a trip like this. So the bargaining begins, and I win, well that is I got the sunglasses for the price I wanted. I am sure I still got ripped off as I am a tourist after all. Tonight is the last night of the group from China being together before we break to go our separate ways tomorrow. I was wandering the streets of Hong Kong alone, they were probably in a pub drinking somewhere. Let's face it, I avoided them for most of the trip so why would I spend our last night with them?

Breakfast was dim sum, consisting of prawn dumplings and internal organ porridge (not joking!). I tried everything, except for the porridge. It was apparently a very famous dim sum restaurant where international stars would be found occasionally. For the life of me I cannot remember the name... It would not be somewhere I would recommend anyway. There are a million dim sum places in Hong Kong so go crazy if you find yourself there looking for some good dim sum. After the internal organ porridge, it was time to say goodbye to our tour guide and the rest of the group. I had booked a fancy hotel and was keen to check into some luxury after all of the slumming it we had just done. I quickly said goodbye to everyone, most of them were continuing on the rest of the day together but I just wanted to get to my new hotel and shower.

Once I had said my goodbyes to the group I headed towards the subway with my bags. I thought I had figured out how to get to the new hotel. I was wrong. I ended up in a cab after realising I was totally lost. I wanted to check in straight into my room but the room wasn't ready as I was too early for check in. I got so angry with the guy at the desk. This isn't like me, I work in hospitality and I hate people like that. It's not his fault that the room isn't ready and I should know better. I literally felt so overwhelmed with anger I had to walk out of the hotel to catch my breath. The blood was pumping through my veins,. I was hot, sweaty and pissed off!! Why bother paying for a fancy room when I cant even check in until later that day? I know, I should be calm, but

I couldn't calm myself. I was close to punching the guy behind the counter. Again, very unlike me. I was at my wits end. I was confused, alone, scared and tried, overwhelmed and in need of a very big hug, preferably from my sister.

What was happening here? I have just broken away from the group and had the freedom to do what I wanted. I was scared. I was scared to be alone and have to go alone, and figure out everything from here on out all by myself. I didn't have a guide anymore and I failed at the first hurdle, finding my hotel. Oh shit, what have I done? What have I gotten myself into? I thought I was a strong independent woman, but I was breaking. I was beating myself up for smoking, but couldn't stop, I was beating myself up for being weak, but felt I had no control over that either. I had to keep moving and ignore what was happening, it was the only way.

I left my stuff with the concierge and headed into the city. I needed to find somewhere to do my washing. Hotel costs were way too high in that regard. I was told exactly where to go and was lost within seconds. This was not helping my anger, which was really anxiousness, but I couldn't tell the difference. I walked around in circles for about half an hour and no one could tell me where I was going. I actually started crying. I found a coffee shop, had about five ciggies and then headed back to finally find the laundry. Phew, now I can get going again.

I put on a brave face and started walking in the extreme heat. I walked and walked until I finally figured out what I wanted to do. There was actually so much to see in Hong Kong that it was difficult to have to choose what to do. I think I chose pretty mainstream - IFC shopping centre, the toilets were definitely a highlight. I had already seen Temple street markets, Nathan Road and Queens road, so on my list to do I still had Victoria Peak, the Giant Buddha, Kowloon walled city and Times Square. I thought that was a good mix and also very achievable without putting too much pressure on. I knew there was a Disneyland which I would love to see if I had time too. For now I chose to go for the most spectacular view in Hong Kong so I wandered off to find Victoria Peak. There were lots of escalators, then a super steep tram and you were at the top. Granted a truly spectacular view of Hong

King, you could see almost everything, you feel like you are on top of the clouds because you can see the tops of so many skyscrapers.

I didn't stay long, I am the kind of person who conquers fast! This is, I see what I need to see, take a photo and move on. I never "soaked up" anything, I was constantly moving and constantly had another million things to do, even if the things were nothing to do. I headed back to the hotel hoping that I could get checked in.

The hotel staff were so kind when I returned, even after me being a bitch. They gave me a free room upgrade with a huge bed, I was feeling like the happiest girl alive! Such a contrast to only 2 hours ago... If only I could have my baby (Jason) with me right now, that would be the best! There I go again, not truly appreciating what I have and always wanting more. I didn't even notice that the highs and lows were coming fast and strong. The lows were bad, and all I could think about was what a failure I was. The highs were breathtaking moments where I generally ended up crying with joy. I had to keep going, I had no other choice. I had to just slap a smile on my dial and keep trying to make every moment count.

Next on my list of things to do was the world famous Hong Kong evening light show on the harbour. It's the world's largest permanent light and sound show, which involves over 40 of Hong Kings skyscrapers. I jumped on the star ferry and headed over to the mainland to look back at the island where the light show was held. There was a massive build up to the show, and as it's also the world's largest sound show, there are literally thousands of people. There is music, lots of sponsor announcements; lights that go from one end of HK to the other, they even had lights on the buildings on the mainland. The music was a huge part of the sound show too. It's a really cool concept; it spreads across the island nicely but not so much that you can't see it anymore. While I was very glad I went and caught the show, it was nothing like the last one I saw in China. Maybe I have been spoilt from that?

I headed back to HK island and try to find Times Square. Surprisingly it's not as easy to find as you would think. Once I found it I couldn't believe the size of it, but then again what else do you expect in Hong Kong? The place makes it feel like daytime even though it's now 9pm. It's so bright, incredibly busy and just like in China, the shops were all super-sized! Once again I decide not to spend my time or money shopping and just take it all in. And by take it all in, I men walk through the streets at a steady pace towards my hotel and not stop for any shopping. I literally did not go into one shop.

When I get back to the hotel I checked my emails and saw an email from my real estate agent back in Ireland. I was trying to sell a house I own back home. When I bought it, it was my dream home. I was 26 years old and I bought it all by myself. I was so proud at the time. I loved it. It was my pride and joy, beautifully decorated, so much love and attention went into that house. It was everything I dreamed of for so long. Every room was lovely decorated by me. I spent hours upon hours on each and every detail. I put all of the furniture together and every week I would buy something new. I had no idea that I would move to Sydney when I bought the house, I thought that it was my forever home. I gave up so much so I could have this home, but it was worth it as I loved it so much. It was all mine, no one could take it from me, it was my safe place.

After living in Sydney for five years, the house no longer felt like my home. The emotional attachment is gone, or so I thought. It was time to sell it. House prices in Ireland had gotten so bad because of the global financial crisis, my house was literally worth half of what I paid for it. I had an offer from some buyers for it and I was just waiting on the banks to agree to the price and hand over the deeds. Even though I thought I had let go of the emotional attachment it was still a very difficult process to go through. The back and forth with solicitors, banks and real estate agents, all while a million miles away was much more difficult than I thought it would be. I honestly thought that I would be bale to sign it over and be done with it. My emotions said otherwise.

The estate agent who was selling the house for me had emailed me a picture of my house, it had been covered in graffiti. I was furious and devastated at the same time, who would do this and why? I immediately called my tenants and asked them what happened. Apparently it was their daughter's ex-boyfriend had done it after they had a fight. I was disgusted! How could someone do this to my house? And what kind of tenants did I have that would have this happen?

The agent went onto to say in her email, that my potential buyers were starting to get frustrated as it had been five months since they put in the offer and they wanted to get the deeds. Unfortunately this was not my decision, as there was so much negative equity, the banks were in control. The agent was getting a bit angry with me even though there was nothing I could do. She kept saying that I was trying to make things difficult and that I needed to sort myself out or the buyers would be gone.

I called my solicitor to see where he was with the banks on my behalf, but there had been no further developments. I started questioning if I should sell the house or not. I had not been entirely set on selling it, but I've been waiting for the banks to say they would hand over the deeds. I would have taken this as a sign to give it up. For some reason though, something was telling me to hold off. I was torn; it was such a big decision. I wanted to sell it and be done with the constant managing of the property, but my brother was listed as a guarantor so I was afraid the banks would chase him if I just walked away. I could potentially just walk away as I lived in another country but I couldn't face the guilt that was attached to that. I had to either sell it at a loss and continue paying the negative equity, or keep it and try and sort something with the bank regarding payments.

When I spoke with my tenants I had reminded them about the fact that I was selling the house. They already knew. I had spoken to them the last time I visited Ireland and the estate agent had been doing showings of the property ever since. All of a sudden they seemed shocked. I wasn't asking them to move now. I needed their rent to pay the mortgage. I was reminding them that once the house was sold they would have four weeks to move out. I think they took this as they had to move now. I kept saying, "No, you don't have to move now, only when the house sells." I started to worry that they would move now and that would be a huge financial burden for me having to pay a mortgage if they were not paying rent.

My head was starting to doubt things. Should I be doing this trip? Should I have stayed in Vietnam? Should I be bringing Molly over? Should I just go home? What should I do with the house? Am I brave enough to be alone? I felt so stressed out and couldn't sleep a wink.

I also had to call the bank as I was getting emails from them about the sale. Even though we live in an age where communication was easy I found it all very difficult to finally get through to them. I was told that they needed lots of paperwork and that they were not going to release the deeds until they had everything they needed. Fair enough, I mean it's a big call, but this just put me into a further tail spin. I was in Hong Kong and rarely had access to the internet, let alone all of my files. I ended up spending about four hours communicating with the banks and my family in Ireland as well as Jason trying to get things sorted. Ideally this would not have happened right now.

I went to the hotel bar. I needed a drink. I ran into a lady who was in a similar situation as me. She needed a drink. We got chatting and ended up staying up very late, drinking, smoking and chatting. It was just what I needed.

Hong Kong | What was going through my head

I was afraid. I never thought I would be saying it, but it's true. When left to face things alone, I wanted to run again, although this time I have no where, or no one to run to. It's almost like my unconscious mind was saying, yes, you have been in similar circumstances but you never learned what you needed to. This time I needed to learn that drinking or taking substances won't make things easier; figuring things out was what I needed to do, but I had to figure out what I needed to figure out first!

I couldn't make a decision and be happy with it. I was questioning everything. Hong Kong was where things really started to fall apart. I wasted precious time by not making decisions. I needed to make a choice regarding my house back in Ireland but anytime I thought about it I literally broke down, so I put that decision on hold. I wanted someone else to make that one for me. I wanted someone to come and rescue me from it all to be honest. I felt overwhelmed, tired, alone and I couldn't see how lucky I was to be on this trip. I couldn't see that I was ruining my own trip with my constant negative chat. I was on a massive downward spiral to negative town. Although this was just how I had programmed my mind. This is the only way that I knew to make sense of the world.

Depression was setting in and I was laying down the red carpet for it. There were no positive thoughts going through my head. It was all negativity, doom and gloom and I thought it wasn't fair that I had to deal with all of this, I just kept thinking, why is this happening to me? I was furious that I bought the house in Ireland at all, how had such a happy thing turned so sour for me. This always happened to me. SHIT! Shit always happened to me and I was getting tired of it. I was tired of having to be strong. I was tried of fighting. I was finding that I had no fight left in me. I didn't want to face a battle with the banks, with the real estate or anyone else for that matter. I didn't want to face life! I wanted someone to come and take me away. I wanted someone to tell me everything was going to be ok and mean it. I wanted someone else to make decisions for me. It was all too crippling for me to handle.

I was terrified to spend time alone. Every thought I had was convincing me that I was going to die. When I crossed the road I thought I would be run over by a bus or car. While walking down a street I thought that I would slip into sharp glass, even when there was none around. I was obsessed with all the different ways that I could die. I was catastrophizing everything. Even when I would have shower I would think of all the ways I could have slipped and bang my head, I would imagine the blood pouring from my head and down the drain.

I was overwhelmed, to say the least, by every single decision I had to make. What to have for breakfast was a life changing decision for me. I started to think about why making decisions was so hard for me. I was a strong independent woman, right? What was happening here? We are brought up being told what to do by our parents, our teachers, and our peers. Then we go into the workforce and are told what to do by our employers. To keep the peace in relationships we often let our partners tell us what to do. We tend to go about our lives being told what to do, where to go, what to say, when to say it, etc. We are even told what happiness should look like. This I find the most alarming. The shopping centre down the road from my house always has advertising promoting their centre which states 'find your happy' indicating that shopping there will make you happy. People believe this, people believe that happiness can come when you buy a pair of shoes. I believed this for so long. I believed what I was told. But here I am, not being told what to do, not being told what to say, and not being told how to be happy, and I was stuck. I didn't know what to do. When I was given the freedom to do what I wanted I had no idea what to do. Crazy, but true!

Some people were happy to go along through life with being told what to do. I thought that I was one of the people who didn't like being told what to do, but here I was wanting someone to tell me what to do. I did not want to take responsibility or accountability for myself, for,my life and definitely not for any decisions. My thoughts that I was a strong and confident woman were 100% wrong. I was completely the opposite. And this brought about an even bigger crash. I don't even know who the hell I am anymore. I was desperately seeking help, but not actually asking for it. I was feeling alone, isolated and in despair. Instead of going back home where I should have gone, I was stubborn and stayed travelling around in 'unsure world'.

I had spent my life moving countries and I hated it. I wanted stability, but I had gone and done this to myself. I made the decision to leave, I made the decision to travel. I decided to leave my home, to leave my job and to leave my boyfriend. It was me that was strong and made that decision, but now I have changed. This trip has changed me, and not for the better, which I was hoping that it would. I then I realised, I didn't know anything anymore.

I couldn't blame anyone for finding myself in this horrible place, but oh boy did I try. I wanted to blame my parents, my old boss, the chef where I used to work, my brother, the real estate agent, the banks, anyone who ever gave me bad news I thought had contributed to my depression. I thought that my life and what had happened to me in my past made me depressed. I was totally cool with that. I was totally cool being depressed as I thought that it was bound to happen considering what I had experienced. I remember a few years ago, being completely baffled by a friend of mine who had both her parents die at a young age yet she managed to do very well in life. She was never negative or bitter. I really could not understand how she could be so happy when she had experienced such misery. Goes to show how my mind was working back then. I associated pain with sorrow, which in many cases they do go hand in hand but in many other cases, when you open your eyes to it, pain can bring so much more than sorrow. I was a misery guts, a girl who knew such doom and gloom. I let it follow me, I actually brought it with me everywhere I went. I wanted people to feel sorry for me. I wanted people to know that I had a shit fucking life. The things that I experienced when I was a little girl no little girl should ever have to experience. I was bitter, not better. And no matter how many shrinks I saw, no matter how many happy pills I took, I couldn't get past my past. It was stuck to me like glue and I was happy for it to be who I am.

I was starting to see that I had lost myself, not in China or Hong Kong, but in life. I was starting to take my thoughts seriously. I could no longer tell the difference between a thought and reality. My own thoughts were sabotaging me and I couldn't tell what was happening. I had been here before, but I hadn't yet learnt the power of my mind.

Decision making was back to me and I had lost the ability to do so with confidence. Every thought that came into my head was a question and it was starting to drive me mad. My teeth grinding was back on super charged mode, my diet consisted mostly of coke, cigarettes, and chocolate. A health disaster was on the horizon. Maybe a change of country will help?

4

Vietnam

Arriving in Hanoi was hassle free, and seemed like any other border I have crossed, organised, secure and procedural. You have to get into a small line to go through customs, get your passport stamped and off you go to collect your bags. It was all very easy, and quite boring really. The only reason I am pointing it out now to due to the crazy borders that I cross later in the book, horrid, unorganised, stressful and far from boring! I have again arranged a hotel transfer, this time he was nowhere to be seen, I go back and check my emails to ensure I have actually done this before panic sets in. It's really late, there were not many taxi's left, and the ones who were left were trying to charge me triple what I paid for my transfer, and I was tired and hungry, not a good combination!

Eventually some guy appears from nowhere, how do they do that? He had my name on a sign and looked at me as though he had been waiting for me forever. Clearly he wasn't and he knew he was late but he hadn't a word of English so there was no point in me asking what happened. To the hotel please! The drive was much longer than I would have expected - almost two hours and once we got there I was so exhausted I almost want to cry. Naturally before I even check in I had to stop for a cigarette and a drink of coke. Then I finally got to sleep.

I was awakened early the next morning by a call to my room - its Lisa, the girl who was helping me via email to book my trips while in Hanoi. She told me that I have to transfer hotels and meet her to give her payment. I was supposed to have breakfast included in my room but I didn't even have time to shower. I literally had to get up and get downstairs immediately. I was quickly rushed off in a taxi, it was as though there was some undercover thing happening, no one could tell what was happening and I just had to keep following some random people that kept being pointed out to me. I was a tad confused but went with it, although my anxiety levels were pretty high. For all I know, I could be being kidnapped! Maybe a bit dramatic but hey, that was where my head was at. I was still tired, hungry and had no idea what was going on.

The other hotel was about a two minute drive down the road - I could have walked it in about five minutes. What was this taxi about? I was starting to get annoyed... Lisa runs out and pays for the taxi and explains that the hotel I stayed in last night was a sister hotel and that where I was now was actually the place where I should have stayed but they had no rooms left, which was fine, but once I was here I realise that this was far nicer than the previous place I get annoyed again because I feel that I'm being ripped off here! It didn't matter that I had somewhere to sleep, I just felt angry that I had been lied to in some sort of way. I didn't realise that in South East Asia this is standard, people dance around the truth or simply forget to tell it to you and then somehow you find out and feel a bit foolish...

Luckily Lisa feeds me, the breakfast in the new hotel was awesome - I literally can't stop eating, but then again it has been a while since I have had a proper meal. Once fed, I get the breakdown of what my itinerary was and how much it's going to cost. I also get told that I can have a room in this hotel for the day as my train leaves at 8pm so I can rest here, which was nice as usually you have to check out of a room by midday and I haven't paid for an extra night. It all feels very rushed though, and I am not sure why everyone always seems panicked? Apparently they are like this all of the time, and it is not panic, they just deal with speed, in everything they do!

Once all cash transactions have been completed and I have my itinerary along with a map of Hanoi and a full belly, it's time to shower then get moving and check this city out. I only have a day here so need to get moving. I had a look at the map I was given and decided to hit a couple of the main spots that I could walk to. First up was St Josephs Cathedral. I'm Catholic so I was drawn to this. Once I got there I was disappointed, while it's a beautiful building, you can't enter it and it looks much unloved. Moving on!

Next stop I decided to visit was the Hanoi women's museum. This has won trip advisor travellers choice award in 2013 so I figured it would be a good spot. Of course you begin on the first floor where you were brought through how women were raised in Vietnam, born – how they dress – how they were then trained to be a wife & mother – the wedding – the birth of their child – how they cook – etc. I initially was very annoyed at how they portrayed women - we were basically just born to serve men and have babies? I almost didn't want to go to the next floor, but I did and then you realise why the first floor was how it is.

There were five floors that go through three different areas – women in family, which the first floor was as explained above, obviously far more interesting than what I had first pictured. Women in history was the next two floors which showcases Vietnamese women from 1930-1954 then Southern and then Northern Women from 1954-1975, Unification, Vietnam's Heroic Mothers and Portraits of Contemporary Women. And then you have women's fashions, which I thought was fascinating! I took so many pictures of the pictures. They were so colourful and I want to just try everything on myself. It really made me want to go shopping.

I left the museum and started to wander around the shops. There were quite a number of locals that came over and tried to talk to me and offer directions etc. but I was warned when leaving my hotel to hold onto my handbag tightly as many people have had theirs stolen right off their shoulder. This made me feel a little hesitant to stop and chat to anyone. At this stage I was so hot and bothered, I just want to get back to the hotel. I had a room so I may as well use it.

I got back to the hotel, took a quick nap, showered, had dinner and got the call for pick up. We got to the train station 2.5 hours early for our train. We were told to wait here, and as usual given no other direction, or any clue as to where the guy had gone or what he was gone to do. As we had no idea what was going on we had to wait, you are left with no other choice. After about thirty minutes, a young guy came back and started shaking tickets in our faces, these tickets have our names on them, so people were going over and looking for their name. I found mine and in the process met an English guy who was also travelling solo so we started chatting.

The people who were on the pickup bus with me were worried that they would miss the train, even with 2 hours left until departure, they all started heading towards the train to board. The communication, or complete lack of, would cause you to be concerned. The English guy that I met seemed to know what was going on, or at least appeared confident that we would not miss our train, so I stuck with him. We went for a beer, over a beer we realised that he, Michael, who just left his job as a teacher in Thailand was moving to Kuala Lumpur to teach in the school I went to when I was 14! What were the chances?

Once we finally boarded the train I was two carriages away from my new mate, Michael, so I wandered down and found my bed for the night. I was sleeping with three French girls, one of who lives in Hanoi and speaks great English and her sisters, who were very young and don't speak much English. All of us were very relieved that we were not sharing our carriage with a smelly old man who was in the cabin next to us. I was amazed that the two young girls were only 16 & 18, and their sister was only 22. They were travelling around Vietnam, so young! Anyway, there isn't much conversation, well in English at least, so I got into my bed and tried to go to sleep. They soon got the message and do the same. Before you know it morning came and we were almost in Sapa.

On the bus on the way here, we were given a card that said, "When you disembark the train you must to go the person holding the hotel sign. He will be inside the train station. If you leave the train station and do not speak to this person then we were not responsible for what happens to you," right oh, I thought, that's reassuring. I will be making sure that I find Michael and follow him.

The train stopped, I walked towards the hotel sign, and they sent me to another bus. I turned to look for Michael and he was about to get onto another bus. I shouted over to him, asking who he was going with and it was lucky I did, as he wasn't paying any attention and just kept walking behind someone else, he was about to get on a bus to goodness knows where and with who?

We arrived at our hotel in Sapa, the Sapa summit hotel, that's the name of it and this place literally churns people through. You arrive, get told to move to the left, then move to the right, then hand over your passport, then wait outside, then you have to have breakfast as the room was not ready, the food was free as your ticket was all inclusive meals, but seeing you haven't showered they have set up large shower rooms where you can take numbers and shower before you then go on a hike and THEN when you get back from the hike you can get your bags and check into your room. OK!

I do as I was told, had breakfast, then had a shower, left my bag and ventured out into the rain to hike to I don't even know where, as no one has really explained what was going on. Any answers we got were in broken English and followed by a strange look, then whoever you were trying to talk to, walks away. I was utterly confused but so was everyone else who was in my group. I now had a totally new group, Michael was with another group and we now have about 50 people altogether but broken into smaller groups of five or six.

And we were off... heading down the twisty road in the rain and I have left my umbrella in my big bag in Hanoi so I was left with no other choice than to purchase a raincoat from the hotel which was a white plastic poncho. It has a very pointy hood, oversized and was so long, even for me that it's trailing on the ground. I looked hilarious but luckily I was not alone as many others have also forgot their umbrella and have purchased this horrid rain ponchos.

I wasn't exactly have the best time, trekking in the rain, with no one to talk to, I never in my life ever imagined that I would trek anywhere and here I am again trekking up a freaking mountain. What has happened to me? Where was the glamour? I needed some high heels and a day spa! When I looked up from my fury, through the rain, the view was pretty spectacular, the greens that you see were the same from the Longji rice terraces in China, the landscape was almost identical. We walked further into the hills and we soon have a group of older woman wanting to carry our bags.

This was all looking very familiar, they were dressed exactly the same as the women in China and when I question the guide he said they were from the same minority nationalities. There were several ethnic minority groups such as Hmong, Dao (Yao), Giay, Pho Lu, and Tay live, as well as by smaller numbers of Tày and Giay. These were the four main minority groups still present in Sapa district today.

Clearly this was an extremely touristy town as the place was just covered with foreigners and souvenir shops which was strange as I never heard of Sapa before actually coming to Vietnam. It was definitely worth the visit but I did hear later in the trip that there were more just as beautiful places, with far fewer tourists. We kept on wandering through the rain, down the mountain, through some extremely poor towns and villages to a waterfall. The beauty is breath-taking, but the poverty is very confronting. The waterfall is self is magnificent, this is where we were told to take a break. Within ten minutes we were then ushered into a small hall, again, no one had any idea what was happening but we just did as we were told. We sat on some tiny benches that seemed like they were made for dwarfs. Next of all there was dancers, but more like dancing umbrellas, it was strange and beautiful all at the same time. There was entertainment arranged for us, some local children performing their local dance. What a nice surprise. It went for about 30 minutes and then the trek back home began. The clouds opened up and the rain came pouring down just in time to walk us up a very steep hill. Needless to say the smile that I had on my face for the 30 minutes of dancing was wiped off now and nowhere to be seen!

Some of the others from the group rented motorbikes and went exploring. I really should have gone too, but I just felt so tired, and I am scared of motorbikes, my mother drilled it into me from an early age. I could feel myself starting to get super grumpy. Again, I missed out and I regret it now. I took the time to what I thought was 'recharge' but what it all boiled down to was I was scared people didn't like me.

The next day I was fresh, ready and excited for the next hike! Who am I kidding; I was trying to figure out a good reason to not do the hike. I was over hiking. I never liked it and have done more than enough to last me a lifetime over the past few weeks. I never imagined how much hiking I would be doing and in all honesty, hiking is not very glamorous, I preferred spa days... not hiking hills and getting covered in mud. I wasn't even losing lots of weight, but I must be grateful... or so I kept telling myself.

After breakfast we had to check out, they had to turn those rooms again. It was six AM breakfast, followed by seven AM get out of the room. Some people were furious with the quick turnaround. In fairness, what else would you expect? I couldn't stay in the room anymore. I either had to go on this trek or I would have to stay in the hotel lobby, with a book and nowhere to sit. I had no choice but to go.

It was really raining heavily, and I had to wear my stylish poncho or I would be soaked. The road we started on was easy, the guides kept telling us it was going to get hard. All I saw was the flat road so I started to think they were just trying to scare us. Then there came the turnoff. Oh my goodness, this pathway, if you could call it that, was literally a slide of mud! The very first step I took my foot slipped and I grabbed hold of the gate to save myself which luckily I did. There were people ahead of me that were just walking down this "path" with ease. Luckily, there were also people beside and behind me that were falling all over the place. And of course the local women who were leading us were wearing flip-flops and carrying babies on their backs while walking down. I was amazed, but also felt a bit foolish.

I literally made it five minutes down the path and wanted to cry. All of a sudden, as in true Asian style, some young kids came out from nowhere selling bamboo walking sticks. They were just cut straight from a tree but were steady enough to keep you up and I bought one of them. A young English guy also bought one. He, at this stage was covered in mud from head to toe and every time he fell I could not stop laughing, even though I knew it could be me any second. Shockingly, I didn't fall, thanks to my new best friend, the bamboo cane!

I had met two Dutch girls at the start of the trek but they seemed to have totally disappeared. I kept asking everyone where they went but no one knew, and everyone was just concentrating on just keeping vertical. When we did stop for breaks the group would thought the whole thing was hilarious, but when we were back on the trek and trying to walk down through these muddy paths, it was far from funny. I was pretty sure almost everyone fell, and most people were shocked by how clean I had ended up. Your shoes just get ruined but my bum was clean – I didn't fall. I was shocked myself, I think I was too grossed out to fall, so it played in my favour.

I eventually found the two Dutch girls, they got lost from the group and just keep walking until they found a place to rest, which ended up being where we all had lunch. I was incredibly glad that I was on such a time restraint and had to head back to Hanoi tonight, the rest of the group were going to do a home stay that night in the mountains. Ha-ha, no way could I have done a home stay if it was anything like China the way I was feeling - It was probably the smelliest, wettest, dirtiest part of my trip so far and when I finally made it back to the hotel that shower was one of the best I have ever had.

Halong Bay

Back on the overnight train to Hanoi. I got into Hanoi about 5 am and it was dark and raining. I went straight out to get a taxi and was looking for the reputable names. I had been warned that they will do everything to rip off tourists. I found a guy who was pleased to have a meter running so I got in the car with him and told him where to go. We were literally two minutes down the road and I noticed the fare was already five times what it should be - the meter must be dodgy!

I started yelling at the guy and demanded he let me out, and, of course, he wants some sort of payment but he knows I know he was in the wrong so I just give him a small payment so he won't do anything to me or my bags. I got out of the taxi, its pitch dark, raining and I have no idea where I am. I started to walk and found another taxi but there were no available taxis as the train had come in and filled all of them. I walked for about 20 minutes and was getting really scared. I just wanted to call home to at least have someone to talk to, but I needed to focus, so I just kept walking until I eventually found another taxi to take me to the hotel.

Why did I want to call home? I always did that. The slightest bit of 'drama' and I would be on the phone to my friends or family looking for sympathy from them. As I mentioned earlier in the book, this is how I got attention from my mother, and this is how my mother got attention too! Dramatising things, everything! When I find myself in 'situations' I love to call a friend... I want them to feel sorry for me, or to worry about me. When I have someone worrying about me, at least I know they care. This is something that I have only recently figured out though. At the time I wanted someone's support. The fact was though, I didn't even have a free hand to call, and the last thing I needed was for someone to steal the phone right out of my hand.

When I finally got to the hotel, the door was locked and the security team were asleep on the floor. This is common practice, so I just knocked on the door as they knew me already - they even made me coffee as breakfast wasn't going yet. Three hours later and I was on a bus going to Halong bay. It's a six hour bus ride I found out - good lord, I just want to sleep but of course with my luck, there were three young kids and a baby on the bus - not one single traveller, all families. This should be fun!

I was excited to see Halong Bay as I have heard so much about it, and the pictures on the internet looked amazing. I spent a bit more on the boat that I was going to stay on so that it would make the experience all the better, or so I thought. When you get to Halong Bay the number of boats in the water was actually astounding – all of the boats have to be painted white as per government regulation. It had something to do with the number of accidents there were due to the sheer number of boats.

The boat that I paid extra for was a huge disappointment; it looked absolutely nothing like the website. It was an old, run down, smelly junk boat, that is what they are called, junk boats, makes sense in this regard. I don't eat much seafood, so when I was asked on the bus if I did, I said no so they had prior warning. This then meant that I got to eat cold rice for breakfast, lunch and dinner, sometimes with a bit of pineapple thrown in. I was pretty furious, I do not deal with hunger well at all. The food was included in the trip price but drinks were not, this is where they made their money, the drinks were an absolute robbery! Electricity on the boat was only turned on at night, so if you wanted to escape to the air conditioner at any time, you couldn't.

At one stage a local lady came to the back of the boat on her small canoe and I bought beer form her - you can get it much cheaper, but you have to be sly and not let the crew see you as they would get annoyed. After dinner I sat at the back of the boat trying to fish, there was nothing else to do. I was in need of some more alone time. I was using this time to write in my journal, I was also using a lot of my 'alone time' for playing games on my smart phone. I constantly had my phone on me so I could play 'fling' or 'candy crush'. I look back now and think, really, Jessica, you were terrible. You had such beauty all around you and all you wanted to do was look at a stupid game on your smart phone? Not smart!

Vietnam | What was going through my head

With regard to Vietnam, I didn't actually enjoy it nearly as much as I thought I would have. I had planned to spend the most part of my trip there and travel down the coast, but I wasn't in love at all with Vietnam. I enjoyed myself, but not to an extent that I would return. Sometimes we can make things appear a certain way in our heads without even seeing them. We can idolise them, or we can tear them down; we really can do anything. Our brain and our imagination are incredibly powerful!

There were thousands of people, tourists, in Hanoi, Sapa and Halong Bay. I could have at any time made an effort and gone to hang out with these people. Instead I chose to sit alone in my room. I had reached the pinnacle with my sadness, I was now blaming cities for my depression and not recognising that it was all happening in my head. I was annoyed by everything, shopping, people, streets. I would literally burst into tears over spilt milk!

I missed out on seeing things, missed out on meeting new people, making new friends, hearing about experiences and learning from what others have done. I was beginning to let the voices in my head take control and they were telling me that I wasn't fun!

I was freaking out about the money I was spending, even though I was sticking to a tight budget. I was worried about my house back in Ireland and what I needed to do with it. Should I sell it, should I not? I was worried about leaving Jason – will he stand by me? Why wasn't I going out and making the most of this trip? I felt sad most of the time, and even though I was getting to see so much, I wasn't really enjoying the experience. I wasn't having fun. I was wishing the whole time that Jason had come with me. I was missing my friends. I was questioning everything. I felt tired all of the time. I wasn't eating properly. I wasn't sleeping properly. I was beginning to not even feel safe. I was so angry and felt ripped off by everyone. I really needed to see my mate and was looking forward to giving Rebecca a hug.

I was putting my hopes and happiness onto someone else. I thought that once I saw Rebecca I would feel better. I thought that time alone just didn't suit me and that one I had someone to share it with I would be better. I was in complete denial that my head was calling all the shots and it was on a downward spiral. I began reflecting back on my childhood, I always thought that my childhood didn't really impact my life, but I had very little memory of it. If I couldn't remember it, how could I know that it didn't affect me?

What I do remember is that my childhood was chaotic, both my parents drank heavily; there was a lot of abuse, both physically and mentally. I think I block out most of what happened as my mind is trying to protect me. Your unconscious mind is very powerful and it can make beliefs that you will hold for life through a simple comment. Drinking heavily was very prominent in my life; hence why I ended up doing it. It was normal to me. The constant yelling that surrounded my childhood made me so afraid of confrontation. The neglect in my youth led me to work hard to try and gain any sort of attention in any way I thought possible. Good or bad, I wanted it, or my unconscious did anyway.

I had grown up in such a negative environment and I couldn't figure out to see the light. My parents split when I was very young but I do recall the fights, they were pretty full on. We had the police come around quite a number of times. My mother did the best job that she knew how to, but she drank so much that her judgement was not the best. I don't want to go too far into my childhood, as I said. So I'll cut it off there.

I really had not learnt any valuable lessons from my trip. All I knew was that I was miserable. I was not having fun, but I was too stubborn to go home. I still had so much more pain, heartache, denial, and shame to experience before I hit rock bottom. The way I felt in Vietnam I thought was pretty near the bottom, but little did I know, that I had so much further to fall. I had no idea that my trip would end up in my suicide attempt. I had no idea how easy it was for me to fall. I had no idea how easy it is for anyone to fall, to fall into a deep, dark depression. A depression where you feel like the best, and only way to move forward, is to end your life.

I think my mother tried to end her own life, on many occasions I might ad. I have been told, but I have no specific details. Maybe that is where I got it from. The depression. It can be hereditary you know. For me it felt that I was the only one out of my brothers and sisters who suffered so badly. I was the only one who had life pauses. Who had to stop working because I was just too sad to do anything. This is what I was thinking about. I spent so much time in Vietnam thinking about depression. I was thinking about being sad. I was bringing it all to me by attracting it with my thoughts and energy. I had no energy because I gave it all to me depressing thoughts. I was obsessing over depression. I was obsessing over everything.

I was 24 when I had my last breakdown. I could feel my world collapsing, not literally, but I knew that someone was wrong. I had just broken up with my boyfriend, whose mother had just died. The fact that I got to watch her die and not watch my own mother die upset me. It upset me that he got to be by his mothers side during her pain, while my mother suffered alone. Obviously the fact that she died upset me too. The break-up was the icing on the cake. I couldn't eat, sleep or make sense of anything. My anxiety was causing me to shake uncontrollably. I self-harmed. I found myself in my bedroom bashing my head with my hairdryer. My head was bleeding and I had a pounding headache, I have no idea how long I was doing this for but I had a hell of a lump on my head. This was when I called my sister. I don't think I even said any words. I was inconsolable on the end of the phone. She knew immediately something was wrong and drove 2 hours to be by my side. She literally came in, took one look at me and bundled me up into her car and back to her house 2 hours away. She minded me, she took me to the doctor. She didn't force me to eat, because I just couldn't stomach anything.

I always considered myself a strong human. I considered myself tough, but that really shook me, it made me realise that I can actually break, and that life will keep throwing shit at you until you STOP. I needed to stop, I needed to slow down, I couldn't keep up at the pace I was going. Partying hard, working 2 jobs, at the time I was trying to maintain a long distance relationship which didn't work out. I was trying to pretend everything was ok, after all that is what I have done for most of my life, I have pretended that I was fine, that I could take it, whatever life threw at me. But that time I couldn't. That time the damage was too severe. My wounds were weeping, my whole life was catching up on me and my mind was collapsing. It took weeks before

I started to talk to anyone and months before I felt "normal" again. I thought that was my lowest point. I didn't think I could get lower than that time when I was 24. Little did I know that I could find myself in an even more fucked up situation.

Back to Hong Kong… I must have made my mind up, and then changed it again a millions times about my house back home. I called my brother a hundred times to ask him his opinion, which he gave me but it didn't help. I was desperate for someone else to make the decision for me, but when they gave me their sound advice I would ignore it. I knew that I had my own intuition, it was still there, I just couldn't feel what it was telling me to do. Even though deep down I knew what to do. I was back and forth on what to do so many times I actually feel sick now just thinking about it.

5

Laos

Next on the itinerary was another flight - this time it was on a very small plane, by far the smallest I have ever been on. When checking in for my flight in Hanoi they asked if I had a forwarding flight from Luang Prabang or even from Laos, which I didn't as I was planning on making my way through by land and continuing on to Thailand. Apparently you need to prove an onward journey in order to get a visa on arrival in Laos. I never knew this, and so my bags were pulled from the desk and I was handed back my passport with no boarding pass.

I was asked where my ticket out of Laos was about 15 times, even though I kept explaining to them I was travelling by land, it went back & forth with the same story. I didn't have a ticket, so the stress was starting to set in and I didn't know what to do. Eventually the manager told me to go over to their flight sales counter. I thought I was just going to have to buy a ticket just so I could get a visa, but she instructed the woman to give me a fake ticket. "Fabulous service," I thought, now I hope this will work!

As soon as I got off the plane I literally ran through to passport control and started filling out the appropriate forms. Rebecca was waiting for me outside since she landed over 4 hours ago, so it was important to get through fast. I filled out the forms, went to the counter but then realised that on the plane I was given an entry card for Cambodia. Why on earth they gave me the wrong entry card I have no idea. I had to run back and fill out an entry card for Laos. They never asked about any forwarding journey so I never had to show them my fake ticket. I grabbed my bags and headed for the arrival hall. It was a huge relief to know that I was through and I was going to see Rebecca, I just couldn't wait.

The 'arrival hall' was tiny, the airport was tiny, and poor Rebecca had waited four hours for me after getting off a long haul flight from Dublin, bless her, she was a sweetheart! We had booked an airport transfer as knew not to try taking a taxi, the ride to the hotel ended up being about five minutes done the road. Seeing Rebecca was such a highlight, just seeing her face was so good, I was thrilled to bits.

We spent the next few hours just catching up on life in general, I showed her all of my pictures from the trip so far. I couldn't believe that I was sitting next to my best friend since I was 4 years old in Laos. I felt that I had been through so much in the past few weeks, but now felt so relieved to have Rebecca by my side. I felt exhausted and so did she, although I had done nothing in comparison to Rebecca. My flight was super short, she had travelled thousands of miles. She also needed some time to adjust to the intense heat - this was something that she was definitely not used to.

We didn't know where to start in Luang Prabang so just hit the streets with no idea of where to go, with Rebecca I was excited, if I was alone, I would have been afraid. We headed into the 'town' if you could call it that and saw lots of temples which we wanted to check out. We went to Mount Phou si, which was up a 100m high hill, which consisted of 100m high steps. We got to the top and nearly collapsed, but once we caught our breath it was definitely worth the trip.

By the time we got back down the hill we were parched and starving so headed for some wine and dinner. Oh wine, I do love thee. Habing a glass of wine and a catch up with a friend was like winning the lottery. I was so happy to be sitting here, with my best friend, drinking wine and having a good time. After dinner we wandered through the night markets. You can't miss them when staying in Luang Prabang, they are just fantastic and an absolute must do. Everything is handmade - so authentic, so beautiful and there are just so many colours, so many things to buy, so many adorable things that you simply can't live without. The stalls seem to go on forever, I got so caught up in the moment, and was in awe of the bargaining, the traders, the children, the sheer number of items for sale. I wanted to buy everything!

After our shopping excursion we went into a tour office and made some decisions on what to do for the next few days. We booked a trip for the next day as I had read about the Pak O Caves and Kuangsi Park Waterfalls, so when we saw a trip for both we just booked it. The 2.5 hour boat ride, well it's more of a tiny tin boat with some wooden planks that you can sit on and a make shift roof made out of different plastic containers, was not the most comfortable, but it definitely made us laugh. The traditional Mekong river slow boats are how many people, even tourists, travel for much longer than our 2.5 hour trip. Keep in mind we also had to return, so that was another 1.5 hours. It's much faster going back with the tide. So all in all, a 4 hour trip in a tin boat, in a very dirty river, but with some seriously beautiful sights to be seen. Just getting into the boat was traumatic, we had to jump across from the mainland to some sort of floating thing, then grab hold the tin roof of the boat, which obviously is not a stable thing to grab hold of. Then you have to somehow manoeuvre your tall body into the tiny boat with a roof. If I made it sound easy, it wasn't! The first stop was to a tiny village where we were told to get off so we could buy from the locals. We went to use the toilet, which was the smelliest, dirtiest toilet I have seen so far go. We got harassed and told we had to pay to use it, all whist being offered some free scorpion whiskey to try. I turned down the scorpion whiskey and also ignored the request to pay for the toilet use, Rebecca ended up paying for us both without me knowing. We walked through the town, it was so poverty stricken, it was actually very confronting. Rebecca and I rushed through as we wanted to get back to our tin boat ASAP. After another 30 minutes on the boat we got to the PakOCaves. It was then the disappointment hit.

The caves were noted for their miniature Buddha sculptures. Hundreds of very small and mostly damaged wooden Buddhist figures were laid out over the wall shelves and you can see this from the river. It really was nothing special and definitely not worth a 2.5 trip up the river to see. As usual there were a lot of steps to get to another part of the caves where you could walk inside but only slightly, it was very slippery and dangerous so we only went in as far as we could see before turning back around to go back down the hundreds of steps we had just climbed. The highlight was really the actual river cruise in the tin boat, so if anyone ever asks you if you want to go and see the PakOCaves, politely decline.

The trip back was so much faster as we were going with the river. We hit the mainland and went straight back to our tour office for the second part of the trip. No time for lunch once as we were headed to the Kuangsi waterfall. I wasn't expecting much after this morning's trip. The drive to the falls was a very bumpy and windy one, I was almost going to throw up at many stages but I talked myself out of it. Besides, I had nothing in my stomach to puke!

When we got to the falls I was blown away by the beauty of the place. The waterfalls had a walkway through a forest which looked like an enchanted forest, I honestly thought I would see fairies pop up. There were so many lagoons that made you want to dive right into each and every one, the blue colour of the water was something that I thought you only saw in the movies. At the end of the walkway that was covered in lagoons and fairy like rain forests was the big waterfall with a three tiered 200m drop – such spectacular sight.

We saw a walkway to the top of the waterfall and decided that we could give it a go. The walkway turned out to be not much of a walkway, more like a vertical hike uphill on slippery, muddy terrain. We started to go up, but after 10 minutes I decided I didn't like the thought of having 15 heart attacks. I had been through enough of them in Sapa, so we turned back and headed for our favourite pool which we picked while walking to the waterfall to take a dip! Oh so refreshing! It was so good, I wanted to stay all day but we had to get back to the bus to get back home. We were so in love with Luang Prabang - our hotel was so pretty, the village was incredibly quaint, the people were lovely, the markets were divine and the food was delicious. We figured if all of Laos is like this, we will never want to leave, we couldn't wait to go and check out some more of this amazing country so we could compare.

We planned another day in Luang Prabang to just relax and do the girlie stuff, like have our nails done, get massages, drink wine, etc. On our last day in Luang Prabang just before we caught the bus to our next stop we decided to go elephant riding. I have always wanted to do it, so figured why not now. We went to the tour office and were shown to a tuktuk (a form of transport, pretty much a motorbike with more seats and a roof). We were told to go with our driver to wherever we were going, this was standard for trips around Asia, you have no idea where you were going, or how long it would take, but you need to trust the stranger that was taking you into his tuktuk and hope for the best.

After about an hour we got to a river and were told to get into another tin boat, which we did. There was literally no one around, the only people that were here were our tuktuk driver and boat driver, we were a little freaked out. It felt like we were in the middle of nowhere with two strange men and we were not feeling confident. The tin boat had no roof this time, and I saw a dead scorpion on the floor, I was shitting myself, but I didn't dare say anything to Rebecca as I didn't want her to panic too. I figured it was dead anyway, so it couldn't hurt us.

Soon we crossed the river to a small park where we saw lots of people so our fears disappeared. We got straight onto our elephant and brought through the jungle. I have always wanted to ride an elephant but now that it was actually happening the guilt was setting in big time, I wanted to get down off the poor things back and just feed him bananas. But it's too late, we were walking through the jungle and even though I was the one who insisted on doing this, Rebecca was the one who was calming me down. Panic set in on top of the guilt, and then the elephant was instructed to go down a ramp into a lagoon, this was when the terror set in. Here we are, sitting on an elephants back, wading through water.

We got off the elephant and bought him all of the bananas in the shop, then stood there feeding him until he couldn't eat anymore. There was a small lagoon where you could go and wash off the elephant smell, we did have a big bus trip ahead of us so we wanted to feel a little fresh. Elephant small is intense, and not so easy to wash off you after you have been sprayed by them. We didn't have long before we needed to go back on the scorpion tin boat so it was a quick dip, some happy snaps and we were back on the river crossing.

Van Vieng

On we went for our five hour bus trip across the worst roads I have ever been on. I have never experienced travel sickness before, ever, but the roads in Laos were so bumpy and windy that your stomach had no other option than to be mad at you. It was quite hilarious, the roads that we were travelling on from Luang Prabang to Vang Vieng were still being built, as in they were under construction. In any western country the roads would have been closed off, but not here. Our van literally drove around the workmen building the road, the gravel may have been laid, but there was no tarmac on top, which of course doesn't help the bumpiness. We drove up hill until we were literally in the clouds, our ears popped and we couldn't see 10 feet in front of us from the fog. Again, if this were in a western country we would not be driving at the speed our bus driver was going. It all started to get too much for me, and I needed to sleep. Luckily my travel sick tablet helped me doze off easily enough.

We arrived in Vang Vieng (VV) a little earlier than planned and looked around for a tuktuk that would take us to our hotel. We agreed on a price and off we set only to again realise that the journey did not qualify transport. We could have walked it easily but the price had been agreed to so you have to dish it over. Seriously, there is no one here that give you a honest answer. At this stage we just had to laugh.

The hotel looked nothing like the website, NOTHING! We were already annoyed before we even got to the tiny room that was no way meant for two. Naturally after the strenuous bus trip and the hotel being far from our expectations, we decided to turn to alcohol. I had barely been drinking the entire trip so decided to give it a go under the circumstances. A few drinks did ease the pain I must admit, not that I was turning to alcohol for support, it just felt good, and tasted good too! After drinking we were so exhausted we went to bed.

On day two in VV we walked through the town to see precisely how big it was - that took us all of five minutes, so we turned around and headed back to the visitor centre to find out the top things to do. We were thinking we should hire a moped to get around to see the sights - we heard that the Blue Lagoon was a must, so we asked about that. The guy at the visitor centre gave us a map and told us NOT to get a moped as they were very dangerous, so we opted for push bikes instead, which I thought was a good idea at the time. Off we went with our map on our little push bikes. We were told which road to initially take and we kept on that road looking for a sign to turn where the Blue Lagoon was.

After a while we realised we must have missed the sign, so we stopped at a petrol station in the middle of nowhere and asked for directions, they had no idea what we were talking about, so we figured we must have been far from where we needed to be. We turned around to go back towards where we came from and whilst on route saw a sign for a cave, so we headed in. The road to the cave was not very push bike friendly, the pot holes were so bad that we had to get off our bikes and walk. We walked up the 200 steps to the cave where we were delighted to get inside and out of the heat. The cave was cool, Tham Chang, it was called - the floors were all so wet and slippery so we had to be careful. There was a spot where you could go take a look out of the cave and it had the most spectacular view over the countryside.

Most of the cave was closed off as it was just too dangerous and slippery, so we headed back down the steps and back to our bikes – we really needed to find the Blue Lagoon and get in for a refreshing swim. We headed back towards VV and eventually found a sign pointing to go over a bridge towards the Blue Lagoon, hooray! We went over the bridge and onto more dreadful roads on our pushbikes. This time we didn't get off and kept on pushing through until we saw another sign for the Blue Lagoon. We were determined to find this place, very determined.

After about 45 minutes we finally got to the end of the road and got off our bikes, out of nowhere a little man came over and told us we would have to pay for him to take us to the Blue Lagoon. We had got this far alone, albeit it the long way, so we decided to keep on going solo, we figured it couldn't be that far from where we were. We asked him to point us in the direction of the Blue Lagoon and he did, it was into a stream and he told us to keep walking up the stream. We still had to pay him a fee to go there but nothing had been easy, or free so far, so we thought this was standard.

The stream had such a strong current, it was very deceiving! We lost our flip flops a couple of times so we tried walking without the flip flops, but it was too painful, the stream was full of rocks and stones that were cutting our feet so we had to keep them on. The water was very cool, it was refreshing and we were happy to be doing something totally different. That was until we hit the 20 minute mark and we still couldn't see anything: no signs, no people. Where were we going? And again, out of nowhere the guy who took our money at the beginning popped up and said he would show us the way - great we thought. It took another 20 minutes before he stopped and pointed "in here." We would never had found the 'entrance' to what we thought was the Blue Lagoon as it was literally a step into the bushes similar to what we were walking by the whole time!

As soon as we stepped in I got stung by something, the pain was intense, naturally I started freaking out and looking for the thing that got me but I couldn't see anything. I thought it was a spider bite, a big red rash appeared immediately and I thought that I was going to die. Thank goodness we had the guide with us at this stage as he took a look and told me not to worry. Within seconds the pain started to subside, if he had not been there I probably would have assumed myself dead!

After I got over the shock of my bite, or whatever it was, I was getting excited to finally see the Blue Lagoon. We saw three guys come out of a cave and they were covered in mud. Our tour guide said "this way" and pointed to where they just came out of, I'm thinking WHOA! I stopped for a moment and said "is this the way to the Blue Lagoon" and the three guys said to us, "we thought it was too, but that's not the blue lagoon in there." It was a cave that you have to crawl through; hence they were covered in bat poo. And all you do is see the inside of a dark cave. That was enough for me to decide not to go in, but Rebecca wanted to go on, and so I stayed behind to watch the bags.

I had seen enough caves to last me a lifetime and I wasn't too keen on crawling through bat poo. I mean, who would be? I really want to go back home, to Sydney where we don't have to hike or climb through bat shit, where we have decent roads, and taxis, and white wine – luckily before I could really start feeling sorry for myself Rebecca and the guide came back, thank you God! The hike back down stream this time was easier and at least we knew where we were headed. Once we got back to our bikes we were hungry, angry, sunburnt, tired and still no bloody

Blue Lagoon. So we got on our bikes and cycled like the wind back to the hotel. We didn't even notice any pot holes this time as we were so focused on food and a shower.

Once we had eaten and showered we thought, ok, let's actually go somewhere else on our list. We gave up completely on the Blue Lagoon. We hired a tuktuk - no way were we getting back on those bikes. We headed to Kaeng Nyui waterfall; it was about an hour in a tuktuk but we heard that it was a beautiful sight that must be done, plus it wasn't like we had much else to do in this town. We were so excited about finally having a swim but once we got there we were surprised to see that there was another hike to the waterfall. I say surprised, but really we weren't that surprised after the day we were having. We put on our big girl pants and just did it, knowing that in the end it would be worth it all, so we set our hearts on the refreshing swim we would finally have today in a magnificent waterfall. This walk wasn't so pleasant, the path was steep and slippery and we were starting to lose faith about being able to swim in this waterfall. When we eventually got to the waterfall... drum roll please - we can't swim! No one else was around, you can't get anywhere near the actual waterfall. We just wanted to cry, but instead we both looked at each other and cracked out laughing! Back to the hotel, a strong drink was needed, and we toasted the end to a very long day.

The next day we woke up and poor Rebecca's shoulders were burnt to a crisp! They literally had blisters, so she was out for the day - no way can we let her in the sun. We were pretty annoyed with VV anyhow, so we just hung out and chilled watching moves etc. I did consider trying tubing out, it's quite a talked about tourist attraction, but I didn't fancy it solo. Tubing in VV has changed dramatically since it began years ago due to the fact that so many foreigners were dying! Apparently you got a tube and would head down the Mekong River to all sorts of pubs that fill you full of drink until you can't see anymore - very popular with the younger generation. My little sister had told me about it actually. I didn't go in the end, and I was thankful when we later on saw some of the guys coming back and they were so drunk, it was gross.

We spent the day trying to plan out the rest of the trip. Where would Rebecca and I go? Where would I bring Molly? There were too many choices and it's actually tough to decide what to do. My trick for checking out what a place was like was Google pictures. I was told to go to Pattaya in Thailand with Molly, but as soon as I typed that into Google images I saw, well, try it yourself and see. It is not where you should bring a 16 year old.

I was dying to get to the beach and I really wanted to chill out by the sea for a few days, so a beach stop was a must. I had already been to Phuket a few times when I was younger so didn't want to go back there. I did want to see Koh Phi Phi but that would involve a flight. As I had already paid for Molly's return flight from Dublin to Bangkok, I didn't want to have to fork out more, I knew she wouldn't have been able to afford the flight herself so I needed another option.

Rebecca and I ventured out into the tiny town of VV to try and entertain ourselves. We went and had lunch in one of the backpacker places where they have reruns of the TV show *Friends* playing all day long. We sat on one of the beds and enjoyed a few episodes. We found a cute little jewellery store and bought lots of nice pieces. As we were walking out of the store, Rebecca started screaming, I looked over to see that a gecko had literally fallen from the sky onto her shoulder. I couldn't stop laughing, things like this always seen to happen to her. I have never seen a gecko fall from the sky ever before, she should count herself very lucky! We got an early night's sleep as we were off again tomorrow to the big city, the capital of Laos, Vientiane.

Vientiane

The bus to Vientiane was four hours, and my travel sickness was in full force on the trip, the only thing that made me feel better was the other people who were on the bus with us that were literally green with sickness. They were so hung-over, one of the girls were in tears. I guess it was a little sadistic but I felt better knowing they felt worse than me!

Once we got to the hotel and showered, we went to try and find somewhere to eat. We walked down the road about five minutes and it started pouring down rain. We were soaked to the bone within seconds - this was a super tropical downpour! Laos was turning us against it pretty rapidly. It was a shame we started out so well in Luang Prabang, we thought that we would love the rest of the country.

As we were soaked and still no sign of a restaurant we flagged down a tuktuk and asked him to bring us to somewhere we can eat. He took us back past our hotel and to the area where we found plenty of restaurants. We just ran into the closest one, nothing fancy, in fact it was a hotel lobby that served greasy chips and soggy sandwiches, it was going to have to do. We had no choice but to stay put until the rain cleared. Once it stopped the roads were completely flooded, it looked more like a selection of swimming polls than any sort of road. You would think somewhere that experienced such tropical downpours would be prepared for heavy rainfall! Clearly it was not.

The next day we needed to go and get my visa for Thailand. I needed a visa as I had no proof of exit from Thailand just yet. Rebecca had her ticket back to Dublin from Bangkok so she didn't need one. Once we got there the cue was huge, I got my ticket and waited in line but then realised you had to have the exact amount of cash in Thai baht, I hadn't gotten any baht yet so started to panic, luckily a lovely Dutch guy swapped me some baht for some local currency. I handed over my passport and was told to come back the next day, easy!

We jumped into our private tour bus and headed to the Buddha Park which was miles out of the city but I thought was definitely worth the trip. We stopped for lunch in a very local restaurant where no one could speak English. Everyone was starring at us thinking we were lost. We tried the speciality (as we had no choice) noodle soup – they serve you a huge amount of fresh vegetables, sprouts and herbs and throw it into the soup. The chicken was in balls and you can't really be sure its chicken. But once you fill the bowl with a LOT of spices and sauces it tastes good.

Next, onto the temple run - we saw six different temples and I really couldn't tell you the names of them all, pretty bad I know, but my interest in temples was starting to fade. I had been seeing quite a lot of them on my travels and I still had no more idea of the Buddhist religion so I started to feel bad just traipsing through all of these temples as a tourist. We did see the Great Sacred Stupa, Pra That Laung, HoPhra Keo, which was so old and fascinating, including Patuxai, Wat si Sacket and the national museum of Laos - this was where I started to lose interest. I was over my sightseeing for the day and wanted eat!

Our driver took us to Chinatown, Laos style - wow, nothing like any other Chinatown I had ever seen. It was a big mall, selling heaps of crap really -terrible fake designer handbags, gaudy bedspreads and curtains, clothes I wouldn't put my worst enemy in, and various other knickknacks. Needless to say we didn't buy a thing and didn't stay very long either. We were being followed the whole way around the mall, we felt very uncomfortable - clearly they didn't like tourists here and didn't trust them either! We got out of there quickly and headed back to the safety of touristville. Next, we tried to score some bus tickets to Chiangmai, Thailand.

We walked into a tour office and asked for the ticket on the VIP bus, which basically was a sleeper bus. It's a 10 hour journey so we wanted to be able to sleep. NOPE - all of the buses were full, so we asked about flights. The only flights were first thing the next morning but I had to collect my passport so we couldn't make them, we really did not want to stay another day here so we walked out and decided to try other tour agents, they were all the same, bus full! Eventually we found an agent who had a small minivan that could bring us. It left at 4 pm the next day and took 15 hours to get to Chiang Mai – we booked it and went and bought some tamazepan to help us sleep through it. We found out this was easy to just buy over the counter and was only $5 for 10 pills. Wow!

The next day we got to the embassy very early, luckily, as the cue gets very big. I got my passport and headed back to the hotel to eat before our mammoth 15 hour bus journey. The bus came to the hotel to pick us up and Rebecca and I settle in and make ourselves comfortable as we were going be here for 15 hours, right? WRONG!

We were on the bus an hour when we arrived at a train station and got told to get out of the bus. Our bags were handed to us and we stood there very confused. I asked the driver what was happening and showed him our ticket to Chiang Mai. He handed me his phone and someone was on the other end telling me to get on the train to cross the border. After this we would get picked up on the other side by someone else. We were so confused. We were under the impression that we were going to be sitting in a mini bus for 14 hours...it was unreal! We had no clue that this was going to happen - why didn't they tell us this when we bought the ticket? We had no choice but to get on the train. But before we did, we had to pay an EXIT fee for Laos. Where on earth do you have to pay a bloody fee to exit the country? Another surprise. We paid it and swore we would not be returning.

Again we settled in our seats ibn the train this time not knowing how long this journey would be. It's about five minutes in total. We couldn't believe it, we got off the train in Thailand and passed through customs. When we got outside to try and find the someone who was there to pick us up, there was no one there. We wandered up and down for 20 minutes with no one there to tell us what to do. I got really angry! I called the number on our ticket to try and find out what was happening but no one spoke English. I called back again and asked for someone who spoke English but this time they hung up on me, GRRRRR!

After a further 20 minutes of pacing, an old guy walked over and asked me if I was looking for the bus to Chiang Mai. Finally! Off we went in another van to be brought to a shop where we were told to get out and wait an hour. Then we would get onto the bus that would bring us to Chiang Mai. Well, at least now we know what was happening and can go and got a coffee at the 7-eleven down the road.

Being in Thailand was so different to Laos. It was such civilisation in comparison. Even though we were in the middle of nowhere in Thailand, they had road markings, traffic lights and even a 7-eleven! Very different from Laos and what we had just come from.

Lao | What was going through my head

The roads really are really that bad! I read about them, but didn't believe it. Stay longer in Luang Prabang, its beautiful, I wish we could go back. Don't stay longer than a day in Vientiane (even though you could easily buy prescription drugs over the counter). Laos's food isn't the best. The people are beautiful, so stunning, so kind.

I was starting to rely heavily on medication to sleep. I wasn't eating properly, so much junk food and little to no fruit and vegetables. This combination is not good for the mind, body or soul. My body was taking a bit of a beating. With hiking for hours a day, as well as not feeding myself any nutrition and not sleeping properly I was starting to get seriously run down.

I am worrying over money when I shouldn't have been, again. I began, again, a Jessica conference in my head about my spending and how I need to track and curb it. I haven't even been spending much and have been super careful - must stop this mindless chatter! STOP! Worrying was fast becoming my one and only thought process. Oh worry, doubt and panic, which I guess are all very similar. I would worry about the most ridiculous things. I was wasting my time, my life worrying about things that I had absolutely no control over. I had no idea that my worrying and energy that I was putting towards my worrying was in fact attracting what I didn't want to happen into my life. I was obsessed with what could happen, instead of enjoying what was happening.

I kept focusing on what I didn't have, instead of focusing on what a wonderful trip I was on. I was thinking about what I shouldn't do, far more than what I should do. I would be checking my Facebook feed and seeing my friends enjoying themselves and wishing that it was me who was enjoying myself. I was only focusing on external things, people and places. I was obsessing over what others were doing, I was wanting to know Jason's every move. I couldn't be bothered to live my own life, I wanted to live someone else's.

Even though I had my best friend by my side, I was sad. I was sad about everything. I felt overwhelmed with every decision that I needed to make. I began to think that Rebecca hated me because I wasn't happy.

The voices in my head were totally in charge and I was fighting hard to keep them at bay – it wasn't working.

I felt that the trip was turning into a bit of a nightmare and I just wanted to go home, but then when I thought about going home I would also freak out. I didn't want to go back and face reality, but I couldn't face the reality that I was in either. The texts and calls from my friends back in Sydney were getting fewer and fewer and I thought that they had all had enough of me.

My patience was wearing very thin and I was getting angry at anyone who was coming across our path, no matter what they had to say. I was beginning to blame my frustrations on Rebecca - anything that I got upset about I would keep telling myself, 'it would be different if Molly was here'. Here I was blaming others for my grievances, again, something I appeared to do often but had never realised before.

I grew up thinking that everyone had it easier than I did. I never enjoyed having sleep overs when I was younger because I hated to sit and watch my friends families be happy together. I was so jealous. I couldn't stand it. I would always try to sleep over but in the end make some excuse and call my sister to come pick me up as I was feel physically sick by what I thought was my friends perfect little family. Of course I had no idea what went on behind closed doors. I had no idea that everyone has a story. I had no idea that everyone has pain, heartache and things to hide. I was so consumed by my own pain that I could never see anyone else's. Empathy was not something that I was taught about. It has literally taken me 33 years to find my empathic emotion, and now I cannot feel anything but empathy.

So here I was in the situation have been longing for. No work, travelling Asia with my best friend and I was miserable. Fuck!! I had no idea what to do here. This was not part of my plan. I hated when things didn't go to plan. I was a control freak, I only went with the flow when I was in charge. I was giving up and putting what little faith I had left into my niece's part of the trip. I figured I couldn't argue with her as much as I had been doing with Rebecca. Or at least in my head anyway. Losing my mind. Most of the arguments I had with Rebecca were solely in my head. Oh shit, I was losing my mind.

6

Thailand

We enjoyed the tastiest iced coffee from the 7-eleven down the road and headed back to the tour office where we were getting the bus from. We waited patiently and watched the others arrive who were taking the same bus as us. Just as we were to get on the bus, Rebecca ran to the toilet and I waited with the bags. Because of this, we missed out on getting a good seat and ended up squashed in the very back beside all of the luggage. This meant that any time the bus turned all of the bags would fall on top of us! We couldn't put our seats back at all as we were right up against the back window and we had no leg room whatsoever. It was going to be a long trip.

We both took our tamazepan and tried to shut our eyes, but after trying for an hour to sleep we gave up and decided to start playing 'remember the time'. It's a game where you start a memory and the other person finishes it. We knew each other so well we couldn't catch each other out. It helped pass the time and we just chatted the whole 10 hours. It was actually so good and it felt so amazing to have such a true friend, and even though we live so far apart we're still so close. When we finally got to Chiang Mai and to our hotel, we were so tired and hungry that we wanted to kill each other, luckily we both know it's a short lived feeling and we will get over it. Pulling an all nighter on a tiny crowded bus was not fun no matter what we tried. BED – STAT! Gone were the days when staying up all night was fun, we were exhausted and needed sleep so we could see straight.

As soon as we woke up we decided to go to the train station to book the train from Chiang Mai to Bangkok, we didn't want to endure that minivan experience again. When we got to the train station we were told "all trains were full" – we couldn't believe it. What were the chances? Why the bloody hell did this keep happening to us? Our tuktuk driver told us that it was Thailand school holidays and that was why it was so hard to get tickets.

He suggested that we tried the bus station so off we went, but then we were told, it's FULL. So he brought us to another station, and again we were told FULL. Finally the 3rd station had a VIP bus available so we paid for that tickets. We couldn't believe our luck with the trains and buses, but we were thankful that we had went so early to get the bus tickets, otherwise we could have been stranded. We also booked a tour for the following day as we wanted to see the white temple.

The tour left at 6am the next day so we were up super early. We stopped off at the hot springs for coffee before we headed for the White Temple in Chiang Rai – it's a three hour trip to get there and once we arrived, we were so delighted we made the trip. It is so freaking awesome. It was designed by Chalermchai Kositpipat in 1997 and whilst we were there, we were lucky enough to see him driving around on his motorbike. He was very friendly and loved to chat. His works have been exhibited worldwide, and he was known for his use of Buddhist imagery in his art.

The White temple and the building are still being built to this day. "Only death can stop my dream, but cannot stop my project," Chalermchai was quoted as saying about the temple, adding that he believed the work will give him "immortal life." His attention to detail was out of this world, as was his imagination. The inside of the temple was painted in various East vs. West, he had paintings of spider man on one hand and then temples and Buddha's on the other. Even the toilets were extravagant, all in gold, and sparking in the sunlight!

The White temple simply takes your breath away, it's dazzling, intricate, mesmerising and the rest. When you are there you can buy a silver heart and use this as a wish and place it on one of the many trees. There were millions of these, apparently when they have enough they will melt them down and make a Buddhist statue. I wanted to stay longer to sit and stare in awe, but we had to move on quickly as we had a long day ahead. Next stop, the ancient city of Chiang Saen built in 129! The pagoda was the oldest I have seen. We didn't stay here long as the next stop was the Golden Triangle, and lunch, thank goodness!

The Golden Triangle used to be one of Asia's two main opium-producing areas. It overlaps the mountains of three countries of Southeast Asia - Burma, Laos and Thailand. After lunch we headed to the opium museum, then jumped on a board so we could see Burma. We then took the boat to Laos where we jumped off to do shopping. We both ;laughed as we swore we would never go back to Laos again and here were only 2 days late. The people who were with us on the trip bought up on the fake designer handbags whereas we just wanted to get back to Thailand. The bus back to Chiang Mai took almost five hours, it was 8.30pm when we got back, such a long day, but as we were leaving the following day we decided to get dropped off at the Sunday markets to get a cheeky MacDonald's meal before hitting the stalls. The Sunday markets in Chiang Mai are overwhelming – you just cannot expect the size of them. They go on and on for streets and streets, and it is hard to find your way out. The merchandise was wonderful - all authentic local made items, but we were spoiled with the markets in Luang Prabang and had bought up there, which left little room for more. We ended up frustrated by the size of the markets purely because we couldn't get out of there fast enough.

The next day we just had to kill time before we got the night bus to Bangkok. We checked out of the hotel, had our nails done, saw more temples and wandered aimlessly for a bit. Whilst on our wander, we found a cute little cafe to take shelter from the rain, the owner told us about Warorot markets; it's where all of the locals shop and you have to go there if you found yourself in Chiang Mai. It was full of local food with some very interesting stalls with smells that get into your bones, delicious, fabulous and so colourful.

We didn't have much time as we had to get back to the hotel and collect our bags to get to the bus station. Once we got to the bus station we realised that we had the best seats on the bus. We got to sit downstairs right at the front of the bus which basically means you got to have empty seats opposite you for your feet, we were treated like VIP's and got water and food handed to us. The new James Bond movie was playing on the TV right in front of us. This was such a far cry from our last overnight bus and we loved it! I took a sleeping pill and was fast asleep before you could say boo. Best bus ride so far!

Bangkok

We woke up in Bangkok and got off the bus about 5 am. We were totally disorientated, half asleep and we were surrounded by people who tried to sell us a ride into town. I found a guy, told him where we wanted to go and he grabbed my bag and started walking, Rebecca was a bit dubious but we kept walking as we couldn't see any sort of taxi area. Once we got to his car I asked how much he was going to charge us and he told us some exorbitant price. Our jaws dropped and we quickly took our bags off him and started walking away. I mean seriously, they take you for a fool... but people must actually pay the prices. It would have cost us the same price to get into town than to get from Chiang Mai to Bangkok!

We found another cab driver who offered a reasonable rate and he took us to our hotel. Breakfast and bed – boy, I needed a break from all this moving around, bartering, sleeping on buses, trains and I feeling home sick. My niece Molly gets to Bangkok in just two days so that meat that Rebecca only had two days left!

Here we were in Bangkok or 'Bangers' as it's called. I've heard so many mixed reviews about the place but I wanted to make my own judgements. We wandered outside of the hotel and came across a tuktuk who offered to show us the sights: one hour for $1 so we thought great, sounds good, let's go.

The first stop was the lying Buddha, a must see tourist attraction and one that was on our to do list. Toni the tuktuk driver then dropped us off at a silk tailor, a bit random and also not required so we quickly entered and exit the building. The tailors really try to push products on us but we just headed out and asked our tuktuk guy Toni to bring us back to the hotel. He insisted on bringing us for lunch, as we were hungry we went along. The food was good but we got ripped off BIG TIME, clearly he was getting a big commission cut for bringing in the tourists. I started to hate this guy Toni the tuktuk driver. This time we really wanted to go back to the hotel, but once again Toni stopped off at a tour office, he encouraged us to go in and take a look, which we did, and ended up buying tickets to the floating markets (as per Rebecca's parent's suggestion) and tickets to Siam Niramit, apparently the greatest show in Bangers. Sucked in yet again... Toni the tuktuk driver then brought us to another jewellery shop on the way home. I almost punched him. He was lucky to get away unharmed.

We were trying to figure out how to get to Siam Naramit, the show we we booked that night, as the stadium was pretty far away and apparently the traffic in Bangers gets pretty chaotic, so we decided to leave an hour and half early to ensure a timely arrival. Luckily we did. First of all, any taxi's we hailed wouldn't bring us there as the traffic was too bad and they didn't want to go. We literally hailed down five cabs and not one would take us. Eventually we got back to the hotel and asked them to help us. They called a taxi and he told us he was going to charge us twice the actual rate because of the traffic –we had no choice at this stage as we were running out of time. My anger towards the taxi man was probably a little unjustified; I mean he was just cashing in on the tourists, something that everyone around here does.

The traffic was infuriating. It was as bad as everyone had said. Actually, it was even worse because one light took 15 minutes to change. I'm not being dramatic - this is fact. Rebecca and I couldn't even talk to one another as we were both so annoyed. We eventually got there half an hour after it started, so it took us just over two hours to get there, when it should have taken 20 minutes.

After many dirty looks we made it to our seats and it was spectacular! Not as good as the light show in Guangshao, but good old family fun with lots of sparkles, real elephants, and a love story. It was really good stuff and we needed it after today. When we walked outside after the show it was pouring down rain. Luckily the event people were very organised and had plenty of taxis waiting, so it only took us 20 minutes to get back to the hotel.

The next morning was another extremely early morning, a 6am start and we were off to the Bangkok floating markets, although they aren't really in Bangkok, they were about an hour's drive away. We were very excited to see them. We got dropped nearby and a boat then brought us to the markets so we could travel through the canal and see some of the houses along the way. It was cool to see but make sure you bring a scarf to cover your face - the smell was pretty intense – in a bad way. We got dropped off at the markets. I wandered around and noticed that there were a few boats which were selling food. It was pretty amazing, they literally have a gas stove and are cooking Thai curries on a tiny tin boat. Most of the markets were in stalls on solid ground, but there were a few actually "floating". There was plenty to shop for, and we made our way around the stalls wanting to buy almost everything.

We had some famous Thai coffee, bought some dresses, had a massage, and bought lots of spices. We could have stayed longer but our group was going to see the elephant park. We hadn't booked this tour but we just had to join in as that was our bus and we needed it to get back to Bangers. We were tired and keen to get back, but happy to see some more elephants. After that we got dropped off at a tourist shopping area for furniture, then got dropped at a jeweller, and then got dropped at a silk tailor. I mean it's just so annoying - they insist you get off the bus and then they will follow you around hoping you will buy something, anything. The tour guide get commission for bringing you there and for anything that you buy, so they can be super pushy. The prices were three times what you would pay elsewhere, it's embarrassing for tourists! Peeps, do not buy from these stores. They were set up to rip you off. You might think it's a good deal but you were in Thailand, EVERYTHING was a good deal.

We met a gay couple on this trip who had gotten the same tuktuk driver as us the previous day, tuktuk Toni but they paid him $20 for the exact trip we paid him $1 for. Clearly they looked richer than us.

Finally the day trip was over and we get dropped off at the Golden Mount. As soon as we walked all the way to the top of said Mount, a huge black cloud came over obstructing the view and it poured down raining. Oh yes, we really do have such fabulous luck. At least we were in shelter. We had reached the top but now we couldn't get back down until it stopped raining - yet more fun filled time wasting in Bangkok. It's Rebecca's last night so we wanted to do something nice. I remembered one of the guys from my China trip had told me about a restaurant in Bangers called 'Cabbages & Condoms', strange name for a restaurant but worth a shot. It's a tough place to find, but totally worth it.

As you walk in they have life size police men made purely from condoms! The philosophy for the restaurant is based on the belief that local people were best suited to build and maintain their own development. They use the money they made to teach locals on family planning and they have helped lower the population by 2.2%. The place was so super cute and I was really impressed. The service was fabulous, the food was delicious, we had a great night and I would definitely recommend this place. When we got the bill delivered we got a male and female condom with the receipt. Even though it was Rebecca's last night we didn't hit the red light district, or even any bars - we just jumped on the train and headed home.

7

Changeover Day

The next day I awoke feeling tired, neither Rebecca or I slept. I think I got to a stage where my body was confused by when and where it should sleep. I constantly felt exhausted - all this moving around, sleepless nights, walking for hours, constant haggling; it all starts to wear thin. Anyway, excitement has me all jittery for Molly's arrival and after breakfast I started the train trip to the airport to collect her. I managed to get on the wrong train, twice, but then found my way there with time to spare. I wanted to go online and book accommodation for us the following days as I had booked a bus to Koh Samet the next day.

I couldn't find an internet point anywhere in the airport, so I headed down towards the gate, as I definitely did not want Molly to walk out and not see me. I stood there staring at the gate trying to work out where each person who walked out was coming from. It said her flight landed 20 minutes ago so where was she? I waited, and waited, and finally my phone rang, its Molly – she needed an address for her stay while in Bangkok so I gave her the hotel address. When she finally walks out, about an hour and a half after landing, the tears were flowing down both of our faces - my thoughts were, finally I HAVE HER! I quickly texted my sister to let her know. The poor child had never travelled so far and she did it by herself. I couldn't have been prouder.

We got back on the train to the city and instead of all the train changes and walk to the hotel we jumped into a tuktuk from the airport express to the hotel. Molly was in awe by it, clearly she had never been in, or even heard of a tuktuk before. The hustle and bustle of Bangers along with the intense heat, left her mouth hanging. This was a totally new phenomenon for her and miles from what she has ever seen.

Is wasn't long before we were off back at the airport express station, this time with Rebecca for a goodbye; I HATE goodbyes. There were lots of hugs, kisses and tears and then off she went. Molly and I trot down to find the sky bar which was filmed in Hangover two; it supposedly has great views of this crazy city. We walked, and walked, and asked directions, then walked the other way. Molly started to get hangry (hungry and angry at the same time) so we tried to find somewhere to stop and eat. We kept walking until we started to see tonnes of stalls and we got excited and distracted by shopping. There were all kinds of things and we couldn't help but delve in for a look, before long the hanger was taken over and so then we had to find food. We did so in sweet donut and iced coffee style - good job Jessica, so responsible on day 1!

We gave up on finding the sky bar and decided that we wanted to find the night markets. Apparently these were the ones to hit up when in Bangers so we headed towards where we were told they were. We even stopped off to ask at a tour desk if we were headed in the right direction. We had to get on a boat and sail down the Chao Phraya River to what we thought were the night markets, but it turned out to be Asistique. This is not the night markets. It had a huge Ferris wheel, and while I got all excited Molly is terrified of heights. "Well it's time to overcome it" I said.

Asiatique is a riverfront tourist hot spot, filled with restaurants, activities, and shops - lots of shops. We headed straight to the Ferris wheel and got in our pod, and again I'm so proud of Molly for facing her fear and doing it. It was such fun and you got a great view of Bangers. That was a BIG day and we were exhausted and had yet another early rise the next day for our bus journey to Koh Samet. I would finally get to lie on a beach and chill. I cannot wait!

Moving On

We checked out of Bangkok and headed towards the Thai beaches. The reason I chose Koh Samet was because it was so close to Bangkok and on the way to Cambodia which was where we wanted to go. If we had flown down to the infamous Phuket beaches it would have taken a huge chunk out of Molly's spending money as I only paid for her ticket to Bangkok. So we were left with little options as to where to go.

Koh Samet seemed perfect. Once we arrived at the port we were dropped at a tour office where we were told that we needed to buy a return ticket to Bangkok right there and then. We were told that all buses only leave from Bangkok and we would need to go back there no matter where we were going. Of course I was trusting and listened to what they told me. I assumed it was the way it goes. I handed over the money feeling very pressured – we weren't sure when we were leaving KS but we figured they knew the deal with the buses. I shouldn't have trusted them.

We got on the ferry over to the island along with the rest of the locals and their shopping. We were surrounded by raw fish and meat, it seriously stank. Molly and I pulled our scarf's from our bags to cover our faces. We looked at each other and thought, was this the island escape we were expecting?

As soon as we got to KS we jumped into a taxi to the hotel. We had no idea how far it would be but it was only five minutes away. We checked in, dumped our bags and headed to the beach, and YES, it was perfect! I just wanted to roll around in the sand naked, but in reality that's not a good idea as the sand would just get everywhere. It already started to get dark and we took in the sunset sitting on a swing nearby. It was total bliss...

The next day we took an island hopping trip. Molly had never been snorkelling and told me that it was on her wish list for the trip, so we got very excited. We got to the first island and off the boat and headed to shore. I grabbed all of the gear so we could go snorkelling. I brought Molly with me through the water until we reached the point where the coral was. We both put on our masks and before I know it, Molly was panicking and had turned around to head back to shore. I popped my head up to see what the commotion was and she looked terrified. She was totally freaked out because there was fish swimming beside her. She hadn't realised what snorkelling really meant, and was not prepared to swim with fish. Ha-ha! I thought in my head, but didn't let her know I thought the whole thing was hilarious! I just said, 'are you ok?' I quickly joined her back on the beach and we sat down for lunch and forgot about snorkelling for a while.

The next stop on our day trip was another island where we just laid on the sand like a beached whale, half in the water soaking up the sun. It was so relaxing and peaceful, and I wanted to stay all day. Now this is the life, relaxing on the beach, getting a tan, feeling the sun on my face. No bloody trekking up or down muddy mountains. I was feeling totally Zen, I was delighted with myself. And I was super happy to have my niece by my side.

The next stop of the tour we got to jump off the back of the boat into deep water where we could snorkel. Molly turned to me and said 'This is how I imagined snorkelling to be." As in, she wanted to jump off the back of a boat, not walk into the fish... So off we went, but it only lasted about two minutes before I could see the terror in Molly's eyes. I just brought her straight back to the boat. Not a very successful day of snorkelling for us, but it wasn't a great spot anyway. Back to the mainland, it was time for cocktails. Of course I was being responsible and only letting her have two.

We had to book our trip to Siem Reap so we wandered around asking different tour operators what the deal was. We found out you don't have to go back to Bangkok to start this journey, you can go straight from KS. That silly cow on the mainland lied. I should have known, don't buy tickets until you were SURE about your route - this was now the 2nd time I have done this and wasted money.

We didn't want to go back to Bangers so we just sucked up the wasted expense and booked the tickets to Siem Reap. When we went to the bank to get the money to poay for the ticktes, in the five minutes we were gone, the seats that we wanted suddenly became unavailable. REALLY? You have no choice but to believe what they say. The tour agent made some more calls and we eventually got our tickets, but of course we had to pay more.

We were both a bit frustrated and returned to the hotel room to shower before dinner. We needed food stat. we were hangry and tired. Just as we were about to leave the room Molly's phone broke – if you don't know any 16 year old kid, then you won't understand the enormity of the situation - losing her phone and therefore camera, was the same as losing a limb. I talked her into coming down for dinner where she calmed down; meanwhile, I'm praying that a miracle would happen and the phone would come back to life.... About six hours later, it did, phew!

Thailand | What was going through my head

I was so terrified that I was responsible for Molly. I could barely keep things together myself, and now I have to not only entertain a 16 year old, but also be responsible for her. Of course I loved having her and I was looking forward to bonding, but I thought that it would be easier. I figured that she would just go along with the decisions I made and I wouldn't have to worry about what she wanted. After all she was young and used to being told what to do, right? I spent my time with Rebecca wanting to have the power to make decisions solo and not have to ask for opinions or compromise, yet here I was with the power to call the shots and I was freaking out.

When I was then in charge of making all the decisions I was overwhelmed by it; I didn't what to make a wrong decision. I had Molly to help, or so I thought. Have you ever tried asking a 16 year old what they want to do? Molly was so easy going and was happy to do anything I wanted, but I needed support. I needed her to say "yes," or "no," not "I don't mind." Every time I asked her anything 'I don't mind' was the response. This was equally as frustrating for me. She was trying to be obliging and sweet, little did she know that I was not actually the responsible adult that she thought that I was. I was in fact quite the opposite. It wasn't her that I was getting annoyed with, it was myself, but as usual I was not ready to admit that. It was so much easier to blame anyone or everything but me for my frustrations. Molly was actually being a dream child, her optimism was astounding, and I was so incredibly proud to be her aunt and godmother.

When I started to think back on the part of my trip with Rebecca, I felt guilty for being so miserable on Rebecca's last night. I hadn't seen her in years and it would be years again until I see her, yet a quick dinner and early bedtime was how we finished off the trip. Says a lot about the trip really, we should have gone out and celebrated, we should have had the most amazing night out of the whole trip but again, I just wanted to go home to bed. What sort of friend was I? We could have made it a night to remember but we didn't. And off they go again, the voices in my head telling me that I was no good, a bad friend, and that I was doomed to make Molly's trip shit too! What was I doing? I was dwelling on the time I had spent with Rebecca and how much better it could have been. Again with the negativity. I couldn't see the stars from the clouds and couldn't even remember the good times we did have. All I could remember was how much of a bad friend I was to her, and how I wish I could turn back time and go through it all again.

I had to get it together. I didn't want Molly to hate me. I didn't want Rebecca to hate me either. I needed to get happy again. But how do I do that? What can I do? How can I force myself to enjoy this? Listen to yourself Jessica, it needs out come naturally but it's not. How can I learn to appreciate what I was seeing? I was starting to get over Asia completely, I was over the constant haggling, seeing the poverty, being harassed, being ripped off, all I could see was the bad stuff.

I was taking everything personally, from being over charged for tickets to how the waiter would look at me. I was letting the little devil on my shoulder take control. It seemed like every move I made was wrong, every thought I had was wrong, and every decision I made was doomed! I was fighting to try and stay in control but the little angel that should be on the other shoulder was clearly not there - maybe she decided to stay on the beach? All that what was going on in my head was self-doubt and self-criticism, it was all negative and I couldn't get out.

I couldn't face talking to my friends back in Sydney. I thought I was not cool, and I felt that my friends had forgotten about me. I was comparing myself to others and I was being seriously tough on myself. I was jealous, so jealous of all of my friends, I was sure they had such an amazing life, and I was sure that I was doomed.

I mean we are all human, and we can all get hit with by the green eyed monster every now and then, it can happen to anyone. The annoying thing is, jealousy seems so much more intense when you are feeling like shit. It creeps up on you like a thief in the night and before you know it you want to unfriend the so-called friend on ALL social media, punch them in the face, wish them unwell and generally never see them AGAIN!! Here I was feeling like absolute crap, and here I was letting comparison be the thief of my joy.

8

One hell of a trip...

The morning that we left to go to Siem Reap we were up so early that there was no one in reception, we walked around trying to find someone to hand the hotel key back to as I had left a deposit. Just as we found someone, the electricity went out so she couldn't open the till. Typical!! Here we go with more scamming, although the electricity going off probably wasn't anyone's fault. Just in the nick of time we get refunded back our deposit and are left with little time to run for the ferry. It's far too early for taxis, so we have to walk to the pier. Once we had made our way down, Molly realises that she had left behind her most treasured item, (not her phone) her soft teddy! She has had this teddy since she was a baby and simply couldn't live without it. The look of terror in her eyes this time was nothing like the snorkelling look, she was devastated and needed to have it back. I told her to RUN. She took off down the road back to the hotel where she tried to find the staff to let her back into the room. She couldn't find anyone, so she ran to our room where luckily she found some staff. She asked for the teddy, but they had already taken it elsewhere. I believe there were raised voices before eventually she got it back.

I stood on the pier beside our boat with all of the bags praying that she was ok, and that she makes it back before the boat leaves. Clearly, I was not going to leave without her, but if we miss this boat we have to stay here another night and buy new tickets to Siem Reap. It had been only about 10 minutes but my heart was pounding, I was getting worried about Molly, was she OK? Finally I saw her in the distance running as fast as she could. Once she reached me I give her a big hug, she was soaking with sweat. I passed her the water bottle and told her to grab her bags and we both jumped on the boat just in time for departure – phew! It took Molly the whole 40 minute journey back to the mainland just to get her breath back. She really did run the fastest she has ever run. I guess when your teddy bear is at stake you will do whatever it takes.

Once we got to the mainland we tried to find the tour office where we would be getting our bus from. We wanted to dump our bags there so we could grab another drink for Molly and go back to the last place I was forced to buy the tickets back to Bangkok. Clearly I had no use for them now so I wanted to get some money back. I took the time to run around to the initial tour office asked for a refund. The manager got very angry at me for not booking our trip to Siem Reap with him, but I show him the emails I had sent them as well as the number of times I had tried to call the office, so he begrudgingly hands me back half of what we paid. I was happy with myself that I went back to ask, at least we got something back.

Before we set off on our trip I asked at our tour office how we would know who to meet at the other side of the border. The guy assured me that he himself would be dropping us at the border, and that he would introduce us to someone at the border who would then walk through with us and continue the journey to Siem Reap. I thought that sounds much easier than the Laos- Thailand border crossing and my nerves dissipated.

For the first leg of the journey we were ushered into a super fancy four wheel drive, it was just the two of us. Molly and I were delighted with our luxurious mode of transport and the fact that we were in safe hands, plus the fact that we would have no hassle crossing the border. We couldn't actually believe our luck so we sat back and had a little sleep.

We were happily dosing for about two hours before being rudely awakened by our driver who told us to wake up and get out of the car. I questioned where we were and why we had to get out. We were at a petrol station in the middle of nowhere, so I was a bit suspicious. We got out and he threw our bags out of the boot and told us that we needed to change vehicles.

There were no other vehicles there, so we were very confused. Another bus soon drove up and our driver pointed to it and told us to put our bags in the boot. The boot was full so we dragged our bags onto the bus with us, but there was very little room. There were three seats in the back so we took two and used the 3rd for our bags. It was far from comfortable and much more like we actually imagined we would be travelling. In Asia, if it sounds too good to be true then it probably is. Strangely enough, our driver from the four wheel drive sat in the driver's seat of the bus and started to drive while a female took the car we initially arrived in. At least we still had him and he was going to help us cross the border, or so we thought.

We met two lovely English girls on the bus, who warned us about the 'scams' we regarding crossing the border from Thailand to Cambodia. There were lots of stories about being dropped at a restaurant before the border where they tell you they would purchase a visa for you and save you time, the reality though is that they charge you three times the price of the visa. We all laughed and said "we won't be sucked into that".

We arrived at what we thought was the border and were told to get off the bus. We all soon realised that this was not the border, this was a restaurant... I asked the driver where the border was and asked him "why aren't you brining us there?" he replied, "no, no, you go with this man" and so the frustration began. We went with some guy and within seconds had lost the two English girls we were chatting to from the bus. This guy asked us for our passports, but there was no way I was going to hand our passports over so I questioned why he wanted them. He got very angry and raised his voice and told me again, "hand me your passports!"

Molly and I said NO! I asked him again to take us to the border. He walked away. So we sat there chatting about what to do. I tried to find the two girls but couldn't see them anywhere. We could hear other people talking about how they shouldn't have handed their passports over to those guys, and we started to worry. The guy eventually returns and tells us to fill out some forms, again, we asked "why" and he turned to us and told us to just "GO" and he showed us a van get into. I asked him who would meet us the other side of the border as we needed to finish the journey we paid for, but, no answer. We just drove off and hoped for the best.

We got to the border, got in line to go through Thai customs and got stamped out of Thailand, that all seemed relatively easy, on we went to the next part. We walk through to Cambodia but there were no signs for customs or passport control, we felt a bit silly as surely it was obvious the point of entry into the next country? We were obviously looking very lost when a nice gentleman turned to us and pointed towards passport control to show us the way. We walked into border control and handed over our passports. It started to pour down with rain, but we were under cover so happy about that. We got our visas sorted out with no problem and walked back outside to the rain, now what? We stood there waiting for the rain to lighten up but it didn't. We were also hoping that we would see someone, or someone would see us and we could finish the trip to Siem Reap that we paid for, but there was no one there. We still had no sight of the two English girls who we thought would were on the same trip. We were starting to freak out just a little.

After about 20 minutes of standing there waiting for something to happen we started walking, we thought we were just going to have to get a taxi somewhere. I was stressing out big time but Molly was as calm as a cucumber and calming me down! How did that happen? I was supposed to be the experienced traveller and the responsible one, I felt that I had let her down.

We walked about five minutes down the road, both ourselves and our bags were completely drenched at this stage. We saw a guard who told us to line up to go through passport control. Apparently, where we had just been was the place to buy the visa only, not be stamped into the country. We started to get hope again that someone would be on the other side to pick us up, not too much, but enough to put a smile on our face.

The line was so long, there were so many people, wet people! No one was smiling, or talking, it seemed like that everyone else, like us, was so confused and frustrated. It took us almost two hours to get through to the top of the line to be stamped into Cambodia, we even had to give fingerprints. I have never had to do that on entry to any country before and thought it was pretty strange. When we finally reached the exit to

Cambodia one of the guys from the 'restaurant' was there ushering us to come with him. He said "I thought you were lost, I have been waiting for you" Ha! It all worked out. We took a deep breath and smiled at each other, we were so relieved and excited to soon be in our hotel drinking a very strong cocktail!

We started to dry ourselves off on this bus and settle in for our trip to Siem Reap which should take about five hours. We had already been on the go for 9 hours, add the stress we had faced to that and we were pretty exhausted, it had been a long day. After just 10 minutes on the bus we pulled up to a bus station and were told to "get off the bus!"

I thought, "are you f**kin serious!?" Yep, they were serious and boy they were seriously rude too - when another Dutch girl questioned them and what was happening they started screaming at her and asked her if she wanted to walk to Siem Reap. We decided to keep our mouths shut and just listened to what everyone else was saying. There was a currency exchange in the bus station and seeing as we had no local currency we gave them all of our Thai Bhat to change over, but little did we know that in Cambodia hardly anywhere accepts local currency, everything was priced and sold in US dollars!

After about an hour of waiting, someone asked what was happening with the buses and he was told that we had to wait another three hours for more people to come so the bus would be full in order to start the trip. This was not what we wanted to hear. There were families with young children who were getting seriously annoyed. I was sure we had at least a bus full of people that we could get going with but they were in charge and they were in no hurry to go anywhere.

We were so tired, hungry, wet and just wanted to get going, I walked over to ask the 'mean' guy to ask if there was any way we could get a taxi or another bus? He told me that if I got 15 other people and we all paid US$3 extra, that we could leave straight away. Some people were super pissed by this as we all had paid to get to Siem Reap but this guy was clearly trying to make an extra buck! For Molly and me, $3 was totally worth it and we easily got the other 15 people to join us.

Once we got on the bus to go, the 'mean' guy got on and thanked us all for our understanding, he also told us that once we got to Siem Reap he would supply free tuktuks to our hotels. That was kind of nice, but he was still ripping us off and he was very mean, so it didn't change my opinion of him. He also told us that this bus was a express bus and that we would be in Siem Reap in only 3 hours, so much faster than the other bus we were waiting for. I felt sorry for the people who stayed behind in protest against spending the extra US$3. We were finally off. We went only ten minutes down the road before we stopped again!! This time to let on a few local families who were obviously going our way, even though the bus was totally full!

They jumped on and started throwing our bags out of the way and using them as seats. No one was impressed but everyone was too scared to say anything. Molly was very worried as it was her bag that was being used as one of the seats for the big lady who appeared to be passing wind quite often... They all looked very suspicious and the bus kept stopping every so often on the side of the road so these people could hand over money to various people for I don't even know what. We stopped half way and I was busting to use the toilet, so I made a run for it at the pit stop, as I was on the loo I was being yelled at to 'come out' - they told me that I have to buy something before I use the loo, seeing as I was already half way through my business I just yelled back at them. I couldn't believe it, how could they expect me to pay while I was on the bloomin toilet? In the end I bought some Pringles at an exorbitant price.

I was seriously pissed off at this stage, how could they actually charge people to use the toilet, they were so incredibly disgusting. I had no choice but to use the horrendous facilities but when I came out the rest of the people from bus were standing looking at me in shock that I actually did. I didn't care! Hangry didn't even begin to explain how I was feeling right now. Three hours past and we kept thinking any minute now we were going to be there. No chance - by the time we got to Siem Reap it was a five hour bus journey.

When we finally arrived, some guy gets on the bus and said "so sorry for the inconvenience but the tuktuks that you were promised are no longer available" apparently the heavy rain has caused big floods and most of the roads were closed. He told us that a tuktuk could bring us to our hotels but through a much longer route than normal. And of course, this would cost extra. The entire bus starts roaring at this guy and telling him just what they think of him. Molly and I slowly walked off the bus and headed towards a tuktuk, as at this stage we don't care how much it costs - we just wanted to get to the hotel, pronto!

We got into a tuktuk and he tried to start it up and it wouldn't start. We looked at each other and laughed. Meanwhile the others from our bus journey were still yelling at this guy - this went on for about 10 minutes and we still haven't got our tuktuk started. Our driver insists we stay on board and promised he would get it going. The rest of the group started to walk off from the bus terminal - well it's not really a terminal, it was more a shed in the middle of nowhere. They all started to walk down this long dark alley with their children in tow. I couldn't believe it, I know it's frustrating but just pay the money and mind your kids. Suddenly our tuktuk started.

Our hotel was about a 10 minute drive and there doesn't seem to be any road closures. No surprise there, just another scam. One we got to the front door I didn't offer any money to the tuktuk driver, we just walked off didn't look back. I think at that stage if he chased us for money we would have punched him in the face. He didn't ask and didn't follow - those families were walking for no reason! We didn't have to pay in the end.

We dumped our bags, - it's been a 15 hour journey with some f**ked up stuff to deal with, all we wanted was food, NOW! We were both so hangry (hungry and angry) we couldn't even talk to each other.

9

Cambodia

The rain didn't stop the following day. We hired some push bikes and thought we would get by as it wasn't heavy rain. As soon as we got far enough out of town, it started pouring down so badly that we can't even see two feet in front of us. We had to pull over and wait for almost an hour until it eased off a bit. We made it back to the hotel and were left to sit by the pool undercover chatting and reminiscing.

After a few hours we were so bored we gave in and bought those horrid looking plastic ponchos. We hit the markets again, Molly was now a professional at haggling – I loved it. We found a nice tuktuk driver who would bring us around all of the temples for only $10. This was a great price as the tour offices were charging around $25 so we booked him for the next day and hoped it didn't rain.

I started to think about going back home. Molly was to fly back home in 2.5 weeks and I started questioning if I would want to continue alone. I have started to feel so overwhelmed by the thoughts of travelling alone after having both Rebecca and Molly by my side. What has happened to me? I started this trip full of energy, passion, excitement and was more than willing to spend time alone and meet new people. I think I have now convinced myself that it's too hard to meet new people and that I won't be able to continue the trip alone. I started then freaking out at myself because I had let this happen. I had let myself become so shy. I have done a complete turnaround from the start off of this trip and all I wanted to do was go back to Sydney and to my boyfriend but at the same time I can't face going back!

I eventually decided to fly home the same day Molly left to go back home. I looked up flight prices from Ho Chi Minh to Sydney and I was planning to fly about the same time as Molly so we can go to the airport together. When looking at prices there was a flight that leaves the same time as hers for $1000! That's just for one way - I was shocked! So I looked into other flights and there was one for $500 but it's at 4pm and Molly's flight was at 9pm. Instead of talking to Molly and making a choice I over analysed every detail of what I should do. One minute I wanted to pay the $1000 so I could spend the extra five hours with Molly and she won't be alone in the airport but the next I was saying, NO, she would be fine by herself once I brought her there. This started to go round and round in my head until I almost had a panic attack. Molly luckily was level headed and calmed me down and reassured me that she would be fine to wait alone and that I should save the $500 and book the earlier flight. What was happening to me? I can't seem to make a simple decision without panic!

While I was away I was chatting with my old boss. I made an agreement with him to come back late September and manage a big project for him. This made me feel better, I figured I was almost over travelling, and this way I could come back to work and not have to worry about not having work. I had also somehow managed to agree to come and help cover some holidays for other managers in the venue that I just left. I wasn't keen on doing this at all, but figured I needed the money after my trip and to have a job lined up on my return was a massive bonus.

It should have been a comforter that was why I was doing it. I was very stressed out when it came to money. The fact was though; the thoughts of going back to work there were stressing me out. I was dreading it more than anything and this was starting to weigh very heavily on me. I began to get very anxious and would regularly talk myself into a panic. This lead to not sleeping, and I was relying on sleeping pills pretty much every night just to get a couple of hours sleep.

The next day we were up early for our Angkor Wat excursion. As we were getting into our tuktuk Molly said she was not super excited about going to see an old pile of bricks but told me that she would go for me as I was so excited. It's the largest religious monument in the world. I kept my laughter inside as clearly she has no idea the significance of it.

It doesn't take us long to get to the magnificent Angkor Wat, and WOW! The place was simply breath taking, I look over to Molly and she was in awe. She quickly retracts her earlier comment and was now keen to write about Angkor and all of its temples for her final year school project. Now that was a giant turnaround, we haven't even walked over the entrance. Apparently Angkor Wat was a miniature replica of the universe in stone and represents an earthly model of the cosmic world (I read that in a book we bought when we were there to help Molly with her project). Now I could write a whole book on Angkor Wat but history was not a big fascination of mine, although I do appreciate one of the 7 wonders of the world.

The heat was unbelievable and we felt our skin burning as we walked through – but at least it wasn't raining. I had told Molly to cover up and wear pants as you cannot get into the temples if you were showing too much skin. We both did, but I was wearing a singlet top which didn't have sleeves, so when we came to the actual temple inside we could not go in as I didn't have the right sleeves. I put a scarf over my shoulders but they were very insistent that it wasn't sufficient. Why were we wearing pants in this heat if we can't go inside? Grr.

We took our time wandering around as we didn't have a guide and we were going at our own pace which was nice, although it would have been nice to have someone explaining a few things along the way. We had bought a book so that Molly could use it for her project so we had that to use as a reference and we took so many photos so she could have her very own pictures to use.

After Angkor Wat we went down to Bayon temple. I loved this one, it was my favourite. While walking through we knelt down and prayed to one of the Buddha statues. I was trying to tell Molly all that I have learned about Buddhism since my travels started which was not much, but I knew more than she knew, which was nothing!

While we were knelt down a girl came over and wrapped a thin red bracelet made from wool around our wrist. Apparently wearing one actually has many positive effects on one's mind and body. It was believed to have magical powers and a person who wore it would see his/

her life changing for the good. The girl who gave it to us told us it was for good luck. We continued on our walk through the temple and while walking through one of the woods, I tripped and cut my toe. It started bleeding pretty badly and all of the dirt got stuck inside the cut. Molly stepped into parent role and started looking through our backpacks for something we can clean it with and wrap it up with, and I'm sitting there thinking, I thought these bracelets were supposed to bring us luck! We washed the cut out with water, then threw on some hand sanitizer and wrapped it with tissues and ripped off plastic poncho, perfect!

We continued on to see Ta Keo, Ta Prohm, Pre Rup, Banteay Kdei, the six temples, they were all huge. We climbed to the top of Ta Keo -the steps were by far the steepest steps I have ever climbed. We had to take off our shoes and place our foot sideways just so we could get up. It was pretty scary as the top of the temple was very high and if you look down while trying to get a foot grip when walking back down its daunting!

Don't forget Molly was afraid of heights so it took her much longer to make the trip. I was a believer in just get it over with and rush to the top even with my cut toe and make shift bandage. The sun was still beating down and we were now covered in sweat and dust from the steps. My feet were 'red' as the dirt was red not black.

Ta prohm was built in 1186. It was a Buddhist temple dedicated to the mother of Jayavarman VII. It was one of the few temples in Angkor where an inscription provided information about the temple's inhabitants. The temple was home to more than 12,500 people including 18 high priests, while an additional 80,000 Khmers, living in the surrounding villages, were required to maintain the temple. This was another favourite of mine. It was covered with huge tree roots and it was very fairy-like. This was also where the move Tomb Raider was filmed. It's the 2nd most visited temple in Angkor after Angkor Wat.

After we left Ta Prohm we were exhausted. Six temples, a cut toe, added to that, it's starting to rain, all of this combined totally equates to a long lunch needed! We asked our driver to bring us somewhere to eat. He stopped in the nearest place and Molly took one look and said "no way." The place looked so dirty, and the sign for the toilet made us want to vomit. So we continued on to the next place which looked far more approachable.

The food was terrible and so expensive, again, ripping off tourists. We got back in our tuktuk after lunch with full intentions on seeing more temples but as soon as we got to the first temple it started raining again. We both looked at each other and shaked our heads. It was time to head back to the hotel. We took photos from the tuktuk of all the temples on the way home. There were really quite a lot of them and we did well fitting in six in one day. For the temple lovers out there is a temple pass that you can get for an entire week!

Phnom Penh

The next morning was another early rise so we could catch our minivan to Phnom Penh. We decided to take a day bus because we didn't want to face a bad night's sleep in a bus when it's only supposedly a four hour trip. We were always told it's a shorter trip than it was. This time it ended up being six hours and we got in just after 2pm, on average 2 hours extra was starting to be the norm.

We checked into our hotel and to our delight our room was on the 9th floor. The hotel has no lifts, so we had to carry our 16kg back packs up 9 flights of stairs! The fun just never stops. After refuelling with our usually healthy snacks of hot chips, we headed off for a city excursion, we assumed being the capital city of Cambodia there would be a lot to see.

We got chatting to some other tourists over lunch and they started telling us we have to go visit the 'killing fields.' Molly looked at me and I give her the 'no fucking way' look back! This is trip advisor's number one tourist attraction. Am I mad? Did I miss something? Clearly it's a memorial, but I cannot understand why so many people would want to visit this place, the name alone was upsetting.

In 4th place for tourist hot spots Tuol Sleng Genocide was listed, and apparently people go and look at the children in the local orphanages for something to do? This was just so incredibly strange to me - children were not tourist attractions. After looking into some more 'attractions' on the web we saw PP has many cinemas and movie houses, lots of temples and wat's but most importantly it's markets were listed as a must see.

This may sound shallow to some, but all I wanted to do was check out the markets, central markets, as they were definitely worth a visit. We shopped up a storm! Molly had really taken to this haggling situation and we were getting super deals, even for tourists.

Since we started the trip Molly had been looking for a particular cover for her phone that she couldn't find even after trolling the internet at home. We found it at these markets plus many more things that we never even knew we needed. Once we left the markets we tried to find a place to buy our next bus trip tickets. We wandered around for a couple of hours and were told many times to go to places that didn't sell bus tickets - we even tried to hire a private car and driver to take us to Sihanoukville as we didn't much fancy another bus trip. It turned out it would cost almost US$500 for that, a little over the top we thought.

Eventually we found the bus station which was actually right behind the markets we started off at. We bought our bus tickets to Sihanoukville for next to nothing.

That night we headed to a nice Indian restaurant around the corner from our hotel for dinner. They had some great wine, I wanted to stay here forever. Wine was the only thing that could calm me down. The owner of the restaurant came over to talk to us, and for some hilarious reason he wanted to help Molly with her future career choice. I thought it was very entertaining, but Molly was quite perplexed. Clearly he was a savvy businessman and saw Molly as a youngster who may have needed guidance. He was trying to tell her to get into medical device marketing as this was the way of the future. He may have a point, but it's not really what a 16 year old wants to hear.

We had one day of rest in PP before we were off again to Sihanoukville. We literally just hung out by the tiny pool in the hotel and drank cocktails as soon as it was a reasonable time to drink. I mean 2pm was more than a reasonable time to start drinking when on holidays, right? I kept saying holidays but this trip does not feel like a holiday! We had been on the move so much, with so many overnight buses and trains. Every day was an early start, lots of frustrations and no sleeping. My brain was starting to break down and I knew that depression was kicking in. I know exactly the warning signs as I have suffered from depression before. I have battled with anxiety, been on anti-depressants, talked to many counsellors, so I knew I was getting close to needing my doctor.

I kept trying to look on the bright side of things. I was on an amazing trip and had my beautiful niece with me. I didn't have to work and I knew things were good but the good feelings started to feel further and further away and the anxious feelings were what I was feeling the most and the strongest. I kept trying to put on a happy face for Molly but inside I knew I was struggling.

Sihanoukville

The bus to Sihanoukville was a coach and we were at the front so had plenty of leg room: a must for us tallies. While driving though I was shocked by the poverty I saw. I never thought Cambodia was a wealthy country but wasn't expecting what I was seeing while leaving the capital city towards Sihanoulville. It almost reminded me of India, with so many people all crammed into small spaces all doing whatever they can to stay alive. It was quite confronting. The place we stopped for lunch on the way was so dirty and the toilets again were unusable. The "shop" if you could call it that, only sold lychees or cold cooked rice; that was it. Luckily we had packed some cheese sandwiches and ate them along with a large bag of M&M's, which Molly was now consuming on a daily basis.

We got to Sihanoukville after five hours on the bus and got dropped off at the bus station, which of course was in the middle of nowhere. Naturally there were about 20 tuktuk drivers all bidding for our fare and once we told one of them where we were going they told us it would cost us US$15 to get there. This was an outrageous price; you should never pay more than US$5 for a tuktuk. So we tried asking other drivers and the price slowly started to come down.

Eventually another couple came and joined us in order to make the trip cheaper. We got to our hotel and it was pouring down with rain and we were drenched by the time we got to our room. At this point, all that we could do was go to the bar, so we did. When the chips were down drinking was always the answer, my mother taught me that from a young age.

With lots of free time we got onto the internet and checked our Facebook page. This was when I posted on my brothers wall. He was just about to get a puppy, he has shared a photo of the puppy and his girlfriend, they had chosen the name Scruffy. We previously had a dog called Scruffy, so I posted a comment asking him why he chose Scruffy again? I really didn't think anything of it, but soon my comment was removed. I was not usually the type of person to get upset over social media, but I was so taken aback by this for some reason. I literally burst into tears and ran back to our room. When Molly came to check on me I couldn't even talk to her - I had to go asleep for a few hours. This was what I do when I can't face the world – go to bed, hide under the sheets, over analyse everything and eventually fall asleep. The silliest of things had tipped me over the edge. I was so incredibly sad that my brother had removed my comment. I felt unloved, betrayed, scared and confused. I kept thinking that he no longer needed me now that he had his girlfriend, and soon their puppy. They were now a happy family and I was going to be alone forever!! This is what I do, catastrophize everything. a very simply gesture from my brother had put me into a tailspin where I could no longer function. Going to bed and covering my head was the only thing that I could do. That is all I knew to do when the chips were down, really down.

When I finally woke up I saw that Molly wasn't in the room. I knew she couldn't have gone far. I went out to look for her, and she was happy just reading her book in the lobby. It took me a while, but I managed to get myself together and head down the road for dinner. I put on a brave face but behind it all I was so upset, so angry, I felt that my own brother was trying to get rid of me. I knew I was right to be worrying about everyone back in Sydney hating me, forgetting me. This was now the proof I needed to assure me that my crazy thoughts were in fact true. As much as I had already convinced myself that everyone hated me, I now knew that even my family wanted me gone.

The next day we just chilled out, I honestly couldn't even think about doing anything, I couldn't organise anything and I didn't want to face anyone anyway. We lay by the pool and had lunch on the beach. We had a private cinema next door to our hotel so we went there and watched the 'Hangover 3'. We had a good walk around the town and did some shopping, had dinner and some more wine, things were looking good again. I felt slightly better and was over the previous day's breakdown. It's funny how responsibility kicks in and takes over. I knew that I had to get up and moving for Molly. If she wasn't with me it probably would have been a very different story. I could have easily stayed in bed for days feeling sorry for myself. I was actually glad she was here, I was glad I had to keep moving.

The following day however was a disaster! Molly got very homesick; she couldn't bring herself to leave the room. One minute she was crying, and the next she was not talking to me. I didn't know what to do - having just had a 'moment' myself the previous day I felt that I wasn't prepared for this and couldn't be there for her. Before I knew it, I was offering her an early plane ride home. Of course I didn't want her to go, but I thought that she missed her Mom so much that she needed to go. I could never be her Mom, I could never comfort her like she needed and I was totally freaking out! She come to the end of her tether. I mean we had been through quite a lot over the past week or so. It really aint no picnic, travelling around South East Asia is hard core. I was breaking, in fact, I was broken, my poor baby niece was feeling and picking up on my negative vibes. This made me feel even worse, more guilt, just what I needed. What the holy hell have I done?

Molly wouldn't leave the room. I called my brother Jamie in Bahrain and asked him what to do. I didn't want to call my sister (Molly's mom) as I didn't want to worry her. I felt like I was totally failing as an auntie and godmother, as well as a sister. Billy was annoyed with me, Vic would be annoyed with me if she found out Molly was upset and Molly was annoyed with me. Oh God, I want to get out of here. Why did I come to Sihnaoukville? This place was a dump. I wanted to go home but I didn't want to go back to that horrible place I worked. I started freaking out about work and how much I hated it.

WHOA! Stop Jessica! I finally managed to calm myself down. Then Molly started to come around. We headed out for dinner where there were a lot of tears, but by 10pm we were back in love and had calmed down enough to go to sleep.

Another exciting bus ride

Before we knew it our mammoth bus trip was upon us, 19 hours to get us to HoChiMinh. We thought we were doing well by getting the 'lie down' bus but we were wrong! This actually meant that you can't lie down if you were tall and you can't sit up either as the seats were made to lie at an angle. The bus was packed. People were eating smelly foods, drinking and being so load and obnoxious.

It was four hours to Phnom Phen this time. We got to PP by midnight and had to get off and change buses. This was never an easy task. It was raining, we had to have our passports checked for visas, but no one knows why we have to do this. Before we knew it there were two guys screaming at the tourists to hurry up, and then they sent us all off in different directions. We got onto our new bus and were left with the very back seats. These were the worst seats as there was no room at all for the seats to move and you had a window at the back of your seat. Molly actually slept on the floor as it was more comfortable. We got about four hours of broken sleep and were woken for breakfast at a local cafe before we crossed the border into Vietnam. We stuck to our cheese sandwiches again and canned coffee. Just two minutes down the road and we were at the border. Molly and I were tired, but excited to get to HoChiMinh city (HCM).

We got off the bus, again, and headed over to the Cambodian border control where we needed to get stamped out and of course give our finger prints again. Molly went through before me and got stamped out. Just as I was trying to get stamped through the customs officer said to me 'your visa for Vietnam was for arrival through airport entry only.' I took the letter I had and he was right - I never read it properly!

I was in shock. What do I do? There were two girls at the side saying they had the same letter and had been told they had to stay in Cambodia for another night until Vietnam can process a visa. I couldn't believe it - how could I be so stupid to miss this on the letter? I told them I needed a visa to enter by land, I assumed I had gotten this. Molly was looking worried and the Cambodian customs officer told me to go across to Vietnam and see if they can help, so I ran like the wind with Molly following me. I got to the Vietnam border and told them the story. I was sent to yet another office, so I told Molly to wait 'RIGHT THERE' for me while I got this sorted.

I was literally running between what looked like private housing yelling for someone to come and help me. Finally a girl came out and said she could help. She brought me into a very small, dark hot room which looked anything but official and asked me for the money for the visa. I only had US dollars and only had a US$100 bill. So I handed it over, got the visa and I was one happy lady.

I walked back to where I left Molly but she was not there. I walked into Vietnam customs, but she was not there. I saw our bus driver taking everyone's bags off the bus and headed over to grab our bags but they were gone. I asked some people from our bus if they had seen my niece anywhere but no one had.

At this stage I assumed Molly had the bags and I started running back to Cambodia to get stamped out. It was 39 degrees and I was dripping in sweat. I got to the Cambodian customs officer and he was shocked by the fact that I had the Vietnam visa. He stood there showing all his colleagues the visa I had and was telling them about the story. He said he had never before seen them give a visa with such a letter. I was like "yeah, yeah, whatevs, just stamp me out bro!" I started running back towards Vietnam and as usual a man appears form nowhere on a motorbike. He offered me a ride to the border; it would be a 2 minute ride or 6 minute run. It cost US$2 and it was so worth it. As soon as I got back to the Vietnam border Molly was standing there with the bags looking very relieved to see me. We went through, had our bags scanned and got back on the bus HCM. We were so exhausted by all of the excitement, plus the lack of sleep, that we were comatose within minutes.

Before we knew it the 19 hour bus trip was over and we were woken up as we had arrived in HCM. Of course as soon as we got off the bus there were "taxi" drivers waiting to pounce and rip us off. I was adamant that we get a taxi with a meter and we finally found one only to find out his meter was doggy and yet again we were being ripped off. As soon as we realised this we insisted on getting out so a two minute cab ride cost us almost $10, grr! We found another REAL taxi and it brought us to the hotel which turned out to be a five minute walk from where we got off the bus. Ha-ha...

Cambodia | What was going through my head

Having suffered from depression before, I could tell the signs when it's about to pop up. I knew that I needed to see my doctor. I knew that I needed to take back control here, and that I needed to focus. Instead, all I did was try to keep my mind off what was happening. I tried to ignore the signs. I ignored how I was feeling. I ignored how my feelings were affecting me. My thoughts were no longer just words in my mind, they had complete power over me. If anyone looked at me I would think they hated me. I was convinced my own brother hated me. I had even let my thoughts decide that my family and friends no longer wanted me in their life.

Every thought has its own energy, I had no idea I was actually creating my reality. The reality that I was living in was hell, and I was the one who had created it, in my mind. I was living a life of negativity and hate, but no one else seemed to be living the same life. I was convinced that the world was against me, that I had no power anymore. It was a spiral that I could no longer get a hold of. I was depressed but I couldn't admit this to anyone. I had my niece to look after and what would people think if I asked for help? I couldn't let on to her or anyone else that I was suffering. It was nothing to do with Molly anyway, I didn't want to ruin what was left of her trip. I had to somehow figure out how to push all of what I was feeling and thinking to the side for just a little bit longer. I was so ashamed. I was ashamed of being sad, of needing help, I was ashamed that I had nowhere to turn.

Ever since I was a child I would play the 'I am so sad card.' I used to write letters about how much I hated my life and didn't want to go on, from 8 years old! My mom would find them, as I would place it at the end of bed in full view for her. When I did this she would come and sleep with me until I felt better. This was the only way I knew how to get attention when I was growing up. My parents were always so obsessed with being horrible to one another that we never got a look in. This was all I knew, and I was building a life on drama because that was how I thought love was gained.

I was brought up believing that hurting each other was what people did in relationships. I believed that I didn't deserve to be loved. I believed that children should be seen and not heard. I believed that I had nothing valuable to say, that love was a painful, horrid emotion that left people sad and depressed. I believed that being depressed was normal, my poor mother never knew it wasn't, and she ingrained this into my mind at such an early age. I was raised in a negative home, with a negative mother who always focused on doom and gloom. She tried to be a good mother, but she didn't know how to be. I believed that I was doomed to be depressed forever, I was always told 'it runs in the family'. It was expected of me, depression. I would always be in awe of people who were strong and got through tough times, I didn't understand how they coped. I was brought up to believe that hard times were normal, but that one should drink lots and then break down. After my parents broke up my mother rarely got out of bed, she wouldn't even bother bringing me to school. My other brothers and sister could get to their school by bus and managed to escape. I was left with my mother depressed out of her brains as a 6 year old child. Depression was how I learnt to cope with life. When things don't go your way, breakdown.

You know those times when you get from A to B without realising how you did? I was in that state for my whole time in Cambodia. The only reason I remember anything was because I kept a detailed journal. I was over life, and it felt that life was over me. Suicide had not even entered my mind at this stage. I had my niece with me and there was nothing that I would stop me from getting her home safe and sound.

10

Back to Vietnam

First things first. We head straight for the main markets for some bargains, Billytham markets to be precise. This again was where all of the tourists go to get some kick ass bargains. We went there and bought stuff, lots of stuff! While walking back to the hotel looking for somewhere to have dinner we were pulled aside by a lady who was trying to sell manicures and pedicures, it was $4 for each, $4! I couldn't believe it, of course we couldn't say no to that. Molly had never had her nails done professionally before so off we went to get our nails glossed up.

Anytime that I sat down my mind would start racing - why did I come on this trip? Should I stay longer? What about my boyfriend? Does he still love me? What about work, should I go back? Should I call them and tell them I don't want to do it? The questions kept on coming, but I never made peace with them. I never decoded anything and when I did, I constantly questioned if the decision I made was the right one and would go back and forth driving myself just as crazy as before I made the decision. It was horrible.

The next day we decided to go all out on tourist attractions, I needed to keep my mind busy at all times. It was as soon as I stopped that the thoughts would go crazy. We saw the Independence Palace; we lit a candle at the cathedral, walked by the opera house, and explored the outside. We went down to check out the Saigon River. I wanted to take a boat trip but Molly wasn't interested at all. Clearly she was not a fan of doing touristy things, and wanted to shop all day.

We finally decided to go for lunch and get out of the heat. We just needed to sit in a nice air conditioned room. As soon as we found somewhere we liked we sat down, got a big glass of coke and the electricity stopped working, which of course meant the air conditioner was not working. So typical! We sat in the restaurant and ate our hot food while boiling away ourselves. We had three or four ice cold cokes to try and cool ourselves down. And you would never guess what happens as we were just about to leave... The electricity came back on!

Fuelled full of caffeine we hit the streets again on a mission to find me a new handbag. We walked the streets for hours. We went down every little alley we saw and went into every shop we saw with bags. We ended up back at the markets after hours of unsuccessful shopping. We were about 30 seconds away from the market door when it started pouring rain, we tried to find shelter but it just wouldn't stop so we decided to suck it up and run through the rain. The 30 second walk was a 10 second run and we were drenched to the bone yet again.

We didn't want to stay in HCM for too long. We were flying back home from there, but had six days until we left so decided to go up the coast to a beach for a few days. After chatting to the hotel manager he suggested that we go up to Nha Trang. He said it had great beaches, great restaurants, with a fun atmosphere and had lots to do. Perfect we thought. We could get a train there which we wanted to do as we were totally over buses at this stage. We asked him to book our train ticket for us and he said it would be no problem. When we got back from our shopping trip expecting to have our train tickets we were told the train was full and we had to find a bus somehow. How frustrating! It was 5pm and we were supposed to leave the next day at 9am but now had no mode of transport.

We dropped off our shopping bags and hit the streets again in search of a bus ticket agent. It wasn't long before we found one and booked our tickets. Once we had booked and paid for our tickets we were told it's a 12 hour bus journey. GREAT! I was trying to find out if there was a beach closer to HCM that was good to go to as we really didn't want to go so far for a few days, and especially not on a bus. We didn't have much other choice so we just went along with the plan. We had already booked the hotel in Nha Trang anyway.

The bus picked us up from the hotel and we were off. This time the half lying down, half seating bus was perfect. Daytime travel, feet up, ipod on, we could even play cards as it was bright so we could see. It took longer than we thought it would, no surprise there. They never tell you the actual time the bus journey takes - they always under estimate.

We arrived in Nha Trang quite late. We of course haggled for a taxi to the hotel. The hotel was a dump. We thought we had spent some extra money to get a nice hotel, with breakfast and a pool but it's really nothing like the pictures and we were very disappointed. The lock on the bathroom window was broken and I insisted that they fix it before we showered. Molly was starting to get embarrassed but I was starting to lose my patience completely!

My mind went again to my house in Ireland, where my tenants had given me two weeks' notice that they were moving out. This was really bothering me. I had to pay the mortgage and I had to get back to Sydney and get working in order for this to happen. It was stressing me out thinking should I keep or sell the house and after numerous conversations with my brother, I decided to keep it.

Now that I had made the decision to keep the house I needed to find someone to manage it for me. Previously I had my sister and dad manage the tenants and property, but this had been a burden on them and I didn't want to burden them anymore. I also needed someone to help me go in and clean up the property so I could rent it out again to other tenants. Victoria, my amazing sister had agreed to do this. She had also agreed to go over the house and get the keys from the tenants who were moving out and check the house so I could refund their deposit. This all turned into a bit of a nightmare!

The tenants seemed to think that I should refund their deposit before they moved out as they needed the money for security in the new place. Clearly this was not how it works and there were numerous emails back and forth on this until they eventually understood. I was worried about my sister's safety when she went over to collect the keys as the tenants had turned nasty. I told my sister that I was sorting the deposit separately and that she wouldn't hand over cash at the meeting as the tenants had hoped. I thought we were on the same page but looking back I probably left her in the dark about a few things – completely unintentionally. I was trying to avoid getting her involved in the back and forth as she was already doing me a huge favour. Anyway, she got the keys, they didn't leave on the agreed date, and after a bit more hullabaloo they left and I had the keys.

Victoria on the other hand was very annoyed with me. She thought that I was lying to her, she got seriously annoyed at me. This just broke my heart, it was another blow for me, it was another way of my mind telling me that people hated me, my family hated me. Not only was I convinced my brother had given up on me, I was now also convinced my sister had too. I literally broke down into tears and couldn't stop crying. I hated that I was making things hard for her, I wasn't coping emotionally at all. I hated the fact that I was so far away and trying to manage this stuff in my state of mind was so hard. I hated that I had upset Victoria, I never wanted that, I was probably missing things all of the time as my mind was a complete mess. It was never my intention to do anything to upset her.

The few days we had in Nha Trang weren't great. Between me and my emotional stability being so rocky, it was tough to live it up for our last few days together. I did try. And Molly was amazing! She is such an inspirational 16 year old. I turned to drink. I would be drinking at any chance I had. I would never get drunk but I was really enjoying numbing the pain with sleeping pills and alcohol, it helped me get through the days. We weren't doing much at all, in fact I liked it that way. It was easier for me to be miserable when we were bored.

On our second last day we decided to hire motorbikes for the day so we could check out the local attractions. There was no way I was going to let Molly ride a motorbike herself and I must admit I had no self-confidence to ride one myself, so we hired drivers. People do this all of the time - it's cheaper than taxis and more fun. As soon as Molly rode off with her motor bike driver I had a massive panic attack. I started freaking out he was going to kidnap her. I think my driver picked up on this and quickly caught up with them, from then on we never let them out of sight again!

We went to check out a famous waterfall. It was about a two hour ride away. As soon as we got there we were told it's closed as the rain had been too heavy making it a danger for anyone to get close. REALLY? The roads on the way up to the waterfall were so bad that we had to get off the bikes on a few occasions as we just couldn't get though the mud.

We had planned to spend the day there, so we had to come up with new plans and then had to explain our new plans to our drivers who didn't speak a word of English.

At this stage our sign language was pretty good so we got back on the bikes and headed towards Fairy Mountain, also known as Chong rock. Legend has it that one day, an immortal got drunk and went to fairy beach. Once he got there he was amazed to see so many beautiful fairies who were bathing nude. He found a place to hide and stayed there and watched the fairies. Unfortunately he slipped and lost his balance. His hand fell into the rock and engraved a huge hand print with six fingers. You can see this giant handprint when you visit Fairy Mountain.

We also visited Po Nagar Cham Temple. It was a beautiful temple with a fantastic view of Nha Trang. It was dedicated to Yan Po Nagar, the goddess of the country. We saw the fishing village but couldn't stay long because the smell was too strong. Both of us were not crazy fish lovers so we took some pictures and got out of there ASAP! We finally gave up on the tourist attractions and wanted to get shelter from the rain so we headed back to get some lunch and to dry ourselves off.

Once the sun came out we headed straight to the beach. We found a nice spot with some lounges and set up for the rest of the day. We were watching people go parasailing and I said to Molly, "shall we do it?" Naturally her first reaction, as she was terrified of heights was, "NO WAY!" So I started thinking about doing it myself. I needed something to take my mind off things and thought this would be super fun. Molly started having second thoughts and soon turned to me and said "let's do it!"

I went straight over to the desk and booked it so she didn't have time to change her mind. We had to wait about 20 minutes before we headed over to get strapped up. We wanted to go together so we both got strapped up to the same line and were ready with our waterproof camera to get some kick ass shots from a bird's eye view. They really don't give any instructions, typical Asia style, you just have to close your eyes and hope for the best. . Just before we were about to lift off they asked if we wanted to get dunked in the water or if we just wanted to stay in the sky. We said that we wanted to get dunked – so he made the signal to the driver. Once you saw the boat start to move you just needed to run and before you know it you were flying high above the water and beach and looking back to where you left off.

It was such a fantastic feeling. The view of course was spectacular! We felt so free and carefree. Molly loved it, and her fear of heights was completely forgotten about. The straps were literally riding up through your bum and it's not exactly a comfortable feeling but one you just focus on what you were doing it's fabulous! We turned around and got dunked into the water but as my legs were so much longer than Molly's it was more just me that got dunked. We were having so much fun and feeling so great that we didn't want to come back down. Five minutes goes really fast when you are up there. Before we knew it we were dropped into the water, this time though we didn't go back up. We had to swim to shore. Once back on the beach the adrenaline was pumping and we wanted to do it again.

Back at the hotel I had more emails coming through. My tenants were getting super pushy and wanted the full deposit back. I was holding onto it until they hadn't proved to me that they had paid the utilities. There was also some broken furniture that they had originally been hidden from Victoria's inspection. Then Victoria started saying that she didn't have the time to help out. I was starting to think that I needed to go back to Dublin myself and sort this out. That thought absolutely terrified me. Then I would have to see the house, I didn't want to see what what the last tenants had one to it. I would have to see my sister who clearly hated me. I would miss out on the job I had arranged back in Sydney. It would put immense financial pressure on me. I wasn't prepared to do it. So I tried to find an estate agent who would take over managing the property as well as get the renovations underway. This could be a very expensive project. Not only do I need to put all costs in for the materials and painter, but then I needed to pay the estate agent to manage it. I was really starting to freak out! I had organised some flowers to be delivered to Victoria in order to apologise for upsetting her. Once she received them I think she started to realise that I was sorry and never meant to hurt her.

Now that I had decided to keep the house back in Ireland, I needed to tell the estate agent that I was no longer selling. I sent an email to let her know and got a bitchy response in no time at all. She stated in her email that I had been stringing along these buyers the whole time and that I was just trying to make money. How on earth she thinks I was going to make money I have no idea. I have said to her on numerous occasions that this was my dream home, my life savings, my pride and joy and not only do I have a family living in there who have destroyed my belongings, they've had graffiti sprayed on the walls. I have been paying money every month to top up my mortgage as the rent doesn't cover it. I had been in contact with her and my solicitor at least twice a week for almost five months and then she throws this at me? I was furious! And of course when I get upset and hurt, I want a drink!

My head just couldn't see reality anymore; all I could see and hear were angry people telling me off. I couldn't push the feelings of sadness away anymore. I could no longer control my emotions. I really needed help but I couldn't reach out to anyone. I knew I had to mind Molly for another few days and knew I had to get back to Sydney to my doctor. My body was continually shaking with anxiety. I couldn't get a hold of things and was using zanex to just try to be semi normal for Molly.

We managed to book an overnight train to go back to Ho Chi Minh. It was Molly's first train and she was very impressed. It really was a much better way to travel long distances if not flying. We had our own berth - we paid extra to have it. Two beds per berth the same as first class. We settled in with some beers and sleeping pills and we were asleep by 8pm. We arrived in HCM at 4am and took a taxi to our hotel. As it's our last hotel we splurged and booked a four star hotel.

It's an awesome hotel with a rooftop swimming pool, fancy beds and bathrooms. It was much better than what we had been sleeping in over the last few weeks. We just went back to bed for a few hours and set our alarms early to enjoy a four star buffet breakfast.

After breakfast I was back on my emails trying to find a new estate agent to help me lease the property once it's been renovated. Victoria sent me an estimate of what she thought it would cost for all the renovations. I started freaking out and needed to get back to Sydney to get back to work so I could pay her back. She didn't have the money for this and the fact that I was travelling around Asia right now was making me feel so guilty! I started to get cross with Molly for no real reason and I just wanted to stay in bed all day.

We tried to venture out and go shopping but neither of us were in any sort of mood to sight see or shop. My mood must have been passing over to Molly but I was so upset that I couldn't see what was happening and I started to think that Molly was being ungrateful for the whole trip. We both were so frustrated that we just went back to the hotel. Molly watched TV and I went to the bar by myself and drank through 'happy hour.' I was far from happy and hoping a drink could help out, but it doesn't and so I kept trying. It still didn't. I went back to the room but Molly doesn't want to go out so I headed off drunk and alone to try and get some more gifts for friends back in Sydney.

I walked down the road and looked at my map to try and find the quickest way to the night markets. While I was walking a man turned to me and asked me where I was trying to go. I explained to him the markets and he said he was going that way and I could follow him. So I did.

He was American, from Texas but lived in Bali and was in Vietnam to buy bike helmets for his staff. He started talking to me about his villas in Bali and told me that I should come and visit. His kindness and warmth were refreshing. It made me smile and I felt my heart lift a little from its heaviness. Once we got to the markets we parted ways. He didn't pass on any words of wisdom or turn my life around but it did feel nice to have a chat. I started to think why was I feeling so isolated. I was missing my boyfriend and friends but I had my niece and was getting to spend some serious quality time with her. I honestly wish I could turn back time now and go through this all again with my current mind-set.

When I got back to the hotel, I really wanted to chat to Molly so we had a long conversation as we hadn't spoken all day. It felt good to have a chat. I did bring home more beer so I could try and drink myself into a good night's sleep. The sleeping pills were doing nothing for me anymore and I needed a good night's sleep. I prayed to my angels for help with my situation. I knew something had to change but couldn't see what. I was dreading going back to Sydney even though I really wanted to be home. I didn't want to face reality. I didn't want to go back to that job. I didn't want to see my brother or his girlfriend. I was so upset with the stupid Facebook comment being removed and hadn't spoken to them in a couple of weeks.

Billy knew I was upset as Jason told him. He tried to text me saying he had his reasons to delete my comment but at this stage I didn't care. I was so consumed with depression, I hated everyone – it felt like everything and everyone was against me. I kept wishing for something to happen to me so I wouldn't have to deal with these thoughts anymore.

On our very last day we just wanted to chill out. We laid by the pool after we stuffed our faces with as much breakfast we could get in. After pool time it was time to check out and we desperately tried to fit all of our purchases into our backpacks. We threw out anything we wouldn't use again and left any toiletries behind in order to get maximum capacity for all of the new goodies. We had hours until we flew so we went to see the sky tower.

Molly still insisted that she was scared of heights even though she had been on a Ferris wheel above Bangkok and parasailing above Nha Trang. She came up the tower with me but wouldn't walk to the edge to take in the views. It's an absolute must see when in HCM. Since there weren't many tall buildings you could see the city for miles and miles and it looked so beautiful. In fact, it looked so very different from what you would imagine when walking around on ground level all of the time.

After the sky tower we headed back to the hotel to get our bags and go to the airport. My flight was five hours earlier than Molly's and I have to be there two hours before so Molly was 7 hours early for her flight. I thought that I would be able to find an emirates desk and plead with them to let me check her and her bags in early.

Even though we had done this online, I wanted her to have her bags checked in too. Once we got to the airport I realised there was no emirates desk. In fact, the airport was very small. Ho Chi Minh was the capital of Vietnam so I expected something much bigger. There weren't many options for food. There was no where she could check in.

Once I had checked in I sat with her for a while before going through customs. The guilt was building up inside and I felt so bad for not booking that $1000 later flight so I could wait with her. I kept giving her money so she could buy food or shop once she got through to duty free. When it came time to say goodbye the lump in my throat felt like a bowling ball! I was so devastated, and felt so guilty for leaving her and was also terrified to go back to Sydney. I walked away but couldn't stop looking back. My heart was broken!

While I was walking through customs all I was doing was praying to my angels to look after Molly. I keep saying, 'please, if something was going to happen, make it happen to me' keep Molly safe and happy. I just wanted her to feel safe and not get bored. I was willing to sacrifice whatever it was in order for her to feel this. This kept going over and over in my head, 'please take me not Molly'. I don't know why I was insisting that something needed to happen to me in order for her to feel safe and happy. My mind wasn't working at its best.

A few minutes before I was about to board the plane a huge thunder storm came. The rain was pouring down and the thunder shook the whole airport. My mind straight away goes to Molly and I'm panicking, hoping she isn't scared. This now makes me think that something actually was going to happen to me. I'm not sure what but I took comfort in the fact that the angels would make it happen to me and they would keep Molly safe and happy.

My flight got delayed due to the thunder storm and all I wanted to do was go back to Molly and make sure she was ok. The flight wasn't delayed for long and I got on the short flight to Kuala Lumpur on route to Sydney. I had a six hour stopover in KL. As soon as I landed I texted Molly - she was still waiting in the airport back in HCM. She texted me back saying she was fine and that her Mom had gone to the airport a day early to collect her. I had to laugh. She knew Molly was flying out on the 15th and figured that she would arrive in Ireland on the 15th. I texted Victoria - she wasn't very happy as she had taken the day off work and had organised everything around Molly coming back on the 15th. I started to feel guilty again for upsetting Victoria, AGAIN!

This time it really wasn't my fault but I couldn't help but feel guilty. The nerves about getting back to Sydney were taking over; I knew Jason would be there at the airport to pick me up and I was starting to question how I felt about that. My head was spinning. I felt sick.

The flight back to Sydney from KL on Air Asia wasn't fun. Apart from the fact that my head was spinning like crazy. The actual seats on an Air Asia flight were tiny. They don't have any blankets, and I don't know why airplanes insist on making the temperature Baltic! Also, there was no TV, unless you have pre-ordered; you can't even purchase once in the air. I have been on budget airlines before but I wasn't expecting how budget this was. The flight was so uncomfortable and the staff were the rudest I have come across. This really wasn't helping my nerves at all. Angels please help me!

I am about to learn the biggest lesson of my life. Keep on reading!

11

My World Collapses

I arrived in Sydney airport and I was trying to keep calm. I went through customs and headed towards the baggage area. I was standing watching everyone pick up their bags and kept waiting, and waiting, and waiting. There was no sign of my bag - I was refusing to think my bag had been lost. This was a nightmare I continually had before I went on any trip. This couldn't be happening now.

Eventually someone came over to me and said, "Looks like your bag might be lost?" At this stage I'm thinking everything about my life was wrong, it's all too hard. The poor guy wasn't expecting my reaction when I broke down into tears. I got myself together while he went off to get some forms for me to fill out. I filled out the forms and he said I should have my bag back within 24 hours.

I headed towards the exit, I was so nervous and excited to see Jason. I walked out and I could see him right there in front of me - my heart was pounding. As I got closer to him he was looking pretty bad and as soon as I went to kiss him, I realised that he had a massive night the night before. He stunk of alcohol, his eyes were like two burnt holes in a blanket and my immediate reaction was anger! I was angry that he went out and got smashed. You don't go and get blind the night before picking up your girlfriend from the airport having not seen her in three months! I would never do that and I think it's just disrespectful.

I was now questioning if Jason was the right guy for me. Sounds dramatic and it absolutely was. I was in no state to be making any sort of decisions or calls on who should be in my life right now. In the car on the way home I was so angry that I had lost all the gifts I had bought for everyone. I had lost my journals. And of course I'm angry at Jason. I'm hoping he has at least made an effort to clean the apartment. He of course had absolutely no idea how I was feeling. He thought that I was tried but could not see what was happening inside of my mind. If he could have, he probably would have brought me to the doctor immediately.

When we got back home I was so happy to be back! The apartment was so beautiful - I have my very own toilet and shower, I have all of my bits and pieces. I have space! As much as I felt good, I felt confused. I was wishing that I was coming back home to Ireland and not to Sydney. I don't know why I felt this as Sydney was my home now and Ireland felt like a place I used to know.

I went to bed for a few hours, I thought that some sleep could help me see things clearer. It was so good to sleep in my own bed; I never wanted to get out of it. People were calling and texting but I didn't want to see anyone. The last few days of travel I was getting emails and messages asking when I would be home and all of my friends were trying to arrange meetings once I touched down. I started to ignore them. I couldn't face them and didn't want to talk about my trip, I didn't want to see anyone.

After waking I spent the day at home. I just wanted to feel grounded again and needed to be in my space to get my thoughts together. I started cleaning - Jason did try but his efforts were nowhere near my standards because I am a bit of a clean freak! I started to spring clean. I even started sanding down furniture and painting it. I was on a mission to keep myself busy and also not leave the apartment. I was wishing my phone would ring and that my bag would be on the way back – but no such luck. We spent the night in and I started catching up on my favourite TV programs.

I tried to call my GP but it turns out she was on maternity leave. They don't take appointments so I figured I would go in the next day and speak to someone about getting some help. I was really a mess. One minute I was feeling totally fine, but the next minute I was having some seriously negative thoughts creating horrid anxiety for me. I was convinced everyone hated me and that I was unlovable, I was beginning to believe all the negativity in my head and it was all fuelling itself into one huge fire ball.

The next day we went shopping as I needed a few things because my bag still hadn't arrived. We went to Bondi Junction shopping centre and just as we were about to leave, I noticed that I had lost my sunglasses. I loved these sunglasses and had to find them. I made Jason come back and we traced our steps to. No luck. Jason offered to go and buy me a new pair but I couldn't do it. I had to get home and fast!

We got back home and I went straight to bed. Losing my sunglasses felt like the entire world had turned on me. I know it sounds so dramatic but that's how I felt. I went to bed and couldn't get up. I slept for about four hours and when I woke up the tears started streaming down my face. I felt so alone, so hurt, so angry, and so scared. I knew that something was building up inside of me over the last few weeks but I had no idea of how bad it was. I could no longer face the world. I no longer wanted to be part of the world. I thought it was cruel, tough, unkind, unforgiving. I thought I was sick beyond repair, that everyone would be happy to see the back of me. I honestly thought I was completely worthless.

I started drinking. I only had a glass of wine, and before I knew it I was writing a suicide note. Jason was playing his Xbox and was completely oblivious to it all. I went to the medicine drawer and pulled out anything I thought could help. I knew I had some sleeping pills and a whole lot of old prescription pills as well as tonnes of other over the counter pills. I was actually shocked myself to see how much medicine I had. I had thought about suicide many times before when in my lowest times of depression, but I never actually planned anything or went through with it. There was no time to waste planning; I just had to get this done. I felt that every second more that I was alive was actually hurting not only me, but everyone else. I felt that my life was a burden to all and that it I was so much better off dead! I felt a sense of urgency to get this done, I felt compelled to do it and do it right. I was doing this, and nothing was going to stop me.

I Googled how many pills I would need to take for it to be fatal and got started. There were so many articles on the internet about this, which are basically helping people to kill themselves. I was happy at the time for the information but it's quite bothersome now that I look back.

The particular pill I had quite a few off would need to be taken in high doses, I would need 15-20 to do the damage.

I was listening to the same song on repeat, and every time I heard it kept me focussed. I was so relieved that I finally knew the answer to my problems; I finally felt that I was making the right decision. I felt that I had finally seen the light and that this was my destiny.

I couldn't swallow all the pills in one go; I knew I had to take a few at a time and keep on going. I didn't feel scared anymore. I had written my note to my family and was ready to not live this life anymore. To me it made total sense and I actually felt so proud that I was following through. I had thought about suicide so many times before, surely a lot of people have had these thoughts at some stage in their lives? The thing is, I never had the guts to do anything until now. I started with the sleeping pills I had, there were about 8 of them and they were small and easy to swallow. I expected the pain go away suddenly, but it didn't. So I started with the other pills I had - these pills were much bigger and harder to swallow. I took a good few of those and could feel myself getting very woozy. The tears were coming fast and strong. I kept thinking back to my trip and how I had made such a mess of it. I thought how finally my house in Ireland would be sorted without me having to deal with it. I thought about how my family would be happy to not have to deal with my depression anymore. I was so committed to following this through.

I was convinced that Jason wouldn't find me until at least three am, at that stage I would be dead for a few hours. I kept on taking the pills, I could feel my eyes getting so heavy, this was a different kind of heavy, nothing that I have felt before. I kept drinking, and taking pills, I had lost track of how many now, and then, I don't know what compelled me, but I ended up going out to Jason and telling him what I did just before passing out in front of him. It could have been my angels, it could have been my dead mother but something stopped me in my tracks, even though I felt committed to finalising it all, there was something that was stronger than me that pulled the pin just before it was too late. This was my miracle turning point.

I was completely out of it. Apparently Jason called my brother first and told him to come over with the car. He then called 000(emergency) and asked for advice on what to do. They advised him to bring me to accident and emergency. Billy & his girlfriend came with the car and Jason carried me down. The hospital was very close to where we live so we were there in no time. Of course as soon as we got to hospital I was rushed through. They could see that something serious was wrong. Naturally I don't recall much but Jason told me that they were slapping across the face trying to wake me, they were looking for any signs of alertness and they kept asking me what I had taken. I remember coming around at one stage and hearing Billy and Laura's voices and thinking, SHIT! It didn't work! I did not want to wake up and face this. I was devastated it didn't work. Why didn't I take more? Why did I go out to Jason? What possessed me to want to fail? I was so convinced this was going to work, and I was so sure I had done it right. My next thought was, 'how could I get out of the hospital and get this done properly?'

I was in and out of consciousness. I was hoping it was a dream. I kept hearing the heart monitor beeping really fast and I kept hoping, this is it, I'm going to die. But I would be woken by the next time the monitor started beeping. It was such an awful feeling - wanting to die and knowing that I had messed up my chances of doing it right. The next awful feeling was realising that I was in the hospital and coming to terms with the fact that this was now everyone else's problem, not just mine.

It took me a almost 10 hours to come around and when I did open my eyes I needed to use the toilet. I wasn't allowed go. I had to do it in a bed pan. I guess they were afraid that I would try to hurt myself. This was so humiliating. The nurse asked me if I wrote a suicide note. Is this happening? Do I have to face this? I looked over at Jason and he was terrified! I couldn't imagine what he was thinking and to be honest I really didn't want to.

He never let go of my hand the whole time he was there. Any time I woke up to the heart monitor beeping as my heart rate was dropping I could feel his terror. It wasn't until the next day I began to start feeling guilty for what I had done, although this didn't stop me from still wanting to end it. I was a mess.

Jason had stayed by my side the whole night until the nurse told him to go home and get some sleep at about 5am. I was still pretty much out of it so I didn't even notice he was gone until he came back and told me what had happened. He filled me in on everything. I didn't want to hear it. I couldn't even cry; I had no emotion left.

Once they had stabilised me I was moved out of emergency and into a ward. I rarely opened my eyes as I just didn't want to deal with the world. When it came to facing the world it's all just too much to imagine.

I was on suicide watch... The nurse went through all of my bags to ensure there was nothing in there that I could hurt myself with. I couldn't believe this was happening to me. How did I get here? Only two days ago I was travelling around Asia with my niece and here I was having my personal belongings searched through and my every move being watched.

I had to fill out some forms and the hospital staff asked if there was anyone who I didn't want any information communicated to; I wrote down my brother Billy. I felt so much anger towards him! My sister had texted me asking if I was OK. Well clearly I was not OK but I was even more not OK because Billy had informed my family back home. I didn't want that. I didn't want anyone to know yet as I hadn't succeeded, I wanted them to all find out when it was done, completed and they could be happy for me. I was so angry with him for doing that, but really I was just angry at myself.

I texted my sister back saying "I'm sorry, I thought I took enough." She offered to fly over to Sydney if I needed her but the last thing I wanted was for her to feel obliged to me again! She was already doing enough for me.

I wanted to have a cigarette but I couldn't leave the room. Even when I went to the toilet a nurse followed me. When it came time for Jason to go home for the night I cried like a baby! I didn't want him to go. The guy who was in the bed next to me kept staring at me and he was making me feel so uncomfortable. Any time that Jason left the room to go for a smoke he would look over at me and it felt like he was undressing me with his eyes. It was so creepy! I didn't want to be left there. I wanted Jason to stay. I was starting to feel so incredibly scared, my emotions were all over the place.

I wanted to get out of the hospital so badly, but there was nothing I could do. As soon as Jason left I hid under the bed sheets and closed the curtain around me. You have to leave a small bit open so the nurse can see you. I couldn't sleep. The other three people in the room were snoring so loudly. My head was spinning. I was so freaked out! The nurse saw that I was distressed and came and gave me some more sleeping pills to help me sleep. Thankfully they worked.

The next day, Jason was there as soon as visitors could come. The love that he gave me made me want to go on. I started to feel that I could live this life if I only had him and nothing else. I couldn't face work again, or my friends. I didn't want to ever leave my apartment once I got back to it. All I knew was that Jason loved me and was going to look after me. I needed that, I needed someone to take control. I felt that I had used all of my strength over my life, and that I was finally ready to let someone else to be strong for me. I was no longer strong enough myself.

I started to hate my brother for no reason at all. When I would hear his voice on the phone to Jason it would irritate me. I kept saying I didn't want to see him. Now when I think about how mean and so uncalled for it all was, I cry. I mean if the shoe was on the other foot and he didn't want to see me after something like this, I would be so devastated!

My brother Billy has been my rock my whole life, along with my wonderful sister Victoria. Billy and I had been very close since we were kids. We even had our own language when we were small. When someone would ask if Billy wanted to go somewhere, he would always reply, "Only if Jessica does". So cute.

I couldn't speak to him though because I felt he wouldn't understand what was going on. Anytime I had been dealing with depression before Billy would get frustrated and tell me to "just stop!" I had asked him to come with me to my counsellor one time a few years back, so she could explain depression to him, but he refused to go. This kept coming into my head and I was sure that Billy would judge me for what I had done, and that he would be thinking, "Just get over it." At that time, I did not want to face that.

The messages and calls from my friends started coming through, not because they knew what had happened - only my family was told.

They were getting in touch because they knew I was back in Sydney and wanted to see me. I could have turned off my phone but I didn't want to just in case I got a call regarding my lost bag. And even though I didn't want to communicate with the outside world, I still wanted to be able to should I change my mind.

My good friends knew there was something up, one of them even asked if she had done something to upset me. They thought it was strange that I wasn't seeing anyone now that I was back. The only person I wanted to see or talk to was Jason. I wanted to stay in my bubble.

While I was in the hospital, all I did was play candy crush with Jason and sleep. Well actually, Jason played candy crush and I watched him. I couldn't eat, and I couldn't read - I was the most unmotivated I have ever been, not including the motivation I had to get out of there! It felt like I was in there for weeks!

I thought about my bag that was lost. I had been in the hospital for three days, and finally on the 4th day I had a psychiatrist come to see me. Naturally they needed to assess me before letting me out of hospital. I told them my story - how I lost my sunglasses, and then tried to commit suicide. That was the trigger and I had no idea why it made me so upset. The doctor told me that I had issues around being a perfectionist and that I needed to go and see someone to talk about these issues. Were they serious? I know I was a perfectionist; what's wrong with that!? I know I have issues; I just tried to kill myself!

I thought that they might be able to shine a little more light on the situation but apparently they just wanted to know if I planned on trying to kill myself again. I said 'no.' I figured that's what they wanted to hear to let me out, so I told them. I may have been depressed but I wasn't stupid. I knew I had to get out of there in order to be able to do this again, properly! They also told me not to go back to work as it was clear that I had anxiety about going back there. Again, this was not news to me.

They didn't have to tell me twice to go home. I walked out of the room and packed my bag in a flash! I collected my belongings and had to wait for the mountain of paperwork I had to fill out. I suppose they needed to cover themselves if I did try it again. I had spent four days in hospital but it felt like forever. See you later hospital bed! I couldn't wait to get home to my apartment and get into my own bed.

Suicide is usually attributed to a mental disorder such as depression, bipolar disorder, schizophrenia, borderline personality disorder, alcoholism, or drug abuse. Stress can play a factor, financial difficulties, relationships troubles, self-doubt, anxiety; so many factors contribute to it. Did you know that around 800,000 to a million people die by suicide every year, making it the 10th leading cause of death worldwide? For 15-24 year olds it's the 3rd leading cause. On average one person commits suicide every 16.2 minutes. Rates are higher in men than in women, with males three to four times more likely to kill themselves than females. There are an estimated 10 to 20 million non-fatal attempted suicides every year.

These figures are astounding! It was so sad to think that people, like me, felt that the only solution they had was to try and take their own life. When I think about this now, I cry, I can't believe that I reached that place. I can't believe that we make this subject so taboo. Why don't people want to help people? Why are people too busy to help out a fellow human in need? It is incredibly heart breaking, and I for one will not stand by and let these numbers increase, or let people think they are alone.

YOU are not alone.

I want to make this something we can all talk about without having shame attached. We need to stand up and take note of what is happening. Don't brush depression, anxiety, hopelessness under the carpet. Suicide is the world's 10th leading cause of death!

3 years after my own suicide attempt, I lost my brother to suicide. Even typing that brings tears to my eyes. His pain was too much for him to take. My father and sister did everything they could to help him, but he didn't want help. He tried so many times to end his life, he took pills, he ended up in hospital, it was like a bad movie on repeat. It kept happening, but nothing was changing. His pain never changed, his thoughts never changed, he never committed to getting better. I wanted so desperately to help him. I wanted him to read this book. I wanted to

give him hope, but he didn't want it. He never got help, he never really admitted that he had an issue. Even after multiple suicide attempts he couldn't see that something was seriously wrong. My heart will forever feel heavy for his loss. I will forever feel his pain. I know the place that he got to, I was there.

Please if you are feeling sad, hopeless or in despair, GET HELP!! There are so many people and so many ways to get help, to ask for help. All you need to do is reach out. I am sharing my story because my suicide attempt was my biggest and best turning point. Your dark moments can turn into bright ones. I never in a million years thought that I could feel as happy as I do now. If I can change, than anyone can. I am here to tell you to have hope. If you want to make the change to get better you can, but you need to ask for help. You don't have to go this alone. If only my brother had wanted to get better, if only he let someone help him, if only he would have admitted he had a problem. Admitting there is an issue is the first step to recovery. If I had made it to my doctor and she wasn't on maternity leave my story could have been different. If I had bene brave enough to ask for help sooner than my attempt my story would be different. Every day that I wake up alive I feel blessed to be here. I feel blessed to have bene touched by an angel that night and be here to share my story. A miracle occurred that night when I reached out to my boyfriend for help. If I never went and told him what I had done I could be dead.

How much money goes towards mental health each year? How much attention does mental health and suicide get each year? How much press? It seems the only press it gets, is when it's too late. We have seen quite a few 'celebrities' suicide being publicised. It amazes me how we can put a person on a pedestal and think them to be so happy, yet behind closed doors they are suffering, alone, in silence. Depression is an invisible disability, and made so by how we ignore it. We make it a taboo. When I speak to people about my book so many ask "what about when you have children, they will know what you did?" I think that me sharing this story is a powerful message for my children. What if they suffer from what I suffered from? I want them to know that it's ok to feel this way, but it's also ok to ask for help. I want them to know that they can talk about it. That they can get through it. That I can help them and that I understand!

I read an article the other day about a guy who had suffered from depression for years. He finally came out and spoke about his illness and his battle with suicide in order to help others. This took courage, and I admire him. Then I read a comment under his blog that shocked me. Someone had actually posted that he was an attention seeker and that he deserved to die. I believe that no one deserves to die and that if we could help save a life then we have made our lives worthwhile. How can someone say he was seeking attention, and even if he was seeking attention, it was for a reason. People seek attention for help as they don't know how else to ask for help. People aren't out there offering help.

I am telling my story because I believe that we are all on this journey together and we should all help each other as much as possible along the way! Ask yourself and your friends, are YOU OK?

12

Coming Home Again

As soon as I walked into my apartment, I had visions of me taking the pills. My suicide note was still beside my bed, and it felt like my apartment had changed. I wanted to come back here so badly from the hospital, but it felt strange. This wasn't the plan. Billy and Laura still wanted to see me but I couldn't face anyone yet. I was keen to just get into bed and stay there. I was overwhelmed again. I didn't know what to do. Jason was scared to leave my side and to be honest I was scared to be alone. The feelings of wanting to end it all were back and they were strong! I knew that if I was left alone I would try something, except this time I knew what I had to do!

This was exhausting for Jason to be dealing with alone, but it was just as exhausting for me. I had to reach out and talk to someone else. I needed to talk to someone but couldn't talk to Jason. He was too emotional.

This was when I called Sarah. She was a very close friend and she is very spiritual. I had never been not anything like that before, angels, yoga, it was all very hippy to me. I needed a different approach, as clearly my way of getting through things wasn't working This was what I wanted to surround myself with. I knew Sarah would understand.

I called her and asked her to come and visit. She knew something was up but I never told her what. Once she got to our place I told her what had happened. She was shocked, but also had so much love. She kicked into 'mind mode' and really helped to start to get me motivated again. I was still depressed, but her light and energy really helped me. We talked for hours, I felt that I could tell her anything and she wouldn't judge me. That was what I was afraid of most - that people were judging me. Sarah just loved me and wanted me to get better. There was absolutely no judgement no matter what I said. It felt good to talk to her but as soon as she left, I felt lost again....

I think I started to bring up feelings and emotions with Sarah but then held back on getting them out fully so they were left dangling once she left. This was causing fogginess and confusion. I couldn't sleep that night. I was tossing and turning all night and anytime I moved, Jason would wake up and ask me if I was ok. It was breaking my heart watching Jason be so emotional. I needed him to be strong for me, but clearly this was taking a toll on him, of course it would.

My anxiety was kicking in big time now. My whole body was constantly shaking. I couldn't eat, I couldn't sleep and I was starting to feel delirious. Numbness came and took over my mind and body. This doesn't make you feel better; it makes you feel dead. My mind just stopped working. My body wouldn't stop shaking, and I just sat in front of the television for hours on end, having no idea what I was watching.

I had to check in with my GP. The hospital had made me agree that I would check in with her every 2 days if I left there. If I didn't go then they would be chasing me up themselves. When we walked around to book in with the doctor there was a four hour wait at the doctor's surgery, I couldn't sit there - paranoia would get the best of me. Luckily we lived around the corner so we went back home to wait. When I finally got into the actual doctor's office she seemed stressed out. Clearly she was busy and was keen to keep the flow of people fast and steady. She asked what was wrong with me and I told her that the hospital should have sent through some paperwork for her to read over. I couldn't say it aloud myself, what I had done and why I was here, I didn't want to and the words would literally get stuck in my throat if I tried.

She told me that she had no paperwork, and that she doesn't have time to look for it. I started to panic, I didn't know what to do. She could clearly see that I was anxious. Her manner changed when she clicked, she came around and more calmly asked me what was going on, and why I was there. I started to explain to her how I was feeling and she began to warm up to me, thankfully. I got a prescription of anti-depressants. I had been on Lexapro before so I was put on them again. She gave me something to help me sleep but not enough to do any damage with. She told me to come back again tomorrow and she would try to find the missing paperwork from the hospital. This would basically just say that I needed to see a GP and psychologist, or counsellor until I felt better.

I wanted to know why I did this. I needed an answer because all that was going through my head was that I wanted to do it again. If I knew why I did it in the first place maybe I could fix what was wrong and then I wouldn't have these feelings anymore. I couldn't figure out what was wrong with me. I had no answers. Jason kept asking if I was ok. Or what was wrong? I couldn't answer him. The more I thought about what was wrong with me, the more I put pressure on myself that I didn't need.

I started to plan how I would do it, take my life for real, this somehow made me feel better. It was better than the numb feeling. This way I was feeling excitement and had something to work towards, even if it was ending my life. A million ideas would come streaming into my head about ways to die. Slitting my wrists, drowning myself in the bath, jumping in front of a train, jumping off my balcony, I was keen to try pills again too, I had the courage to do this as I had tried it before. I didn't want to get too elaborate as that would be too hard. Something like jumping off my balcony seemed easy, but did I have the courage to do it? I kind of preferred the thoughts of a slower paced death, like with pills, it seemed more gentle.

Another ting waying massively on my mind was work. I knew I had to call and tell them that I wasn't coming back. I was due to start in six days! There was no way I could face that so I asked Jason to call them. I told him to call and tell them I had been suffering from exhaustion, that I had been in hospital and that I couldn't come back to work for a few weeks. But I'm pretty sure he told them the real truth. He said he didn't but I knew by his face that he did. I knew he was trying to protect me. But this really pissed me off!

Even though I was trying to think of ways to kill myself again there were moments when I was focused on getting better too. In these moments I wanted to keep the work relationship open should I need it in the future. Jason had gone and blown my chances of going back to work and I was furious. Why did he do that when I asked him not to? I figured I would just leave it for now and once I start to feel good again I would call them myself and sort it out. I was back and forth with wanting to end it all and making plans for work in the future. One minute I was over it all and planning on how I could get enough pills to do the deed, and the next minute I was stressing about where I would work once I felt better. I wasn't focusing on getting better, I was just focusing on the obstacles I had in front of me. Or at least the ones I set up for myself. I was up and down like a yoyo and it was exhausting. I couldn't think straight, I wanted someone else to think for me.

Thankfully the sleeping pills the doctor had prescribed worked. Well at least for a few hours. Having finally gotten some sleep again I could contemplate starting to talk to Billy and Laura. Although I still felt that they were judging me. Sarah called me every morning. If I didn't answer she would call Jason. She came over almost every day and I loved seeing her. After three days of not letting me out of his sight Jason got some freedom and went out for the night. Sarah came over and we hung out and ordered take out - this was pretty much the first time I ate properly.

When we were sitting there chatting, it felt so normal. This was the first time I actually had forgotten what had just happened. I stopped thinking about suicide and just sat in the moment. It felt so good!

As soon as Jason came he saw a new look in my eyes. As he had a few drinks he started to get emotional. Once Sarah had gone he started to tell me about what happened, how he felt etc. This broke my heart. I felt so guilty for doing this to him. I hated hurting him. He had been so amazing over the last few days, and I couldn't imagine having gotten through it without him. Even though I thought I wasn't ready to hear it, it helped me to wake up. I needed to stop thinking about my next suicide attempt.

I had been calling the airport daily to check on my bag. I had pretty much given up hope that I would get it back, but after a week they called me and said they had it! This was another feel good moment. Once it arrived at my doorstep I opened it up and started crying, although these were tears of joy! I finally had my stuff back and I had all of the gifts I had bought for Jason, Billy, Laura, everyone!

This was a good little pick me up and gave me confidence to finally ask Billy over. It had been a week since 'the event' and I needed to see him. Not so much for me, I wasn't sure if I wanted to see him, but I knew that had to. I was starting to build a situation in my head that didn't even exist, or so Jason told me anyhow. I was convinced Billy hated me, that he was annoyed with me for what I had done. I was sure he didn't want anything to do with me. When I called and asked him and Laura to come over I was nervous he would say no... I was so scared to see him and asked Sarah to be there. I figured that she could keep the conversation going if I was too anxious. I couldn't have faced being left alone. Once Billy came over and we started chatting, it was fine. It was clearly awkward, but nothing like I had imagined it would be. I had almost imagined that there would be yelling, screaming, and maybe even some heads torn off. My head had gotten completely carried away with 'what could have been'. My anxiety before Billy arrived totally peaked, my heart was pounding, my whole body was in shock, it was trembling like never before.

It wasn't long before all that started to fade, the anxiety was still there but the shakes calmed and the feelings of anger I had towards him started to fade away too. Laura didn't come. I guess she figured it was best for Billy to see me first. Of course this made me think she didn't want to see me, the negative thoughts started to come in thick and fast. Does she hate me? Does she think I was stupid? Is she annoyed? Does she think Billy shouldn't be here? Once Billy left I started telling Sarah what I was thinking, she quickly told me to stop it. When you are so unsure about life, a thought was no longer just a thought. It becomes reality, no matter how crazy it is.

As much as I was happy and relieved to have seen Billy, I was still worried about what he thought of me, and now I had to add the fact that Laura hadn't come to see me. Why not? What did she think of me? One minute I felt that Billy wasn't judging me, but two seconds later I changed my mind. I couldn't be alone as my mind would go crazy and go round in circles driving me mad! I couldn't sleep. I quickly took a sleeping pill as my head was starting to spin out of control. I was starting to run out of sleeping pills. The doctor had only given me a couple and she wasn't keen to keep prescribing them. I had to try to sleep without them, I was starting to really want to anyhow. It had been 8 days now and there were moments of seeing the light. I was having moments of wanting to keep living. I was motivated to stay here for Jason at least.

Luckily Jason wasn't working a full time job at the time so he could be in the apartment with me. If he did have meetings, I didn't trust myself to be left alone, so I needed a minder. As I hadn't told many people what was going on we were short on options, but when the time came when we really needed someone I called my friend Cat. She was so supportive and gentle, which was just what I needed. We hung out of hours and she made absolutely no issue around my vicious anxiety. I was shaking like a leaf, even my voice was shaking. I felt so lucky to have such wonderful friends between Sarah and Cat.

Laura was calling and texting almost every day but I rarely replied to her as I thought she hated me for no reason what so ever. At the time it made complete sense. I felt a huge distance between myself, Billy and Laura and I couldn't quite figure out what the issue was, even though it was only in my head. I knew that we would sort it out, but right now I just wasn't ready to talk. This alone was stressing me out. I knew there shouldn't be an issue but I couldn't help what I was feeling.

A whole week past, and all I did was worry and feel guilty. These thoughts kept bringing me back to another suicide attempt. I felt that this was the best and only way to deal with things. I wasn't afraid of dying anymore. I felt that I had a connection with death and that I needed to fulfil this connection. These thoughts would come and go - most of the time I would feel nothing, just emptiness. Maybe this was because the mind works so hard on anxiety that it just needs to take a break and you were left feeling dazed and confused or just left feeling empty. I was happy being miserable. At least I didn't know any other way to deal with depression other than accepting the horrible feeling and letting it take over me. I had no coping skills, was given no direction. All everyone was doing was asking of I was OK? I wasn't OK. I was f**ked!! But no one could help me.

13

The Help

I made a booking to see my counsellor. She wasn't free as soon as I got out of the hospital so I had to wait a few days. I had seen her before a couple of years ago and thought it would be good to go back to her. I thought a familiar face would be better, added to the fact that I had no idea where to turn and wasn't given much direction either. I couldn't go out there and find a good counsellor; I just needed one to be put in front of me.

I stepped into her office and she asked why I was there. I explained to her what had happened but she didn't seem shocked- that's her job I guess. I'm not much of a talker, especially when it came to talking about my problems so I was waiting for her to tell me what the issue was.

This seems to be a trend. I just wanted someone to tell me what is wrong me and I wanted to be able to resonate with their synopsis. She pretty much told me what she thought was wrong based on my previous visits almost a year and a half ago. She explained that I have issues with work and that I shouldn't work so hard and need to find a job where I could work part-time - that was her answer to my issues!

I was shocked! I hadn't worked in over four months so how could work be stressing me out? I was so confused! This didn't resonate at all with me and I left even more confused than when I went in. I wanted to see someone else. I just wanted to know what was wrong so I could fix it. I didn't realise at that stage that I had to figure out what was wrong with me and that no one else could.

I started doing some research; Sarah helped me too. I wanted to find someone who I thought could tell me what was wrong with me and tell me how to fix it. Seeing as I had always just seen a counsellor, I decided to try a psychologist. I had always been under the impression that a counsellor was more of a gentle approach and that a psychologist was more of a medical/white coat approach. Again, I was wrong. I found one that I thought would suit me and I called him up to question him. He was so nice and instantly made me feel at ease. This was who I wanted to see. I made an appointment for as soon as I could.

My first session was great! I told him I didn't really want to talk so he did lots of talking but cleverly asked the perfect questions to get all the info he needed from me. He helped me to just focus on my breathing. My anxiety was still very bad and my body and voice were so shaky. He made me realise that I did actually have control over my brain and thoughts. He told me to 'look at the wall' and I did; this showed me that I was in control. Simple exercise but very effective. I was amazed. Why did I wait so long to see a psychologist?

I needed someone to show me that I was in fact, in control. I was in control of me, of my mind and of my body. I could easily go and take my life, that is the 'easy' way out. No one had actually told me that I needed to take control, that my life was my own. I had completely forgotten this. I had spent so long feeling that I had no control I forgot that it was possible for me to have it in the first place. Everyone had been so sacred for me that they were trying to take over and run my life for me, this just assists the depression. How can I start to feel better when I just don't have to. I can continue to have people mind me and run around after me, but what kind of life would that be? I was scared, was I ready to take back control? Having others look after me was actually nice... Maybe that's why I didn't want to get better?

The doctor had me focus on my breath. I had to carefully breath in and out whilst counting my breath and paying close attention to how I inhaled the air as well as exhaled. At first I wasn't sure what he was doing. Why could this help me? I just tried to kill myself. I wasn't here to learn how to breathe... I decided to stay open to anything. I started to feel better after the breathing exercise. Then the doctor explained that it was called mindfulness, it's being present in any given moment. Not just present but also non-judgemental. This was something I had to work on… Not judging anything was going to be a push, but I was keen to try it.

I had to walk home by myself from the shrink, this brought on some bad anxiety. Armed with my new breathing exercises I managed to get through it. Although, I did walk the long way so I wouldn't have to see so many people. My anxiety was so bad that I was scared people were looking at me, so I avoided them as much as possible.

As soon as I got back home I practiced my exercises. My anxiety was still there and strong, but I had a little hope. I started to read more about mindfulness. It originated from Buddhism and psychologists use it to focus attention and awareness. Mindfulness is all about training your thoughts to do what you tell them. Just stop for a moment right now, and consider just how valuable this present moment is. You are living it right now. This moment is all there truly is. If you can learn to master your mind and stay with this moment, you will transform your life into a far more liberating and joyous experience. When you learn how to practice mindfulness, you learn to view life through the eyes of your true self.

Mental focusing exercises such as meditation not only help you increase awareness, they can also harness your attention in directions that will best serve you. It starts with closing your eyes, relaxing your body, and tuning into your breath. You can then work to quiet the mind and become aware of the present moment sensations. With practice you will learn to quiet the mind and let the random thoughts that may pop up simply pass through like waves, without judgment or attempt to hold on. I tried to imagine my thoughts as bubbles, I would let them float away in the air and watch them go away.

Mindfulness meditation is unique in that it is not directed toward getting us to be different from how we already are. Instead, it helps us become aware of what is already true moment by moment. We could say that it teaches us how to be unconditionally present; that is, it helps us be present with whatever is happening, no matter what it is. I have always said, the present is a gift and that is why it is called the 'present'. Through mindfulness you can begin to appreciate this wonderful gift. We can also begin to train our brains to see a bigger picture and not let ourselves be so controlled by our emotions.

Mindfulness is paying precise, non-judgmental attention to the details of our experience as it arises and subsides, doesn't reject anything. Instead of struggling to get away from experiences we find difficult, we practice being able to be with them. When we are mindful, we show up for our lives; we don't miss them in being distracted or in wishing for things to be different. Instead, if something needs to be changed we are present enough to understand what needs to be done.

It is important to realise that there is a difference between mindfulness and concentration. Concentration is important. It helps you to focus your attention on one thing or another, and in this way it helps you to take command of what goes on in your mind. But mindfulness is another step beyond concentration. Mindfulness is a state of awareness. It is "presence" of mind. Concentration is the tool you use to bring your mind into focus and to close the door on mental chatter, but it's still up to you to "show up" and be present in the moment.

Whatever you experience in this world, whatever you think and feel, breathe it in, then breathe it out. Be conscious and aware of your experience, without judging. Just be. Just breathe. Live freely in this state of mindfulness.

After more and more research plus putting my mindfulness techniques to the test I was in awe. I just wanted to sit in mindfulness all day every day. It became such a wonderful place to be. I downloaded tonnes of mindfulness meditations and guidance and would sit listening to them for hours. I did have a favourite, it was such a simple exercise, no music in the background, no frills, just all about the breath.

I was starting to see that I was in fact, my own worst enemy. That it was my thoughts that had carried me away down this path of negativity. That it was me who was putting all this pressure on myself. It was me who talked myself into killing myself. It was me who was scared of my own mind!!

With depression and anxiety your thoughts take over, and what is actually just a thought feels like reality. Your mind can be seriously mean to you when you let it. The real truth is, that your mind is trying to protect you. Your unconscious mind is there to serve and protect you. Your mind can convince itself that killing yourself is the best solution, as it did mine. It can also convince you that killing people is bad, or that drinking and driving is bad. It can convince you that you don't need to exercise, that you don't believe in Santa, it can convince you that you have nothing important to say. All of what it has learnt is built into a protection model. Therefore if I was told that I should keep quiet and I wouldn't get in trouble, then my mind will keep me quiet throughout my life. That is, until I recognise that this belief no longer serves me and I need to let it go.

What do you believe? Does your mind hold you back from doing something that you really want to? What were you told as a child that still to this day sticks in your head every time you go to do a certain thing? Deep down my unconscious mind knew that I didn't want to end my life when I tried to. I got carried away. I never planned on killing myself. I just jumped straight in without thinking about it. My mind protected me by somehow sending me a message to go and tell Jason what I had done. If I didn't leave the room that time, I would be dead! This is my miracle, this is my second chance at life, this is my time to change. It was time for me to stand up to my demons, it would take hard work but I was dedicated.

My unconscious mind knows that I have so much more to do before I die. I have to help others, I have to have children, I have to share my story in order to give hope to those who need it. There is so much that I wish to accomplish in this life, and I never would have gotten to do any of it if I hadn't told Jason what I had done. If I was my usual stubborn self I would not be sitting here right now. I wouldn't be sharing my story. I would have missed my happiness. I can barely even think about it.

The pain that I felt when my mother died all those years ago, I would have put on my family. The pain and suffering that we are all experiencing now after my brothers suicide I also could have given to my family. I didn't have to leave this beautiful, wonderful Universe. I would have gotten rid of my guilt, my depression, my fears, my loneliness, and swapped it for theirs. At the time I honestly thought they would be happy to see the back of me. I was so caught up in pain that I couldn't see what pain it would cause them. I am so happy that my mind protected me, that it knew there was more for me.

The time came for me to see Laura. Jason and Sarah kept telling me that I was building these thoughts around her and Billy that were untrue, and I needed to stop. As soon as she came over and we sat and had a cup of tea, we were back in our friendship zone within seconds. Of course Laura didn't judge me. She was worried and naturally protective, but maybe I saw this as judging me. We touched on the topic and moved on quickly. She just wanted me to know that she was there for me. I was so happy as the negative thoughts around our relationship literally disappeared.

Although things were looking up one moment, there were still moments of numbness. It was like I had no feelings. It sucked feeling numb. It makes you think there was nothing to live for. When I went to my GP and told her about this she instructed me to increase my meds - she said to double the dose! I really wasn't keen on doing this. My sister thought I should follow the GP's instructions whereas Jason thought if I didn't want to, that I shouldn't. I decided to give it a few more days to see if there were any changes before upping the dose.

I hated the fact that I had to rely on medication to make me feel normal, and I still wasn't feeling normal. I wanted to stop the meds altogether but thought I better hold on and keep looking for alternatives before I just stop. I was still searching for someone to tell me what was wrong with me and wanted someone else to fix me. I never realised that it was me who was the only person who could fix me. Why didn't the shrink tell me that? I think if he did, I wouldn't have listened anyhow. I wasn't ready to be told I had brought this all on myself and I could only fix it myself.

Moving on

Sarah had given me a book to read the day after I came out of the hospital. I couldn't bring myself to focus on anything when I got out so never picked up the book to read it. She had told me over and over again to just start to read the first few pages, and assured me that once I started that I would want to continue reading. Picking up the book became almost impossible for me to do. I realised that what if Sarah was right? What if it did make me feel better? Then I would have to start getting better and face the world but I wasn't ready to face the world. I had plenty of time to read it. I mean I had 24 hours a day, every day!

The issue was that I was scared to see changes! How silly does that sound? I wanted to feel better, or at least I thought I did. But I didn't want to take steps to make me feel better, and I didn't want to face up to what was wrong with me. I was hoping that someone else would put a label on what was wrong with me and I could then just deal with this label. This sounded easier and was generally how I had gotten through my depression in the past. I was getting myself into knots again over what I wanted. Did I want to get better? Did I just want to check out? Did I even have it in me to do what it would take to get better?

Sarah came over and we decided to read my angel cards. She had bought them for me for Christmas and I only ever did a reading once before. I decided some news from my angels wouldn't hurt. When we did my reading my three cards were CHILD, MIRACLE, HEAVEN – these represented the past, present and future consecutively.

The child meant that I needed to pay attention to my inner child. I understood that this meant that it was my child that was suffering and that my child needed to be nurtured out of this depression. The miracle card was letting me know that I was safe and protected and that I needed to let go of how I think, I should move forward and just let it happen. The last card, the Heaven card represented that the Universe was lending me supreme belief in the power to heal and love.

WOW, what a perfect message at this time. I loved to think that I had someone watching over me. I mean the fact that I was still here proves it! The very first time I did angel cards I was 100% positive that my deceased mother was sending me a message and it brought me to tears. This time I was a little more apprehensive. Yes, I got amazing cards, but when you are not in a place of miracles you can't see them from the clouds. I did, however, have faith in my angels and the fact that they were working their magic in their own magic way. And in hindsight a miracle occurred! My miracle journey started as soon as I tried to end my life. I have been reborn, with fresh eyes, a new love for all. For where I am today I never thought possible. I was back and forth between suicidal thoughts back then, and today I am the happiest I can be.

I decided to eventually pick up the book Sarah had given me and read a bit. I had been doing my mindful meditation for a couple of days in a row so was feeling slightly motivational. I started reading the first few pages and it totally resonated with me. It was Louise Hay –The Power is within you – I honestly felt like I was having a conversation with Louise, and that I had known her for years. I was sure many people would say that about Louise Hay. Her passion and motivation were astounding and moving!

Initially I didn't want to put the book down and I could feel a sense of relief really coming over me. Once I did put it down though, I couldn't pick it back up for days. The thoughts of getting better kept coming into my head, I wasn't sure I was ready for that. The fact that I would have to face the 'real' world gave me massive anxiety attacks. What was I afraid of? What was it that made me fear being better?

I was scared that once I was better that no one would love me. I was scared that I would go back to trying to be perfect and not be able to live up to it. I was terrified about going back to work. I was scared of losing Jason. I was frightened about the questions I would face... I was going back to being scared of everything. I was supposed to be getting better, but now I was afraid of getting better. It was almost comfortable, familiar and I was scared to cross over as I knew this time would be a whole new world. I just had no idea how good this new world could be.

It had been two weeks since 'the event' and there were definitely improvements. I didn't want to end my life all of the time - it was getting less frequent every day. The mindfulness was the easiest and most effective technique when it came to handling my thoughts. Reading the book was good also, but required a bit of focus which was hard to do outside of meditation. Feeling good really helped me to sleep easier at night, and when I had a good night's sleep things didn't seem so dreadful. It really is amazing what a good night's sleep can do for the mind. Thinking, planning and worrying put the body in a fight-or-flight state. This state is your anxious state, where I had apparently chosen to live in, but was slowly starting to come out from.

I started to think about seeing or talking to other friends. I was even allowed to be by myself in the apartment now. Every pill and drop of alcohol was taken out of the apartment, so I would have had to go and buy them in various stores throughout the suburb. This seemed like too much of an effort, so I felt safe to be alone at home.

I got a call from my friend Olivia who had just returned from the States. I decided to answer her call. She was keen to come over and see me as we hadn't seen each other in so long. She walked in and we gave each other a huge hug. She knows straight away something was up, she could see it in my eyes. She didn't say anything, and when I asked her about her trip, she continued to fill me in on all the gossip. In between her conversation I blurted out what had happened, "Olivia, I ended up in hospital as I tried to kill myself." It was like she didn't even hear me. She just kept on going telling me her story and all of a sudden jumped in for another HUGE hug!

Good friends really make life so much easier to deal with. If everyone would stop being so bloody busy and just be there for each other we would live in such a more beautiful world. I completely believe that we as humans are missing out on why we are here. You never hear someone on their death bed saying that they wished they worked harder. I always think that 'the greatest of tragedies, is when one is having the time of their life, but they are too busy to realise. People really seem to have forgotten how good it feels to live for the now, be in the moment. We are so caught up with what is about to happen, what has happened, and what may happen, and our time is consumed by this. We forget that we should be helping other people out, we should contribute, we should be growing, together. Do you know how good it feels to be helped, or to be a helper. When did work and going to the gym become more important than PEOPLE? When I read back my suicide note that was exactly what I talked about. STOP BEING SO BUSY! We get so caught up with being busy that we forget to live, forget to love. The greatest thing that you will ever learn is to love, to truly love teaches you to grow, to flourish.

"Busy" used to be a fair description of the typical schedule. More and more, though, "busy" simply doesn't cut it. "Busy" has been replaced with "too busy", "far too busy", or "absolutely flat out." Please stop the glorification of busyness!~!

I can say this now after being on both sides of busyness. I have been that person who was too busy to talk, too busy to listen, too busy to be there. I put work before my health, my friends, and my family. When I tried to listen, I was in fact constantly making lists in my head. I never heard anything that was said to me. I was chasing my tail, thinking that I was chasing the future.

I recently went for lunch with a friend and we realised that we hadn't actually seen each other in two years! How did two whole years pass by and we didn't make time to catch up? It's not like I don't like her; I love her and I love being around her, and her energy. We both had been so busy that we didn't catch up. If you were on your death bed do you think you would look back and wish that you spent more time at work, in the gym or do you think you would wish you had spent more time with loved ones?

Prioritises, they are vital to life. What do you value? What do you make number one in your life? I can say that I used to put work before everything. I can say I put drinking before a lot of things too! I can say that I didn't count time with loved ones important, as I didn't think I had people who loved me. I was so busy being miserable that I didn't even realise that there is in fact so much more to life. I spent my life wanting for more and not appreciating what I already had. I was content with other people controlling my happiness, and not taking ownership over it.

Speaking of a busy life, I had a call from my old boss. He had some potential work for me. This was also the one I was sure Jason told all about what happened. I was surprised, but figured he wanted to sort me out with some work so thought it would be good to chat. He wanted me to come and meet him at the venue. He knew I wasn't going back to work there, but we still had to talk about the event that I wanted to

163

do. I needed the money. I had my mortgage to pay, as well as rent, food, my psychologist bills, etc. I really wasn't ready to go back to work but sometimes you have to do things you don't want to, so I went to see him.

I thought I was going in to talk to him about the event. Instead he called me in to tell me that I wasn't going to do the event. He still was, but I wasn't involved. I still to this day don't know for sure if Jason told him what really happened. Either way, I understood he needed someone who he could rely on, and I had just let him down massively at the last minute. What I didn't understand was why he made me come in person so he could tell me that! Surely he could have told me over an email or phone.

It was so hard to get the courage up to go and see him, and then for him to tell me I lost the job was very upsetting. I decided not to argue my point and just walked away. I do believe that everything happens for a reason. And in all honesty I only wanted to do it for the money! It was definitely not for the passion or the love for the company. Surely there were easier ways to make a buck.

I had to find some sort of work so I started speaking to recruitment agencies about getting back to work. Just thinking about interviewing was making me go crazy, but I went and did them. I knew that I wasn't ready to start the process and that there was no way I could get a job in the state that I was in, but I had to start somewhere. Money was running low and I needed a distraction, from life!

I didn't want to go back into a venue as a general manager. I wanted to go and work in an office somewhere - I just wanted to do something easy because I didn't want to have to try too hard. I figured it would be easy enough for me to make the next move into a group role or head office role within hospitality. The recruiters all agreed with me and all figured that they had something and would get back to me. After about a week, I got a call from one of the recruiters - he had set up an interview with a large hospitality group in Sydney. It was for a role in head office - a new role within the company and I would be head of training and development. This would be my ideal role!

What I loved about my role, any manager role was the training and development side. I loved to have this kind of relationship with my staff. I loved to help them and see them grow. I guess I loved to mentor people.

I should have been super excited but I wasn't. I was terrified to go for the interview. This was a big one and I wanted the job. I thought about taking a Zanex just to get through the interview as I didn't want them to see me shaking from my anxiety – that is not a good look for an interview. Three days later I went for the interview and met the HR manager. She was so lovely and I felt better but I knew I wasn't myself. I was stuttering when she was asking me questions and couldn't get the words out that were in my head.

When it came to the time she asked me if I had any questions, and I had loads. Once I started asking her my questions she seemed annoyed. Was she in a rush or did I ask the wrong questions? When I walked out I thought, 'that didn't go well!' A combination of nerves, anxiety and some serious verbal diarrhoea didn't make good for an interview. Oh well, everything happens for a reason I kept repeating to myself. I never heard back from the recruiter on the interview. That is so unprofessional. He could have at least called me to give me some feedback!

I had completely lost all of my confidence. I was convinced that I wasn't going to be able to go back to work. I thought that I had somehow lost all of the skills that I had built up over the years..? Why on earth I thought this I have no idea. I was over it after just one interview! I was ready to pack it all in again. I knew I wasn't ready to start interviewing, but I went ahead and did it anyway. Now I had to ask myself if I did it to sabotage myself? Did my mind set me up for failure because it wanted me to be knocked back as a test? Or was it that I wasn't ready to fly yet so I needed to be knocked down?

14

The World never stops

In the meantime my bank back in Ireland was asking what was happening. My tenants had moved out. My sister was amazing and took care of the renovations in her extremely little spare time. I couldn't pay the mortgage, or the money to get the work done. Luckily my family stepped in and helped me out with that. I want to thank my amazing sister again for all her hard work on the house, along with her friend Roisin and my Dad. They really took control and made everything happen so the house was ready to let out again within a month.

This was such a huge relief for me. All I had to do was find an agent now to lease the property and also someone who could manage it so I wouldn't have to pester my sister anymore with it. My sister made the place look so fantastic that it was only on the market two days before being rented. Phew! The rent was only covering 2/3 of the mortgage. I decided to talk to the banks to try to work something out. I was very scared but I have to admit they were extremely understanding and very easy to work with.

They helped me work out my repayments in a way that worked for me. I couldn't believe it. So many people have plenty of bad things to say about the banks, but I was blown away with how great they were. That was another huge weight off of my shoulders.

I started to see some changes in myself. I got back to reading my Louise Hay book. I started to go for walks. I even went for lunch with Jason's mom. This was something that scares me even in full mental health! It wasn't that she was scary, it was more because It was because of my social anxiety. I went for lunch and made it through alive. No one was hurt, not even me.

I thought it was time that I meet up with some friends. I was pretty nervous but also looking forward to seeing them. Half of them knew what had happened, and the other half had no idea. My anxiety was starting to ease off so I thought I could get through it and they wouldn't notice my shakes. I also wanted a bloody drink! It had been a long time since I tasted some wine and I had a thirst for it. I know what you are thinking, I shouldn't be drinking when on depression medication! Hey, I am not saying I am prefect, I just needed a wine. It wasn't like I was going to drink a couple of bottles, just a glass or two.

As soon as we organised the meet up and I walked in and saw all of my friends there waiting for me, my shakes came back with a vengeance. Luckily, Jason my little legend, was by my side and holding my hand and ensuring to fill all silences. I just kept completely losing track of what I was trying to say. My heart was so full of love for him at that time, he really was my rock! I wouldn't have gotten through this without him.

Below is a letter I wrote to Jason to say thanks for all he had done for me.

Dear Jason,

I cannot even begin to explain what you have done for me. I will never let go of the gratitude I have for how you saved my life. It was you I chose to reach out to for help after I had taken the pills, it was you that sat beside me through every moment of my recovery, it was you that made me want to stay alive.

Thank you for being my strength when I had none, thank you for being my voice when I had none and thank you for being persistent with my minds repair. Thank you for your humour, your understanding, and your non-judging.

Most of all, thank you for your love. It was your love that made me sleep, wake-up and eat. It was your love that made me look to the future. It was your love that helped me to re-build me. Thank you x Infinity!!

Jessica

A peak of brightness

Sarah had bought me a ticket to a seminar that was supposedly awesome! It talked about relationships, business, spirituality, emotions, health, etc. I wasn't that excited about it, mostly because I don't like being in a room full of strangers, and also because I wasn't in the mood for some bullshit 'let's hold hands' crap! It was almost a month after the 'incident' now. I was starting to come around. I thought I should just push myself and go to this and see what's it's all about.

As we arrived we had to fill out a questionnaire, the only way to get the answers was by asking all the people in the room. BOOM! No time for shyness now. I almost felt like crying, but instead I took a deep breath, started going up to strangers and asking them the listed questions. I was impressed with myself.

The seminar started off with asking what you want to achieve from the weekend. I wasn't even sure exactly what we had signed up for so had no idea what to write down. They kept repeating that "success was 90% just showing up" this made me at least want to stay a little longer. I didn't want to be seen as giving up so soon.

We moved onto talking about personality types. I have done this all before, so got kind of bored. Before I knew it, we were split into groups and I couldn't be in Sarah's group. They didn't allow people who already knew each other be in the same group. This scared the shit out of me and I wanted to go home, but I sucked it up. Our representative was asking who wanted to be a team leader and my hand was up in the air before you could say 'boo!' What? Everyone looked at me and was delighted that they didn't have to do it and they all started clapping. Oh no, I thought, what have I done? I talked myself out of the immense panic that was going through my head; I mean, how hard could it really be?

At break time I had to run down for a cigarette! We had been asked not to smoke for the weekend, so we could try to break out of our comfort zone – ha! They had no idea I was well out of my comfort zone. There was no way I wasn't smoking,. After the break our group had to come back into the room screaming and shouting like maniacs. They told us it would release tension, I thought they had lost the plot, and thought I may lose the plot if I had to keep up this nonsense. It was a real test for me. I not only had to act like a fool, something I would never do, I had to lead a team of people to act like fools.

There were many different exercises and lots of 'looking within' - lots of positive motivation and lots of team spirit! We had to go home that night and come up with team slogans, make team outfits, banners, and anything that would make our team stand out.

It was great to be involved with something again. It made me really think about getting back to work. This whole sitting around feeling depressed all the time was starting to wear off. I noticed that once I had something to do the anxiety was duller, the shakes would disappear and my mind would be still.

When we returned the following day our first task was to fire a team member. As the team leader I lead the team into how we would do this. We huddled into a circle and I asked everyone who they thought should be fired and why? As we went around the circle, everyone had their say but me. I purposely did this so I wouldn't have to make a decision. When we later reflected on how we fired someone I spoke up and said that I never voted. Nobody noticed at the time, as I cleverly covered it. I realised that I didn't vote because right now I had no self-confidence. I didn't have any courage in my decision making.

When I look back, I was bombarded with too many choices to make. With travelling, it was where to go, when to go, how to go, who to go with, and when to come home. With my house it was when to sell or not to sell. Also my choice to go back to work or change industries altogether wore me down. All it was about was making choices and I didn't want to make them alone. This made me feel so alone. I hated feeling alone. Wow! This was such an eye opener. I couldn't believe it was so simple. I had talked myself into absolute panic mode all because of a few decisions that I had to make. It was me who made my life a misery, it was me who decided to be negative all the time and it was me who was letting sadness reign in my life. Yes I had been through tough times, but they should have made me stronger, not weaker!

We had to write a letter to our future self, about how we felt right now and what we wanted to change. Here was what I wrote:

'Let go of anger, hurt and vulnerability. I'm so tired of trying to be perfect, to be what everyone else wants me to be. I don't want to want other peoples validation anymore. I want to validate myself. I'm tired of being angry and judgemental. I want to stop trying to get people's attention in such a negative way. I don't want people to worry about me anymore. I want people to look up to me. I want to be an example to others of who they want to be. I want to ooze happiness, confidence and love. I'm sick of having social anxiety and sick of being labelled with things every time I go and see my shrink! I'm over hospitality. I'm going to change my life and I'm going to be the best girlfriend, sister, friend, boss that I could be! I want to live!'

This is what just came out without me even thinking about it. The words literally wrote themselves, it was weird! It's basically a promise to myself to make changes. I needed to follow the instructions I just wrote to myself. I couldn't believe that this weekend had turned out this way. I had such an awakening. I felt motivated, empowered, confident and ready to make changes in my life. They spoke about success and how your passion should be your compass. Ok, so now I had to find out what I loved to do. I love decorating, Christmas, helping people, and personal development.

Once the weekend was over the people holding the seminar offered their courses and other seminars at a discounted price. There were wealth courses, health courses, sales, presentation, management courses and life coaching courses. There was also a deal that if you bought all of the courses they were basically half price! I was in 'go get em' mode and paid a signup fee to do all of the courses. Sarah was all gung-ho too so we left thinking that we were pretty much going to sign up and figure out how to pay later!

The next day I went into research mode. Since my last 'breakdown' back in 2005 I've been interested in counselling. I even finished a course back in Ireland on counselling for beginners. I thought about looking into that, then I thought about how I had been seeing a counsellor for years and while I thought they were helping me they were just listening to me chat about what was annoying me at the time. I definitely did not want to go down that path. I wanted to do something with more impact! No offence to all the counsellors out there because I still think that they do offer a valuable service.

I started to look into psychology. I thought that this had really helped me over the last few weeks. At least they had some concrete exercises that worked. Again, after much more thinking and searching, I didn't want to end up 'labelling' the people I was trying to help. I mean how does that really help? Ok, you have an issue, and this was what we call it – you have _____ (fill in the blank). I mean, yes, I loved my time with my shrink but I still wanted more. Most people will need a therapist at least once in their life and also every successful person has a coach, right?

I started looking into life coaching. Now I personally think this term was a little fluffy. Who even knows what services they offer? I thought I did, but in reality I didn't! And I'm sure I'm not the only person that thought that a life coach was more of a personal assistant than therapist. But, a life coach could be so many different things. I started researching, and spent days on the internet and hours on the phone trying to find out more. There were so many places that said they taught life coaching, and they offered to help build your company website and help get your business off the ground. It felt like most of the teaching was about how to build a business more than how to be a life coach.

While I was pretty impressed with the weekend seminar and how they had made such an impact on me, that didn't necessarily mean that I needed to study with them. I called them and ask for a refund on my deposit as there was a cooling off period. They really tried to convince me that they were the best place to go with if I wanted to do life coaching but I just had a feeling that I couldn't ignore.

I think I called every life coaching course in Australia. When it got down to it I figured out that NLP (neuro linguistic programming) was the basis of coaching. Now I wanted to be the best coach out there, so if NLP was the basis of coaching then I was going straight to the root and going to find the best NLP course out there.

To my surprise there were quite a number of them in Australia, so more confusion began. I had to make a decision, by myself. This was going to be a real test to see where I was mentally! I spoke to some awesome people. They were so friendly and helpful. I was having conversations with people about their courses and ended up in many 'life' conversations with almost all of them too.

After a week of research I got onto the phone with a guy named Jamie. I'm not sure how I ended up calling him - it must have been a link I clicked through but as soon as I got off the phone to him I knew that this was the course for me. Although when I was later directed to the website for information it didn't look familiar. How did I find this course when I hadn't even seen the website before? I was a big believer in destiny and this was it!

Not only was the course in Sydney, the three courses that I wanted to do were going to be held in the next three months. Many of the others were spread out across a year. I couldn't believe it. On top of all of that, it was being held in Bondi, a 15 minute drive from my place. Amazing! Now I needed to find some work that could work around this. The course went for 15 days in September, 12 days in November and 8 days in December. It was full on, from 9am – 5pm. It's been a long time since I had to study but I was so excited about this.

I had made a decision and was proud of it. When I started to go back out into the wonderful world I would tell people of my new 'decision' to be a life coach and study NLP. A few people looked at me as if I had ten heads and there was one or two that even laughed at me. This time I was happy and confident in my decision. I was confident that I was on the right track.

Once I felt that I was on the right track, I suddenly felt that it didn't matter what anyone else said or thought about me – it's now about what I think of me. I started to turn my thinking around and I was 100% dedicated to getting better, being happy. I wanted to share my happiness and spread happiness. Now, it all starts with me: how I view the world, how I view other people, other things, how I deal with feelings, and how I manage my emotions.

I finally had hope, had passion and had something positive to focus on. I was waking up every day and choosing to be happy. Of course I had moments where I got sad, where I thought that I couldn't do this and where I thought that I needed to crawl back into a hole. Anyone who is 100% happy all of the time is lying. Ups and downs are completely normal to our existence, we need them, how can we have ups if we don't have downs? We wouldn't be able to tell the difference. I was beginning to see that life was manageable. Good times and the bad. I could face them. I was started to be addicted to happiness. I wanted more if it. I craved it. My happiness research was almost like a drug, I was addicted to finding out more. I was addicted to how good it felt to feel good. I don't think that I ever felt this good. I was much more accepting of the bad times. I knew that they were part of me, but I also knew that I could either focus on them, or I could learn from them. I decided to learn, to move on, and to make my life better than it has ever been.

I read up on everything to do with happiness. I searched high and low for anything that I could find. I wanted to feel happier and I was letting nothing stand in my way. If there was an article that told me to stand on my head for hours to feel happier, I would have tried it. I started a daily gratitude list, I meditated daily. I soaked up happy vibes, said daily positive affirmations and smiled as much as I possibly could.

My anxiety and depression did a complete 180! I even decided to stop taking my anti-depressants. I hadn't said anything to anyone as I wanted to see if I could do it. I didn't feel nervous, I had a feeling that I would be fine and I was. I had no side effects of coming off them. I was so excited about my future and it seemed that everything in my life was starting to turnaround.

My relationship with Jason felt the best ever. I loved being around my friends again. I was making plans for the future. Things were looking up! After being off of the pills for a week I told my sister, she wasn't happy and wanted me to go see the doctor and tell her what was happening. I had also stopped going to see my GP. I suppose if you were a million miles away and weren't seeing the changes in me in person, you would get worried. The reality of it was that I was loving life more than I had been for years! I had choices and I loved it. For so long I felt that I had no choices and when given them I freaked out. Now I know I have them and I could make decisions. And I could be happy! I don't need someone to tell me how to feel!

My close friends, and even Jason were still worried about me. I mean I had turned into a completely new person. My sister back home was convinced I was lying to her. She didn't believe that I could be so happy after being so incredibly sad. It was strange, but I knew myself that the feeling that I was feeling was real. I knew that I was committed to getting better. I had made the decision to do this. I had made the decision to change my thoughts, to invite more positivity into my life. This was the turning point, the place where my brain was actually starting to rewire itself. Have you heard about neuroplasticity? It is basically the ability of the brain to rewire itself through environmental, behavioural and neural changes. I figured out that I could train my brain to think positively. After living for years in a negative world I could make the change to live in a positive one. I couldn't believe it. I couldn't believe that it could be done, that it could be so simple.

It was not easy. Every day I had to work hard on my happiness. It wasn't a simple, take a pill and you would feel better. I tried that, it didn't work. It took time before I even saw the smallest change after putting a lot of effort in. The thing was that I wasn't going to give up until it worked. Determination was what I needed. Dedication was applied. Happiness was my driving force. I had my daily routine and I had to stick to it. I had the perfect recipe and I needed to follow the steps precisely in order to turn this around and keep was on that track.

Every day I would be open to hearing new messages and learning new lessons. It's true what they say, when the student is ready the teacher will come, they come in many, many forms. It could have been a person's advice, a quote, a seminar, a hardship, a message, a sighting, I promised myself to be open to love. Once you commit to a life of love, you commit to a wonderful life. I was practicing daily meditations, eating healthily, giving thanks each morning when I woke. I was recognising and releasing my fears. I was surprising myself with my happy vibes but loving every moment of it.

Label jars, not people

I went back to see my shrink again and I told him I had given up the anti-depressants. He was happy. He didn't see anything wrong with it. I told him about the course I had booked, and how I had such a massive turn around. He was excited for me. We spoke about a few things that were irritating me at the time. Mostly silly things but he helped me to put them into perspective.

I didn't need him to tell me what was wrong with me anymore. I didn't need him to put another label on me. I already had enough! Everyone has labels. They make up our personalities - some good, some bad. I don't think they should be used against us and I don't think someone else should put them on you. How well can someone really know you when you speak to them for an hour a week? They shouldn't have the power to 'label' you.

One of my many labels was 'perfectionist.' I know that I could take this to extremes sometimes. But I also know that my perfectionism would drive me, it would make me work harder to strive for something better. I was fully aware that anything that was 'perfect' was only so in my own eyes. The constant struggle for perfect was wearing me down and I was putting far too much pressure on myself, all by myself.

Research from back in the 1930s, proposes that words we use to describe what we see aren't just idle placeholders, they actually determine what we see. In most cases people don't label themselves. For example, I am me and I may know no different as to who I am. I cannot therefore label myself as a perfectionist because this is all I know. How can I call myself a perfectionist when I am just getting through life the best way I know how to. Unless you have done some internal work, i.e. self-help, you will never know what you don't know. In most cases, people still don't know what they don't know. If someone tells me that I am 'negative' enough times, or even the one time that I let it sink into my mind, then I believe that I am negative. If someone tells me that I am 'fat' and I listen, then watch me as I put on weight. If you tell me that I am mean, then see me bite your head off for no reason. Use your words carefully, as your words can become reality.

The long-term consequences of labelling a child "smart" or "slow" are profound, as they are for labelling a child "bossy" or "mean". As I have spoken about earlier in the book, my parents labelled me many things as a child and I only now realise the power this has had over my life. It is only now, at 36 years of age, that I can see that I have power in words also. I can take the words that were inserted into my naive mind at an early age, and I can change them. It is important to recognise the power that words have.

Words can hurt and words can heal, be kind with your words. Choose to use positive words and positive reinforcement rather than negative. Choose to speak kindly of others before going around bitching about them. Every single person in this universe has their own cross to bear and we should accept this. Being kind should be a given for us, not a random act performed for brownie points. Every day I make it my mission to smile at every person that looks at me, I open the door for anyone who walks behind me, I'll shout coffee for my team or the next person in the cue. I share my daily gratitude with others, I share my stories to help people heal, I do what I can to be kind, to be loving and to be generous.

Keep your thoughts positive because your thoughts become your words.
Keep your words positive because your words become your behaviour.
Keep your behaviour positive because your behaviour becomes your
habits. Keep your habits positive because your habits become your values.
Keep your values positive because your values become your destiny.
Mahatma Gandhi

15

Getting back into it

I needed to start looking for work. This time I was looking for a casual job. Maybe I could work as a florist? That would be a nice job to work with flowers every day. I also thought about being a painter. I would like to paint other people's houses. I thought it would be therapeutic. I started to look on gumtree, while looking I came across an ad looking for staff to help decorate shopping malls with Christmas decorations. Having been an avid Christmas fanatic I was super keen to get this role. I would generally start preparing for Christmas in September, I love it so much that I just can't wait until any later in the year. I couldn't believe there was a job as a Christmas decorator, it was perfect! I wanted that job. I emailed straight away.

In the meantime my best friend called me, she was stressed out with work. She asked me to come over to help her out as she needed some extra managers, and of course offers to pay me. It was a three week gig, I was STOKED! This was perfect. I get to work with my friend, I was doing stuff I already know how to do, and I would be finished in time for the start of my course. It may not be Christmas tree decorating but hey, beggars can't be choosers. I was super excited and headed straight over to her.

I was working enough hours to keep me busy. It felt good to be back working. I missed it. Although this was not my ideal role, it was perfect for the time being. When coming up to the end of my three week stint the owner offered me a more permanent role. I was delighted. The universe kept giving me what I needed. I could work part time from home. I explained to him about my course and he was fine with that.

Everything was working out perfectly. I could do my course, work from home and make money to pay the rent. YIPEE!

My thoughts were starting to be consistently good. Now when I thought about suicide I was shocked that I had gone there. I couldn't believe how my life had turned around, and I knew that this was only the beginning. I even gave up smoking again and it was super easy. There was no doubt in my mind that I was going to stop. I made the decision and followed through. That was it, it was done. I was done!

Three weeks flew by and before I knew it, I was starting my NLP course. When I walked in the door and saw our teacher I walked straight over to him and said, "I want to work for you!" He has over 30 years' experience in this field, he was there from the beginning of NLP with the people who created it. Who better to learn from? He acknowledged what I had said but I was sure he heard this a lot so I left it there.

There was so much to learn, so much to know. Every day we were being challenged. We were learning something that I had never even thought about before. Your head does some pretty funky stuff when you put it into situations like that. I was one of those learners who needed all of the information, and where this information could be applied, before it was clear to me. This wasn't an option here. We had to learn and had a lot to learn. There wasn't time to see where it could be applied. I just kept trying my best, kept listening and kept studying my ass off. Every night I came home I was looking up information on the internet, and I was listening to podcasts. I was reading and typing up my notes. I literally submerged myself into NLP for those 15 days. It was intense.

I met one lady who I got on great with. We would go for lunch together and sit and watch the ocean down at Bondi beach chatting about what we learned or what we didn't understand. It felt like I had known her for years. We were instantly drawn towards each other and we are still friends to this day.

I went into this wanting to be the best coach I could be, to be able to help my clients with therapy that wowed them. Now I was seeing so many more possibilities. I didn't know where to start. Initially I was set on having a business with Sarah and setting up a practice where we would offer an array of different approaches for our clients. Now I was thinking BIGGER! I was thinking global.

I wanted to help people like me who needed something other than just a psychologist to label them, and more than a counsellor to talk to. I wanted to help people change their thinking and in turn, see how their world changes. If you believe, you shall achieve. I had no idea how I was going to do this but something along those lines was starting to become my vision. This felt like what I was here to do.

The course taught me about the mind and how we can control it. More of what I had already been learning about through meditation. This was different though, NLP is about the connection between how we think, communicate and behave. I was starting to see that my thoughts were creating who I was. All of my life I my head had been filled with negative thoughts. I had always struggled with life, with my life in particular and with love more than anything. It was because of what I had learnt that love was from my parents, who by the way did not love each other. Well at least in front of me. I am sure they did when they met, but by the forth child it was over!

I was brought up in such a negative environment, that was all I knew. I never knew that I needed to be grateful, I never knew what happiness felt like, I couldn't strive for it because I had no idea how to get it. I had suffered so much when I was younger with so many blows to my confidence. It was as if I had given up on living a happy life as all I knew was sadness. I was learning that life could be so different and that I had the power to change it. All those years I had been waiting for someone else to change it for me. I had been waiting for so long for someone to tell me what was wrong with me so I could look at fixing myself. Little did I know that I was the only one who could make the change. I didn't need to know that I had it in me. I thought that my past owned me and that I would always be sad because it felt comfortable. It was my default.

I was learning that through NLP I could go back into my past and relive any past situations that had caused me issues today and change how they affect me. Throughout the 15 days, every day we were given a specific exercise to complete. I had never wanted to go back to my past because it was too hurtful, but here it was easy. Here is one of the trivial things we worked on, I always had a strange thing that when I saw an elderly person I would cry. I would simply burst into tears by the mere sight of someone elderly. Strange, but it was true. I found out through NLP that this was because when I was just 7 years old I saw my dead grandmother in her coffin. This image then came back to me every time I saw an elderly person and brought on tears. Isn't that incredible? My mind had created this automatic response due to an image it had held onto for 25 years. We did many of these type of exercises and I was able to release so many pent up feelings that I had no idea were even there.

I did so much work on my past, I cried so much during the course but they were all good tears, it was like a release for me. My past was my past and I couldn't change what happened, but I could change how I now behaved. I decided that I was no longer going to let my past haunt me, I wanted to be free from it. One I made that decision my thoughts became so much lighter. I felt so much better, I didn't feel sad about what had happened to me anymore. I didn't want to focus on my sadness anymore, or my suicide attempt. I wanted to be more positive, I wanted to make positive changes in my life and move past the hurt and pain. I wanted to be free.

NLP taught me how to disassociate from things that were not mine to deal with, how to see the bigger picture, how my mind would presuppose things without me knowing. I.e. just because I had experienced something doesn't mean everyone else has. NLP taught me that what I don't know, I don't know, and that there is a whole entire Universe that I know so little about. It taught me to be so much more open to the world and to people. I now wanted to hear everything that everyone had to say, whereas before I never had the time to listen. Suddenly I understood what empathy was, I understood that everyone had their story, it wasn't just me to had a cross to bare. My whole life I had felt burdened with my past, it held onto me like a chain, dragging me down. I finally figured out how to let it go. I accepted it and let it go. This way it had no power over me. This way I could move forward with my life instead of playing the bad on repeat like a horror movie. Now when I work with clients who hold onto past pain I help them to let it go. Our past makes us who we are and we must be grateful for it but we also need to accept we cannot change it and move on.

NLP taught me how to change beliefs that I had which no longer served me. It taught me how to build rapport with people, how to have confidence. I taught me how to see things from another perspective; I was never able to do this before. I started this course in order to be able to help others but this course was helping me more than anything. I couldn't wait to learn more.

16

The next step

I had three weeks off before the master practitioner course in NLP started. This was the next level of the course I had just done. Having become totally confused as to what my next step was once I had finished all of my courses, I totally pulled away from making a decisions. Just so that I wasn't putting needless pressure on myself.

I got stuck back into my part-time work, which had now turned full time role, and was back in the hospitality saddle working for the people who I didn't want to work for anymore, doing a job that I wasn't inspired by. All that said, I had bills to pay and I was very thankful to have it at all. Jason had not worked for almost two years now so I had to look after myself. I was pretty much back to my old self. Back to seeing my friends, back to hanging out and feeling good. I couldn't believe that life was feeling so good. I was committed to feeling this good for as long as I could. I was meditating daily, reading up on all things happiness and focusing on the present moment instead of my past.

I was excited to go to the next level with the NLP training. Just before I was going to start the next course my NLP teacher called and he offered me a job! I couldn't believe it. I just put it out there to the Universe and here it was coming to me. After the first day when I mentioned to him that I wanted to work for him, we never mentioned it again. I was surprised that he remembered.

I was going to be a supervisor for the new venture into online courses. I was absolutely thrilled! I was in the car with Jason on the way to lunch when he called. I almost cried. Jason didn't care. I tried to tell him, but he didn't listen. This upset me. I started to question our relationship. Now that I was feeling better, I could see that we were not travelling on the same path anymore. I loved him so much and he got me through the toughest time in my life but we were growing further and further apart by the day. I didn't know what to do to get us back on track. In a way I didn't want to try. I guess it was because I wanted to be selfish for a bit, I wanted to be able to focus on me and my career, my business. I had the world at my feet and it felt as though he was just dragging me down. It was tough as he had done so much for me, I couldn't just walk away now. I decided to let things be for now. I shouldn't be making big decisions like that as I was still healing.

It had been brought to my attention that you were who you spend the most time with and that surrounding influences were a key factor in your happiness. I wanted to ensure that I was around the right people. I wasn't about to go and dump any of my mates that weren't on my page, not at all. I wanted to make sure that I was around the right people where we all get the support we needed, where we all encourage each other, and build each other up. Who wouldn't want that?

I knew Jason was a sweetheart, I had known him for years and he was always very kind and generous. He was a good influence in the fact that he was always positive, he saw the good in everyone, no matter how bad they were. He believed in everything he thought and he was convinced that he was going to build his health business by being in the pub drinking and socialising. I never noticed how much he drank as I was usually there bedside him drinking too. It was only now that it was starting to frustrate me. We never did anything together but go to the pub. We would never even watch TV together at home. He would play his xbox and I would sit alone watching my TV shows. For so long I thought this was great as I had my own time and he had his. That was because I always needed that time with mindless TV, but now I needed and wanted more. I wanted to be able to go and enjoy life with someone, but not in the pub. I was thinking about having children, but couldn't see this with Jason.

Jason kept on telling me that I was negative, probably because I was nagging him about his drinking. After all that I had done over the past few months for him to say that I was negative hurt so bad. It was like he ripped out my heart to be honest. I couldn't believe after all we had both been through that he would throw that back at me. He was starting to bring me down, I wished it wasn't the case but it was.

Your friends, especially your boyfriend, should lift you up and help you to be the best person you can be. One way to determine if your friends are having a positive effect on you was to gauge your mood after you've spent time with them. Do you leave feeling energized and happy? With Jason, every time we were together we were arguing. I was starting to think it was normal, but this is also because I grew up in a house full or arguments. I wanted different for my life, I just didn't know how to get it. I had the 2nd part of my course coming soon so I kept any feelings of upset or frustration aside as I needed to stay focused.

All my NLP training was continually going through my mind. I loved it and was thinking about it all day everyday. It seemed to make so much more sense now that I had the time to digest it. It all started to come together. I was beginning to see how I could use this in business. I was literally lying in bed and a thought popped into my head about a name for my business, 'The Happy Pill', obviously it's a play on words. Everyone knows that anti-depressants are also named 'happy pills', I wanted to be able to help people feel happier without the pills. If I could do it, then so can others. I wanted to start a revolution to help people to get their happy back. The first place to turn was social media, I started a Facebook page where I wanted to encourage people to share their happy thoughts. I wanted these thoughts to help people feel better when they were feeling down. A little like the chicken soup for the soul books, I always loved them.

I kept dreaming that one morning I would wake up and see that I had thousand of likes. The likes did come in that fast at the beginning. All of my friends were on-board, I mean who doesn't love a feel good story? But then the likes stopped, they dried up and I started to notice some unlikes come through. What was happening? I was filling the page with positive inspiration, feel good stories, as well as information on how to be happier. This was when I realised that people don't necessarily want to know about happiness. They like to talk about it, and they like to say that they are happy, but in actual fact most people have no idea of what happiness is. Don't get all crazy at me for saying this. After the journey I have travelled I know this to be true. I even see it in some of my friends, they say that they are happy, they think it, but they are not. They are trying to convince themselves that they are, but they are not. The reason I know this is because I used to be just like them. I used to think I was happy, that I had it all and that life was good. It is only that that I can look back and say I was living in denial. There is a saying about this because it lies true for so many.

So many people didn't like seeing feel good stories, no one wanted to share what made them happy and people were over inspirational quotes. These days feel good stories annoy people, unless its about themselves. People only ever want to talk about what happened to them! These days the only people that do offer kindness are happy people. We are all too time poor to be nice apparently. I often get asked why I bother speaking to certain people, it is because I want to help them. They have showed to me that they want my help and I will stand by them and help them in every way that I can. I wont give up on people, if they are troubled souls I can relate, I too was a troubled soul. It was becoming apparent to me that we all want to strive for the elusive happiness, yet none of us have any idea what it means.

I was devastated, was this the world has come to? Was the world over 'happiness'? I refused to believe it and continued on with my Facebook page. I continued to try and educate people on happiness, self-talk, on positivity and on how amazing life can be. I looked into starting my own website, Facebook was not going to be enough. I wanted to share my story, share my message and I needed to do something more than just share other peoples information. I needed to start writing my own blog. I had learnt so much over the past few months and I needed to share it. Before my journey started I knew nothing of what I now know about happiness and how to get it. Surely there are many others out there who are in the same boat that I was in. It was then I had a light bulb moment, I was going to start an online course to help people feel happier. I thought back to where I was when I felt alone and in despair, if only I could have been able to find all that I needed in one place, tips on how to feel better, someone to guide me to happiness. I thought that an online course to help people get heir happy back was such an incredible idea.

I started researching online what else was out there in that regard. There wasn't much in fact. Instead of seeing this as a sign to not go for it, I saw it as just the opposite. I felt that people needed to be able to get help online should they need it. I wanted to be a happiness pioneer. I just still was not 100% sure how exactly I could do this or what I needed to do.

I knew that I had learnt some key things when it comes to feeling happier:

1. Gratitude – MASSIVE, we must be grateful for what we have right now instead of focusing on what we don't have, we need to focus on what we do have.

2. Meditation – put simply, we need to breathe, take a breath and feel the moment. Let go of everything else but your breath. By learning to meditate we can train our minds to be calmer and more positive.

3. Affirmations – I am not saying that you ban any negative thoughts from entering your head and only fill it with positive affirmations. I know this cannot happen. But I also know that what you think about, you bring about so try thinking about some good stuff for a while.

4. Self-talk – this was by far the best lesson I have learnt. Your thoughts make up your self-talk, anything that you say to yourself fin your head is self-talk. What you think about others in your head is self-talk. We have this constant chatter that is going round and round in our minds driving us absolutely bat shit crazy.

With this in mind I decided that I was going to start an online course that gave people a platform where they could practice all of the above every day, as well as learn more about happiness and how to let go of what no longer serves them. I wanted to help people re-evaluate their lives so that they could move forward into their happiness journey I had never truly understood what happiness was until now. I thought for years that I was happy, but I had no idea how happy I could be...

That feeling when you know that the Universe actually has your back and that the world is with you every single step of the way?

Many people tend to spend their lives thinking about a life they would live if they had the chance. Many people dream of winning the lottery and what they would do if it happened. What if you didn't need to win the lottery to be happy? What if you knew that happiness was inside of you, and all you had to do was let it out. Would you be fighting to find out how? The sad thing is, so many people won't. They won't bother to look within for happiness, they won't bother to find out more about happiness and they will refuse to open up to new ways of thinking. They will refuse to let go of the past, they will refuse to have faith in the future and they will complain about every single thing until they die. What a sad life to live. I am so incredibly happy, blessed and grateful that I saw the light, that I changed my ways and that I have felt true happiness. For now, I can find true love, I can feel true love and I can give true love.

I now had a massive challenge on my hands. Not only did I want to help people to get their happy back. I had to first convince them that they never had it in the first place. This was going to be a big job. I had to do lots more research, read lots more books, study more about the mind and dedicate my life to this.

So I did. I wasted no time. I spent hours every day researching, reading, trawling through every bit of information that I could find. I found someone to help me with my website so I got that going and then started to build the online course. I spend hours on end trying to write just one days learning's. There was just so much that I had learnt and that I wanted to pass on, I didn't know where to start or where to finish. The strange thing was though, when I started putting pen to paper the words just flew out of me. It was like I was been given what to write from the Angels, sometimes I looked at the words and thought, where did this come from? I knew it had come from research that I had done but sometimes I even surprised myself.

I contacted a friend who would help me make my tutorials. I didn't want them to be a 'taking to the camera' vibe so again I sent hours looking for another way to do this. Then I realised, as so much of my course was about self-talk, I wanted the tutorials to look like I was talking to myself, in my head. I thought it was genius. I wrote the script for six tutorials and picked different locations for each. They took almost a week to film and even longer to produce. They looked so perfect when they were complete and I was so excited to get moving and finish off the course so I could get out there and start talking to people about it.

It took months, far longer than I thought it would, to finish my website and tutorials. I was never happy with my website as I never had a designer do it for me. The guy who did it was purely a developer. I needed someone like that due to the complicated series I needed for my potential new customers. It wasn't going to be complicated for them, it was just complicated to set up. I spent hours and hours playing around with word press myself and taught myself how to use it. I designed the website about seven times. Each time I would change everything and then decide I didn't like it and change it all again. I wanted it to be perfect, of course, I was a perfectionist☺ I still had the site live so I could have people test the course and go to the site. It had a long way to go, but at least I had started.

I was determined to help people find their happiness, to get their happy back and to make the world a happier place! If I can do it, then so can many others. I knew an online course was not the only answer, I knew I had to write my story, this story! I wanted to be able to give others in the same situation hope and to show people who don't understand depression how it can come about so easily. I wanted to be able to write, it is therapeutic for me. I started this book only months after my suicide attempt, I wrote 75,000 words and put it to one side, I didn't read over what I had written, I didn't go back to do any editing, until now. Three years later I have finally found the time, the motivation, and the determination to finish this book. I have learnt so much more, helped so many people and grown so incredibly I wanted to share this story. Everyone has their story, the only difference is with me that I have put it into 89,000 words!

When speaking with a coach the other day about my book she broke down into tears and said "girl, you have to get that message out there!" This was the final kick up the bum that I needed to finish this book. This was the motivational bum tap, the emotional face slap, and all that I needed at the most perfect time to get me going. My story above is the truth about how I went from hell to heaven, no joke! I simply cannot believe how I have turned my life around. I see some of my friends suffering still because they refuse to admit they are not happy, they refuse to let go and they refuse to listen, or learn from me. I will never preach to those who do not want to learn, I won't push my beliefs onto others if they do not want to hear them. I am simply sharing what happened to me, the tools I did daily, to change my life. It aint rocket-science, it aint brain surgery, but it works!

If you are ready to learn, ready to change, and ready to grow, please read on. Simply reading is not enough, you must take action. If I want to host a party and put a guest list together but don't send out any invites, then I guess that party aint gonna happen. If you want to read about happiness, there are a gazillion books, blogs and courses that you can read all about it on. If you want to be happy, then all you have to do is read just ONE of these and put into action what it says to. The next chapter is my happiness recipe, the list of what worked for me. I am human just like you. I have had heartache, just like you. I have been through tough times, just like you, but I have finally stopped fighting happiness and let it into my life, just like you can...

17

My Happiness Recipe

I found 4 key things to focus on when looking to get your happy back, or even to just get happy if you weren't happy in the first place. You may have heard about them all before, now that I know about them I see it everywhere. It is true that what you focus on comes into your life more. I never thought about inviting gratitude into my life, I never knew I had the power to control my self-talk. I thought affirmations and meditation were only for hippies. You can call them all what you like, but by welcoming them into your life you can completely change it for the better. If you don't already practice any of the below, please consider starting to. Start with one for 21 days, and then move on and add another. Just try it because I said so. You have managed to get this far on my book so you must be liking what I am saying.

GRATITUDE!

Below is my letter to the Universe way back when I was starting to feel better after my suicide attempt.

Dear Universe,

I want to thank you from the bottom of my heart for what you have given me and for what you continue to give to me on a daily basis! You never cease to amaze me.

You make me see things I never thought I would see, feel things I never thought possible and know things I need to know. I know sometimes I may try to resist but this was only due to fear. And I promise to try to no longer resist what you so cleverly give me in signs. (*note TRY, I promise I would try)

My intuition is thriving, my love blossoming, my life glowing and it's all due to me opening up to you. I'm not quite the earth angel I know I could be, but hey I am trying. I know I have MANY more lessons to learn, tales to tell, barriers to break down but I also know that you would guide me, hold my hand and give me strength when I need it (you may need to double dose on that!).

I see so many doors opening – a new business venture that only six months ago would never have crossed my mind was now my mission to share. You bring me everything I need when I need it.

I promise to stay aware, to stay aligned and to work towards being the best possible version of me that I could be. I promise to listen, not only to you but to others who you have sent a message through to me.

Please keep me strong when others do not believe, give me the courage to continue, to accept change even when I fear it and please make it worthwhile.

Thank you for being there and knowing me and never giving up on me.

Peace and love Jess xoxo

Gratitude or 'the BIG G' as I like to call it means being thankful for everything! It means counting your blessings, noticing the simple things, the small stuff that makes up the big stuff and praising everything that happens to you on a daily basis. It means learning to live your life as if everything were a miracle, and being aware on a continuous basis of how much you've been given. Gratitude helps you to focus on what you do have, not what you don't have, and by doing this you are opening yourself up to what this wonderful world can offer you. Gratitude puts situations into perspective.

Think of it this way... If you give someone a gift and they don't say thank you what would you want to buy them another gift? By saying THANKS you are opening yourself up to abundance, which is what the Universe wants to give to you once it knows that it's on the right track! Take time and make time to say thanks! Everything in life is a lesson, even the shit stuff. Be thankful that you are here living this life and learning and growing from it.

Count your blessings, notice the simple things, the small stuff that makes up the big stuff and praise everything that happens to you on a daily basis. Learn to live your life as if everything were a miracle, and be aware on a continuous basis of how much you've been given.

Giving thanks makes you happier and more resilient; it improves health and reduces stress. So why won't everyone get on the gratitude train? I have a member's page where I ask my online course members to share what they are grateful for from each day. The 3 same people share every day. There are many other members but no one shares what they are grateful for. Why is this? Why can people not openly admit what they have been blessed with? It is because they do not feel blessed. They feel hard done by. When they have a bad day they blame the Universe, they blame life, they never for one second think that they are the ones bringing back this negativity. By not saying thank you for what you have already been given, why would the Universe continue to give you more. Not having a grateful heart is the same as having a hateful heart.

Research shows that by practicing gratitude you can increase your happiness levels by around 25%. If something bad happens to you during the day, your happiness levels can drop momentarily, and likewise, if something positive happens to you, your level of happiness can rise. A daily practice of gratitude raises your "happiness level" so you can remain at a higher level of happiness regardless of outside circumstances.

What are the health benefits of gratitude? People who rate themselves as highly grateful seem to be healthier in a variety of ways. They have stronger immune systems and succumb less often to illness, fewer symptoms of illness when they do get sick, lower blood pressure, and suffer less depression, envy and resentment. They experience less stress and anxiety, and express more optimism - traits strongly linked to better longevity.

I used to be sick all the time, like I am talking chronic illness. I had so many doctors visits and would find myself back in the docs office every 2 weeks. These days I am much stronger, healthier and the only time you see me in the docs office is for a check up. Living a positive life is so incredibly healthy. In addition, grateful people seem to sleep longer and more soundly, and appear to have stronger relationships with those around them when compared with people who rank lower on the gratitude scale. Kapow!! Now get out your gratitude journal and get writing.

I sleep soundly every night. I eat a balanced diet. I feel more optimistic. I see bad things for what they are, lessons. I have not suffered another bout of depression. I even got off anti-depressants only one month after trying to kill myself. I am living proof that gratitude can change your life. PLEASE listen to this! Don't wait until it's too late. For so many it already is, too late. For my brother and so many others who have succeeded in their suicide attempt. If they could have found room in their hearts for gratitude their story could have been very different. We don't need to find something to be grateful for, we need to be grateful for what we have. It is not about searching outside, its about searching inside. While you may be grateful for the best cup of coffee at the perfect time, it's gratitude that changes your feelings, not the actual cup of coffee.

Every day I now wake up and say thank you for all that I have. I am grateful for the lessons I have learned. I was grateful for my family and my friends because they were all that really matters besides my health. That's all you need. I work every day on training my brain, on talking to and working with my beautiful little angel on my shoulder, and I kick that little devils ass when he rears up for no reason. Your brain is a muscle that needs attention and it needs to be worked out like any other muscle in your body. You need to challenge it. Sometimes it's really hard. Sometimes I have to push myself to be grateful. I am only human after all. Some people think I should be this beacon of light and joy, but hey, I am when I am, and I aint when I aint, OK! Like I said, happiness takes work every single day...

Gratitude is a natural state of bliss, so why wouldn't you want to embrace it? It's a practice we need to engage in daily, and more importantly, we must learn how to express it. Being grateful not only increases our happiness and sense of wellbeing, it also helps us deal with adversity and build stronger personal relationships — it even improves our overall health. Plus practicing gratitude gives us even more to be grateful for. Repeatedly focusing on something positive produces a positive ripple effect in your life. I think gratitude is the absolute best form of therapy and that we should all get on board.

And don't forget gratitude in its simplest form, manners!! Say thank you to your waiter, post man, cashier. To a stranger that smiled at you. Say thank you as much as you can. Be kind, be caring, it is all part of gratitude. It is all part of your brain training, it is all part of your happiness journey.

My happiness levels reached a new kind of high when I started saying thanks! I never knew such a simple exercise could change the way I think, but it did. It helped me to rewire my mind. It gets me thinking about all the simple good things that I have. I used to constantly be focused on what I want and striving for it, which is not necessarily a bad thing, but like I said before, you cant receive the good stuff until you say thanks for the small stuff. Start and finish your day with some gratitude, a simple thanks in your head is enough. You don't have to write it down or share it publically like I do, you can simply say it in your head. Try it for 28 days and see what happens, try it for just one day and see what happens!

MEDITATION!

Meditation is a way in which we can train our minds to be still. It helps to calm the mind and therefore ourselves. It promotes relaxation and an internal peace that we all hold within us. Unfortunately, the world we live in is filling our mind and lives with a constant bombardment of information, most of which we do not need. Think of our ancestors all those hundreds of years ago. They survived without phones, the internet or those Jimmy Choo shoes!

If you can't wrap your head around meditation just yet, try an even easier task. Find a quiet place, sit comfortably, close your eyes and take ten deep slow breaths. Focus purely on your breath and let any thoughts that come into your head float away like a bubble. That's it! If you do this twice a day, it will have the same benefits as meditation.

Meditation helps you in so many ways. Not only does it help you get back in touch with yourself and help you to feel peace within, it helps you focus, experience less anxiety, helps your memory, your creativity and helps you to manage stress. Yup, all of that, and more... just 5 minutes of meditation daily can improve your life tenfold. Meditation helps you to find a peace within your soul. When you can sit in peace with yourself, your world will become peaceful, even amongst all the noise.

Mindfulness can often be referred to as meditation because it is simply being mindful of exactly where you are and what you are doing without judgment. To be mindful you are immersing yourself into the present moment, you are paying attention to what is happening in the moment, such as what you are physically feeling and what you are physically seeing. You can pay attention to the sun, the sky, the breeze on your face and really notice what's right in front of you. By leaving the past in the past, and the future where it belongs, you can be mindful of the moment and enjoy it for what it is.

It is a magical and amazingly powerful practice that you will learn to master. Once you do you will feel the benefits and be hooked! Even if you can't find the time to sit and practice a meditation you can still take a moment to be mindful. Being mindful means leaving all judgment behind and just focusing on the very moment that you are present in.

It is being consciously aware of what is. For example: have you ever walked through the park on your way to the city, and next of all you can find you are in the city, but have no idea how you got there? This is what happens when we let ourselves wander, there is nothing wrong with it, but life is so much better when you are aware. Its almost like a hypnotic state, we miss things in this state and we miss out on life. You could be living a magical life, but you could miss the opportunity to appreciate it because you are too busy worrying about the future or dwelling on the past.

By becoming aware of your breath, your steps, the air on your skin, the sun on your face and the sounds from nature, or whatever is around you, you are ultimately being mindful. It is that easy! Being mindful is being conscious of the life that you are living. Practicing mindfulness helps you:

- to be fully present, here and now
- to experience unpleasant thoughts and feelings safely
- to become aware of what you're avoiding
- to become more connected to yourself, to others and to the world around you
- to increase self-awareness
- to become less disturbed by and less reactive to unpleasant experiences
- to learn the distinction between you and your thoughts
- to have more direct contact with the world, rather than living through your thoughts
- to learn that everything changes; that thoughts and feelings come and go like the weather
- to have more balance, less emotional volatility
- to experience more calm and peacefulness
- to develop self-acceptance and self-compassion

Meditation is another technique that has helped me to turn my life around. A simple breathing technique that takes just minute day has so many benefits to us, yet once again, people refuse to do it. They say they are too busy, they don't have the time and that they can't focus for long enough. Well I say, do you want to continue to feel like shit? It can turn your frown upside down, it can turn your wounds into wisdom and it can be the one thing that can and will change your life, it has stood the test of time and it will forever be the answer to your problems. Can you take 10 deep breaths? If so then you have no excuse not to meditate. Just start with 10 deep breaths, that's all. Simply stop and take a moment to take a moment. Use the time in-between the TV commercials. Please start thinking about your mind's future. If you do not start to take care of your mind right now, you will not live a happy life and soon your mind will be filling you with nonsense. The time to make time is right now.

I used to think it was strange that by focusing on my breath I could feel calmer and more relaxed, but now I get it. By stopping my crazy mind from the crazy talk that used to run freely in there, I can be present in the moment. By being present in the moment you realize that you are safe. No thoughts can interfere or take away from breath when you are focusing on it. Maybe at first it will be challenging to do. I know for me it took quite some time before I could sit and not be bombarded with my minds ramblings. If at first you find it difficult that's OK. Many people do, it is called a practice because you are constantly learning, practicing and mastering your meditation practice!

My meditation practice has helped to heal me. It has taught me to not race into worry, to not waste time wondering about what could be, and to focus on the right now. I am safe, I am here and by focusing on this simple thought during my meditation I have been able to come back from depression, been able to get through wanting to kill myself and I have been able to just sit, silently and feel peace. You can find happiness in peace, a peace that is inside of each of us once we learn how to turn down/off the madness that we fill our lives with. When we stop for just a moment and focus on our breath we can begin to feel grateful, to feel blessed. When we stop and take a look at what we have been through, what we have achieved, we can see how truly magnificent we are. How truly wonderful life is, and how fucking fantastic we are for living it.

Never in a million years could I have imagined the power of meditation, I could never have thought such a simple thing could be so life changing. I wish that everyone would give it a chance, I wish that everyone could understand how freaking awesome the present moment is. Yes, I do have times where I forget and get carried away with worry, but I also know that I can come back home to myself, I can take a deep breath and I can feel a whole lot better quick smart by doing so. Peace is in your breath, it begins with you and only you. You cannot look to others for peace, you cannot look to others to fix your life. Meditation can take you to a place where life is calm, where life is peaceful and where you are in control of it all. Miracles will occur in your mind when you stop for a moment and be still. You can release fears, unlock love and find happiness in your breath during meditation.

Want a simple meditation technique? Try breathing like a dog, stick out your tongue and pant, try it. It feels liberating.

Meditation can be used in so many ways, it can help you to recall memories, it can help you find answers, help you find something that has been lost. It can help you to feel positive, harness empathy, help you to make decisions, and it will help you become more in tune with your gut instinct. Your unconscious mind knows all the answers, meditation can help you to reach your unconscious mind and figure out the best move for you. I have used meditation successfully for so many big decisions in my life. Just close your eyes, focus on your breath and ask the question you need to ask. The answer will come to you once you give it space to.

AFFIRMATIONS!

I am constantly grateful for the opportunities that are presented to me.

An affirmation is what I like to call a self-declaration. It is a positively stated phrase that you should repeat to yourself over and over again. Our brains are hard wired to focus on what we need to focus on. Try looking around the room for something red, now close your eyes take and a breath, then open your eyes again and find something blue. See how your eyes are drawn to the red immediately? If we are continually putting on attention towards negative affirmations, i.e. I am fat, then you will continue to eat and keep yourself fat! When you start focusing on a positive affirmation such as "I am a healthy weight and I eat wholesome foods" then you will notice that this is how your life will be.

Don't get to hung up on the process, what needs to happen will happen once you start to believe what it is that you are saying. Don't let your ego try to tell you that it cant happen, whatever it is that you want to happen. You have the right to be whatever you want to be and you have the power to be whatever you want to be. By affirming to the Universe you are attracting what you need into your life. I am always affirming that I am the luckiest girl in town, and I honestly believe this to be true. I don't have to win the lottery to prove this, I just have to trust that this is true and soon it becomes fact!

Some may say that affirmations are simply you trying to kid yourself, these are the non-believers. I say "clearly you haven't tried it". I used to be a non-believer, I used to listen to my friend go on about them and think, 'you are such a hippie'. Little did I know about the power that they have. When you repeat a positive affirmation over and over again your brain will register this as a goal and it will make you take action to achieve said goal. It also makes us want to be at peace with what we are saying, I.e. if you are saying I eat wholesome and healthy foods, then your body will want to be at one with that statement. It can take up to 21 days for this change to happen, so be patient.

By saying affirmations loud and proud you are helping to rewire your unconscious mind. When I first started saying affirmations every bone in my body rejected them, I had no belief in them, and I felt stupid even thinking that I was abundant, or joyful, or whatever other waffle was listed. I was just trying to replace negative thoughts with positive ones. The thing is, you cannot replace negative thoughts, they will always be there. The thing with affirmations is to remember that what we think about, we bring about. Make sure the affirmation is something that is relevant to you, you need to be able to relate to it. Using above as an example, instead of saying 'I am skinny' you would say 'I eat wholesome and healthy foods and enjoy exercise'. If you continually repeat a positive affirmation then you will soon start to believe it.

Studies have found that people who constantly repeat positive affirmations rather than entertaining negative thoughts have stronger muscles, you heard it here first (well actually you may have heard it before). Research claims that a person's muscles become stronger and more active when the unconscious mind is filled with positive loving banter. The same report indicated that the human muscles tend to become weak when a person thinks and verbalizes that he is tired or that he hates the world or that he cannot do a particular thing. Time to shape up!

The goal of your affirmations is to believe!! They will help to rewire your mind and you can begin to believe anything you want. You literally have the power to make anything happen. Trust your power, it is all within you!

Get yourself an affirmation list, read through as many affirmations that you can get your hands on and soon you will find the right ones for you. When you do set a reminder in your phone to repeat said affirmation 3 times a day. When you wake up, in the middle of the day and before you go to bed at night. Keep at it, Rome wasn't built in a day and affirmations won't work over night, trust in the process, stay committed and then sit back and watch the fabulousness unfold.

SELF TALK!

When I found out about self-talk and how it controlled my life I was blown away. I finally realised that it was me who was sabotaging my whole life!! It was confronting, but also astonishing. How had I let myself become my own worst enemy? How had I become so negative, sad and depressed all in my own head. How had I let my life get so bad? I had simply talked myself into it. The years that I had wasted by telling myself I was worthless, that I wasn't good enough, that I was unlovable, were all my own thoughts that no-one else shared, even though I was sure they did. Can you see how powerful self-talk is? Can you understand that there are few, is not any, people out there who hate you as much as you hate yourself?

Self-talk - We all have it, every single human in the world has their very own self-talk that is continually going. It can be positive, negative, it can build you up, bring you down, make you smile, make you sing, make you cry, make you go completely bonkers but can also make you incredibly successful, happy and motivated.

We make our way through each day with what we say to ourselves in our head. We make lists, recall memories, think, plan, prioritise, organise, tell ourselves off, give ourselves a pat on the back, laugh, it never stops. Our brain never stops this constant self-talk. We need it, it what makes us get up, move, sleep, eat, drive, work, play, it's what makes us live.

Self-talk also determines how we feel. It controls our confidence, self esteem, ability to socialise, our anger, our joy, basically our overall happiness. It's so important that we give our self-talk some attention and take control over it. Your self-talk, like your brain is linked. Every word you say to yourself in your head gets linked to feelings and these feelings, well, they make us feel how we feel.

Self-talk is basically your inner voice, the voice in your mind which says things that you don't necessarily say out loud. Often self-talk happens without you even realising it and can be a subtle running commentary going on in the background of your mind. But what you say in your mind can determine a lot of how you feel about who you are.

Self-talk can have a really great impact on your self-esteem and confidence. There is positive and negative self-talk and they both have an impact on how you feel. There are a few ways you can develop better self-talk including just listening to what you're saying to yourself each day.

Many of us don't realise how frequently we put ourselves down. By beginning to observe your self-talk you catch yourself out, when you pay attention to what is happening in your mind you are starting to take back control over your life. When I found about self-talk I finally realised that I could control my happiness. I was the one who was making my life miserable, and I was the one who had the power to change it.

How you talk to yourself in your head impacts how you think. If you drop something on the floor, what is your first reaction? Do you say, "well done, good job", Or do you say "you freaking fool"? Your mind will always give you what it is that you desire, so if you are telling yourself that you are a fool, watch how you will turn into one. If you wouldn't say it to others, don't say it to yourself.

Here are four common types of negative self-talk to watch out for: Which one are you? I was all of them!!

1. Perfectionism/Polarizing: Things are either good or bad – there's no middle ground. If you're not perfect, you're a total failure.
2. Catastrophizing: You dream up the worst possible outcome, and small issues are harbingers of doom.
3. Rationalization: You blame yourself for everything bad that happens. For instance, if a few friends don't make it to your party, you assume no one likes you.
4. Filtering: You search for the negative aspects of any given situation, filtering out any positive ones. The holiday was mostly great, but you complain to yourself and others about the delayed flight home, rather than sharing the delights of the trip.

Our mind is the control centre... Our unconscious mind listens to our self-talk and gives it power without us knowing. The unconscious mind is a million times more powerful than the conscious mind and we operate 95 percent of our lives off of it. We need to learn to work with our unconscious mind, we need to recognize what it is saying, it is always there to serve and protect but if you have a bad memory from your childhood stored in there it could potentially be holding you back.

Negative self-talk can contribute to stress and even depression, which put the body into terrible metabolic state. I spent years depressed because of what I was telling myself. According to the Mayo Clinic, negative self-talk can induce physical as well as emotional stress, harming your cardiovascular health, gut health and immune system.

I used to think that the critical way I talked to myself was simply me being realistic and honest. I thought that I was simply a truth teller, who could see myself, my faults and flaws clearly. I didn't talk to others in this way. Not a chance, I would never say to someone else what I would continually say to myself.

For some reason I thought I deserved this tough love approach. Mistakes were the end of the world. I dramatised things like you wouldn't believe. My mind was grounds for constant bashing. And I didn't exactly make any effort to look after this precious body, I abused it, HARD! My biggest life awakening happened when I lost my sunglasses and then tried to end my own life! I had hard wired my own brain into a catastrophic state where the tiniest thing was the end of the world for me.

Most of us don't even realise the terrible way in which we talk to ourselves. It's so automatic, so common, it might feel like another part of your daily routine. Like waking up, brushing your teeth or like walking.

Negative self-talk only keeps us stuck, spinning our wheels, sinking deeper and deeper into the mud and muck. Calling ourselves stupid over and over doesn't help us learn from a mistake or see anything clearly. We need to learn to change this negative chatter to a more positive loving banter. Once you master this your life will change dramatically.

The wise man Gandhi said "Your beliefs become your thoughts, your thoughts become your words, your words become your actions, your actions become your habits, your habits become your values and your values become your destiny."

Here are a few ways to challenge your self-talk.

1. Whenever you find yourself feeling angry, anxious or upset, STOP and become aware of what is happening. Your feelings have come about due to what thoughts are going through your head. Ask yourself "what am I saying to myself?" If you are really honest with yourself you will soon find the root of the feeling. For example: Just the other day I was so anxious going to meet my girlfriends for lunch. I knew I shouldn't have been, but I was. When I stopped to ask myself what was really going on, I found out that the anxious feeling was coming from what one of the girls said to me the last time I saw her. I let what she thinks upset me, I let someone else's words affect my own body and mind. When you look at it that way it seems a little silly. What right does anyone have to be a worm inside of your mind? They have none. The only person that lets them be a worm is YOU! Always stop and ask yourself what is happening and soon you will see with such clarity what is upsetting you.

2. Are you sure what you are thinking is real? Have you got any real evidence for this panic or have you gone and jumped to a conclusion. Often we make mountains out of molehills, and often we make an issue when there is none there. You may have conjured up a situation in your head but the reality is very different. To help gain perspective when I get lost, I ask a friend who I know comes from a place of love. Are your thoughts only happening in your head, or is something really wrong? For example: If a loved one is sick in hospital, then you have something to be worried about. If you think that your friend doesn't like you anymore because she said something nasty, then this is probably a made up story. She may have been nasty to you because she is hurting. Most people do not want to cause pain to people they love, they only do it because they are sad, angry, upset or stressed.

3. Ask yourself, what else could this mean? Why am I having these thoughts? Does it make sense? Where is it coming from and how can you find peace the root of the cause. For example: if the

counter has not been wiped down, should I feel hated? I used to feel this because I thought that someone leaving a mess for me was because they wanted to hurt me, I thought that they were testing me to see how perfect I was. I thought that if I didn't clean it up then I wouldn't be loved.

4. "What is the worst that could happen?" Sometimes you have to ask this question. Sometimes the answer is not actually that bad. After you ask yourself that question, ask this one "what is the best that could happen?"

5. What can you do to solve the problem? In most cases you will have to do something, to take action, to change your mind or lifestyle. Or sometimes you may just need to turn on a switch☺ I have been in situations where I have completely lost my temper because I think something is broken, I yell and scream and then realise that the power is not turned on. DOH! Sometimes the answer is easy, and sometimes it is more difficult to find, but the answer is always there.

6. RECOGNISE – your current way of thinking way be self-defeating.

7. CONQUER – if you continually challenge your self-talk your brain can begin to make new links and form new patterns so that you can live a happier life!

By changing how you talk to yourself, you will change your whole life. It was my greatest ever lesson, my biggest ever finding, and I use the above challenges every single day. I have trained my brain to a more positive outlook, but I am still human. I still have negative thoughts, I still get caught up in negative self-talk, but I also know that I can challenge it, I can thank my mind for giving me a warning but then let go of what I do not need.

We have all been given the same abilities. We can all stop our negative thoughts, the very first step in doing so is to decide. Do you want to live happier, more fulfilling life? I am not saying it will be all peaches and roses, but you will see the sour apples for what they are. Everyone needs to have some downs, otherwise we would not appreciate the ups. We all need to have difficulties, and I honestly believe that we choose our paths before we come to Earth. We know what lessons we want to learn in this body and we go about learning it the way we planned it out. Sometimes the shit that we have to go through has been put there for us to use as fertilizer! The times that we are hurting so bad, are the times that we should grow the most. If you are not growing, you are dying!!

You have the right to this worlds abundance, you have the right to a beautiful mind, you have the right to live a happier and more rewarding life and you my darling have the right to whatever you chose to have in your life. It is what you believe that you deserve which will control what you are given. I used to believe that I was a bad person, that I didn't deserve happiness, and that my life was fuckin shit! Now I believe that every single moment is precious, how I look at life, life looks at me right back, and I believe that I have the ability to help make the world a happier place... Are you with me?

18

Believe

We were all born into this world equal, and all have the same rights to prosperity, abundance and love. Society can restrict us by placing labels on us, our own parents and teachers can restrict us, mostly unintentionally of course. All it takes is a few simple words, it could have been a passing comment, it could have been a nasty comment, it could have even been some words of encouragement, but our brain took those words and twisted them and created a limiting belief for us that we will hold onto for life.

When we are born, we are born without beliefs, values, opinions, judgments, perceptions and viewpoints. We are also born without limitation. If only we could hold onto that complete openness, vulnerability and compassion. We have to build on how we see the world. Our beliefs and values are what all of our opinions, judgments, viewpoints and perceptions are based on, and we will defend what we *"believe"* to be true, sometimes at the cost of relationships.

We all have beliefs, things we believe we can do and things we believe we can't. The fact is, what you believe, tends to happen, so it is far more productive to believe you can and then just do it. If you think you can, or you think you can't, either way you are right.! Our beliefs are like the building blocks to our unconscious mind.

Every decision you make in life is based on your belief system. This system works without you even knowing it. Beliefs are judgments about ourselves and the world around us. They are usually generalizations and generalizations are well, general.

Do you believe that you are in charge? Do you believe that life is an opportunity? Do you believe that only rich people can be rich? Do you believe in the law of attraction? Do you believe in fairies?

These are just examples, but you can see how either believing in these, or not, can impact your life. When I was really young I used to believe that everyone lived in Ireland and all other countries were just for holidays. I also used to believe that I didn't have a 'real' job as I worked in hospitality, my father would say to me all the time, when are you going to get a 'real' job.

You can change your beliefs. Peoples' beliefs usually evolve as they gain new experiences. What limiting belief do you have that holds you back from something that you want to do? Do you have any evidence? So many of my friends when chatting to me use words such as ALWAYS and EVERYONE, even though what they were really saying is that one person, or maybe two people told them so. They begin to believe that based on one or two comments from a potentially unreliable source that whatever it is, is. They convince themselves that everyone is following suit but this is not the case. Don't let yourself fall victim to this, challenge yourself, challenge them. Even if everyone is doing it, if you don't want to do it, don't!

Have you ever let someone else's perception of you get the better of you? I had people think that I was too strict at work - they had no idea the pressure that I was under (no excuse for being mean). I may have come across short at times but instead of trying to understand me, they labelled me. Yes, I could have been a bit calmer, but I was so caught up in proving to my boss that I was good enough that I forgot to be human. I was too busy trying to be super woman. I started to believe what they were saying about me, and before long I was doubting myself and letting them dictate who and what I was. I lost myself due to other people's perception of me even though they didn't even know me.

Has anyone ever told you that you were mean, negative or too strict? What they are doing is placing their own insecurities onto you. People are entitled to their own opinions but how we take them is up to us. We could either take it as constructive feedback or we could let it take over us. If someone is mean enough to say something like that to you, then you don't want them in your life. Pay attention to what was happening.

Are they right? Do they have evidence? Be true to who you are. You don't need to explain yourself to anyone, only to yourself.

If your brain has been trained to continually make links with the negatives, it could quickly turn a perfectly sane, normal situation into a scary, unreal disaster. I mean hello, I lost my sunglasses and ended up trying to kill myself! You need to change the links.

Think about anxiety. The truth about anxiety is that the brain makes our fears bigger than reality. But what is really going on? We need to tell our brain to put the anxiety back in the place where it belongs and not right in front of us causing us this distress. Our fight or flight response kicks in when we think we are under attack. When our brain perceives danger it will make us feel anxious. It is actually our safe guard. If we see a tiger in the woods that is about to attack us, we should run. Fight or flight response is the trigger that is sent to our brain is these types of situations. In reality the only thing that humans should be scared of, is loud noises and falling. So in theory we should not have anxiety about anything else, but we do. I used to get anxiety when I met new people, some people would think that is very odd. Some people get anxiety over getting on a plane, which I think very odd. These are all things that we have programmed ourselves to be scared of. We can program ourselves to be scared of anything, but we can also push ourselves to get over these fears. What do you believe that that is making you scared? And it's not getting on a plane or meeting new people. You have to get down deeper than that! Why is this causing you issues?

For example, why do I get so nervous when I meet new people? I have a fear that they will hate me. But why do I think this? I honestly believe that I have nothing worth saying so I should be quiet, this will lead people to believe that I am stupid and then they won't like me. This comes form my belief that was drilled into me at an early age that 'I should be seen and not heard'. For many reading this it will not make any sense, if you think about meeting new people, do you have the same thoughts? These thoughts come about because of my childhood and of course you wont have the same reaction as I do because you don't hold the same belief that I do. Here I am now writing this book, sharing my story and giving myself the voice that I never felt that I had.

When I was younger I was constantly told that I should been seen and not heard. Added to this in my adult working life the company I worked for was telling me that they didn't want to hear what I what to say, combine these together and I was left feeling like if I said anything people would think I am stupid. Now when I know I will be meeting new people I start the day with an affirmation such as 'people love and respect me'. There is no reason why this can't be true, and if someone doesn't respect me than I will repay them the same favour!

You can train your brain to think a certain way. Many people have been brought up believing things to be true, which leads to them being programmed a certain way. Unfortunately no one ever knows what they don't know. How can you? If you have no idea about how to feel happy, then how can you feel happy? If you don't know what it takes to build a solid, nurturing relationship, then how can you ever have one? What if we train our brain a new way? What if we look at things differently? When you open your front door and look outside, what do you see? Do you see this wonderful planet we live on, filled with beautiful things, creatures and how Mother Nature has built this world? Or do you see something else? If we have gotten into a habit of not looking at things, then we won't see what may be right in front of us.

To change your brain pattern you only need to do something consistently 4-5 times. So every morning when I wake up I no longer wake up thinking, 'it's too early', or 'I don't want to get up', or 'give me five more minutes please'!!! I wake every morning without an alarm, with a smile on my face and I thank the world for another day. I thank the universe for all that I have, as I have everything I need. How you wake up every morning sets the mood for the entire day. I honestly believe that I am lucky and blessed. I have trained myself to believe this.

I used to set my alarm for the very last minute that I could wake up. As soon as my alarm would go off I would jump out of bed, run into the shower, get dressed and run out the door. Sound familiar? This is no way to wake up, it is similar to being woken up with a sledgehammer to the head. Your mind and body need time to wake up and kick start in order to be productive, otherwise you are just running on empty.

Here is my new morning routine and how I now wake up every morning which ensures I am in top form as soon as I walk out the door.

1. I set my alarm so that I can have 5 minutes snooze time. Most of the time I don't even take the 5 minutes, but they are there if I want them. Don't hit the snooze button more than once. Set your alarm so you know you can only hit it once. Trying to put off what you inevitably have to do is not a good start to your day. How to wake up every morning

2. I wake up and say thanks! Every morning that you wake is actually a gift, you have been blessed with life, even though at times it can be tough, it is still yours for the making! I wake up and say thank you to the Universe, not only for waking up, but also for the good in my life, and no matter what I am going through I always have something to be thankful for.

3. I ask my Angels "where would you have me go, what would you have me do and what would you have me say?" I expect my Angels to be by my side 24/7, so in turn I must expect that they need me to be there for them too. By asking them this question I am allowing them guide my day, as they will not intervene against my free will.

4. I leave my phone alone after I have turned off my alarm. It will literally stay in it's place until I am ready to walk out the door. There is no need for working longer hours than necessary, and I highly recommend waking up without checking your emails or social media.

5. I move… Yes, I know you don't have time, I don't have time either but I get up earlier and make time because my body is a priority. Get the good endorphin's rocking around your body and kick start your mind and body with some nice movement, whether it be some simple yoga poses, some squats, planks, or a 5km run, whatever you do for movement, do it in the morning.

6. I then take a mindful shower. I stand under the water until I become aware of what is it that I am doing. Sometimes I can jump in and out of the shower and not even noticed that I have just had one. Nowadays I feel the warm water as it rolls down

my back, I feel the soap as it clean my skin, I listen carefully to the sounds that are being made and look attentively at what is around me. By focusing on the present moment and what is happening, I am being mindful. Don't start your day thinking about all that you have to do, you will get through your to-do list, but shower time should be mindful time. How to wake up every morning

7. Affirm. I ALWAYS choose an affirmation for the day and set my mind up with a positive kick start for the day. Some examples: My business is booming, I have boundless energy, I am loved and I give love. The possibilities are endless with affirmations, all you need to do is stay committed to saying it and of course believing it. (ps. if you don't believe it straight away that's OK)

8. I meditate, just for 5 minutes and it works a treat. In fact, if I don't meditate I feel stressed out before I pick up my phone. Even if 2 minutes is all that you have, it will be worth it.

9. I hydrate before I drink a coffee. Coffee used to be the only thing that I put into my body in the morning, now I drink water with fresh lemon and either a green smoothie or berry smoothie, depending on what I have in the fridge. These can be made the night before so no excuses. How to

I know many people have little time in the morning before they got to run out the door, all of the above don't take much time but are so incredibly valuable for your day. In fact it takes almost no extra time at all. Set your alarm for an extra 10 minutes earlier, not including snooze time and try out this new routine. You will soon see how much more amazing you feel and you will be committed to the new routine for good!

Be mindful of what you say to yourself in the morning too. If you drop a bowl of cereal, just laugh at yourself. We must learn that our words have power and you don't even need to say them out loud. The ones that go around in your head can cause pain, that's what happened to me. It all happened in my head. The sadness was all in my head, which transferred to my body, which transferred to my actions.

Your thoughts become your feelings. Remember this!

Stand up and take action against your negative thinking. Studies show that 80% of our thoughts are negative and that negative thinking actually shrinks the brain. That could explain my empty feeling when I was feeling down and out - my brain wasn't functioning properly. When you get caught up with a bad feeling this could take over and cause fuzziness. When you have a negative thought arise, catch it and challenge it. If you think, "I can't do this" stop and ask yourself why do you believe this? By learning to challenge our chatter we could learn how to change our life.

Remember this

"Happiness is when you think, what you say,
and what you do are in harmony"
Mahatma Gandhi

Gandhi is a super clever guy and he couldn't have gotten wrong. It has just taken me some time to figure out what this meant. The secret to my happiness was all within me. I am not going all hipee-ish here, this fact is true. I have heard this many times before, and I hear it all the time now from various people, including myself. We are all amazingly, wonderful beings and we all have the power within us to be happy. What we need to do, is realise this.

Happiness is not defined by money, clothes, bags, shoes, phones, laptops, what you have, what you want, or what you don't want. I used to think being happy meant that I would have a huge wardrobe filled with clothes, shoes and bags but now I think completely the opposite. When I look at my wardrobe now, it's filled with so many clothes that I can barely make my mind up what to wear. How many times do girls go and buy clothes that they never even wear? It's crazy!

The wanting that we have for more clothes is only ever increased by our giving into it. When we want we buy, and then we buy and want more, we are never happy with what we have. Why not? Well a lot of it has to do with society and how we think we should portray ourselves, along with the fact that it's not cool to go out naked... I used to hate wearing a dress a 2nd time, especially to a special event, now I would much rather experience the special event and enjoy it than worry about what I am going to wear.

Our constant wanting more, can cause us pain and suffering in many cases. I have a friend who cannot accept where she is in life. If you asked her 5 years ago what she wanted from the next 5 years you would see that she has achieved that and so much more. She has such an amazing life, yet she wants more. She believes that by wanting more she is never settling and never giving up on what potentially can be hers. She puts pressure on herself to constantly strive and push herself. She wastes time and energy and can get very depressed by this constant wanting more. What is wanting more achieving in this case? Resentment? Anger? Pain? Suffering? What is the point? Her belief that what she has achieved is not enough. When will what you are and what you have be enough?

Life really is not made up of what we possess. Yes, society does play a huge factor, I mean we all want houses, homes, cars, but when we achieve this we want better ones, faster ones, bigger ones, when will it end, when will we finally say, ok, thank you, I have enough? What will it take for us to realise that our possessions do not make up who we are, our wanting makes us who we are, and who we are through this wanting is not who we really are, make sense? You still with me?

I can't say that I don't want to live in a nice big house; I honestly want to live by the ocean in a big white house with a big wraparound porch. But this does not and will not define me. That not to say that I will have it and strive for it. The point I am making here is that it does not define who we are. Possessions are simply things, even though things are a lot more than things.

Be thankful for what you already have! Sit back and reassess your wants, needs and desires. In the end of it all we can't take possessions with us. Don't let your ego take over and make you think you want things that you don't need. Will having a certain object make you a better person? If you answer yes, ask yourself one more time…get out of your head, let go of your ego and see the world in a whole new wonderful light.

I never thought I would be that annoyingly happy person who always has balls of energy and loves to give. I always thought those people were just hippies, but now that's me.

"I choose to live by choice, not by chance, to make changes, not excuses, to be motivated, not manipulated, to be useful, not used, to excel, not compete.
I choose self esteem, not self pity. I choose to listen to
my inner voice and not the opinion of others."

People often ask me how I managed to turn myself around so quickly. It's simple. I made a choice. I didn't need pills and I didn't need someone to tell me what was wrong with me. All I needed to do was decide to be happy and commit to it. I felt like I was a new person and it felt so good. When I was told that depression was simply not wanting to take responsibility, I thought, yeah right, you have NO IDEA! Now that I look back, it's exactly what was for me at that time. I was bombarded with choices and I let them and the fact that I was overwhelmed by it all take control of me. All I had to do was make some decisions, but I was so scared of the potential consequences. I was scared of what I had created in my own head, nothing was really scary or a threat, but I managed to see it that way.

It was all so easy and I made it all so hard. I was my very own worst enemy. My inner dialogue, or Jessica chatter as I like to call it spun out of control and I was living my life on what ifs, can't, shouldn't, wouldn't, etc. Remove the "nots" in your life. And if you change your language and change your chatter, the world would be such an amazing beautiful place to live in. Stop saying 'I have to', and start saying 'I chose to'.

Remember this **'you are NOT your thoughts.'** Your mind doesn't define you, nor does it control you. It is not who you are. The quicker you realise this, the faster you will become happier. What we sometimes forget is that our own thoughts are just that! They are our own, and what we sometimes think to be true, is in actual fact something that we have just convinced ourselves to be true. Your thoughts are NOT facts! They can be wrong, very wrong. We can train our brain to think the worst in every situation, especially when it comes to ourselves.

Just because you thought it, doesn't mean that it is true... I so often hear people try to justify themselves to others, when the 'others' have no idea what they are talking about. We can get carried away with our thinking, and create a situation when there isn't one there. For example, I might think that my friend is annoyed with me over something I feel guilty about doing. My friend is not actually annoyed at all, and I have spent hours justifying myself to myself and others. Waste of time!!

When you find yourself getting into a thought spin just STOP!!!! Take a step back and breathe as this too shall pass. Worrying is simply using your imagination to create things that you don't want. I have wasted so much time on worry and all I got form it was wrinkles!!! No more for me thanks.

When you feel happy it's easy to think more happy thoughts and be happier. When you feel sad or depressed they take over and it's easy to remember sad and depressing times. Once you start climbing down the black hole it's tough to get back up. There was a way out though - don't ever give up. Don't ever keep crawling down the hole. Don't try to cover up depression or sadness. Don't be ashamed to ask for help. Be strong and stand up to your feelings. Stand up and take charge.

You can train your brain to love yourself. You can see the world through a whole new lens. You can appreciate all the little things. You can have a whole new life. Trust me, I never knew feeling this good was even possible and I want everyone to feel this way. I love to learn, and I look at any obstacle as an opportunity to overcome and learn from. I spend my days and nights working on how I could share this energy with as many people as I can.

Don't think I live this unimaginable life. I am an everyday person living an everyday life with everyday people and have annoyances and problems to face like any other person. I look at them differently though. I was teaching myself to reframe what I needed to. I have started my business, 'The Happy Pill' to help inspire and motivate people. I want to help people change their chatter. It works, and it all starts with YOU. You are the only person who can help yourself. Stop looking to others for answers, you have them all.

Start looking up at the sky more often and see its beauty for what it is. Start cherishing the present moment, as you will only ever experience the present moment once. Never let a second go by that you are not grateful. Love with every morsel of your being. Let go of what you do not need! The only thing is this life that is guaranteed is change, yet change is what turns us into a tailspin. Be brave, be kind and be you. Ask for help when you need it. I am always here should you need some advice. And remember 'If you are not growing, you are dying'. Always learn, always change, always grow!

Peace and love, Jessica xoxo

19

What took me my lifetime to learn

Our most profound life lessons can be learnt in an instant, it can be something someone says, it can be a billboard poster, a tough time, a song, a memory, a walk in the park, a lightning bolt of realisation (this happened to me), there are many ways, both fast and slow that lessons can be learnt. The key is to be open to them, and also to know that everything in life is a lesson, even the toughest, darkest times in your life. In fact it is in these times that we learn the greatest lessons of all.

Every day I am learning, and every day I am growing. It is difficult to turn my whole life into just 35 lessons but I am going to share my wisest wisdom with you in a hope that you will learn from them:

1. Life is meant to be fun, not a bitch.

Life is ultimately what we make it. I wandered around for years saying 'FML' and 'life is a bitch!!' I was telling the Universe I hated life, that it was tough, hard and pretty much throwing out there what I wanted back. Now I know that life is a beautiful lesson, the Universe wants us to grow, that tough times don't last. When life isn't fun, then I need to change something!! Next time you are in a tail spin of worry, ask yourself, how can I make this fun? Start measuring your success by how much fun you are having.

2. Don't compare your life to others.

I was a pro at this one. I spent my life comparing myself to anyone else in my life. I was constantly trying to be someone I wasn't, and berating myself for not living up to what I thought that someone else was. In reality, you have no idea about their journey and what they might be going through. You are comparing to what you THINK their life is, not the reality of it. Envy is a waste of time. Comparison is the thief of joy. And by comparing yourself to others you are ultimately letting the belief that you are not good enough sneak in. You will never find peace in comparison. Next time you find yourself in comparison mode just take a moment to stop and insert an affirmation such as 'I choose love instead of this' or 'I honour the light inside of you' (towards the other person).

3. What other people think of you is none of your business.

This is pretty self-explanatory. Similar to above, they have no idea of your journey and what you are going through or what goes through your head on a daily basis. Others peoples thoughts are just that! You have no business letting those thoughts shape your life in any way shape or form. Let them think what they want to, they have no power over you. You are the creator and master of your own destiny.

4. You already have all you need.

The crazy desire we all have for wanting more stuff is insane!! What is ultimately important to you? What would you take with you if you died? Do we really need so much stuff? Sit back and reassess your wants, needs and desires. In the end of it all we can't take possessions with us. Don't let your ego take over and make you think you want things that you don't need.

5. Forgive.

This is BIG my friend, BIG!!!! If someone has done you wrong let it go... be free from anger. If only for yourself. When you release your anger and forgive you will feel a whole lot lighter. Forgiveness helps us to reconnect with our truth and to love more. Drop any fights that you may towards forgiveness, toward others and let love reign instead of hate. By holding onto something old and not letting go you are ultimately carrying a heavy rock that you don't need to. What will holding onto this rock bring into your life?

6. Believe in miracles.

A miracle is a shift in perception. Believe in this and you believe in miracles.

7. Life is too short for long pity parties.

Whatever doesn't kill you really does make you stronger. I absolutely condone feeling your emotions, but feel them and let them go as soon as you can. Negativity breaths negativity so if you are feeling sorry for yourself and telling yourself a "story" over and over again you are blocking positivity from entering into your life. By all means feel sad, but don't let the sadness reign and take over leaving only sadness in your life.

8. Being kind is more important than being right.

You don't have to win every argument. I used to think I had to have my say and be "honest" with my friends/boss/colleagues. The fact is they were not ready for my "honesty" and I pushed them away. Before you say what is REALLY on your mind ask yourself this "is it kind?" what you think is right may only be right for you and not the other person. There is always a solution that is best, but it may not be the solution that you think it is.

9. You have to be your own best friend.

No one else will stay your true friend until you are your own true friend. It took me forever to get my head around this one. I love all of my friends dearly and I often put their needs above my own. In the end

I got hurt because I was the one who was putting myself out there for them without thinking about myself. If I put myself first then I wouldn't have gotten so hurt . You will be a much better friend when you can be your own best friend.

10. Fear will try to hold you back.

Don't let it. This is simply your EGO a play. The only two things that humans are frightened of is loud noises and falling. Most of us don't like to admit we are afraid, especially to ourselves. Most of us don't even realise that it is actually fear that is holding us back. I have been trying for years to stop smoking, and have made up infinite excuses as to why I should keep smoking and why I can't stop. I didn't realise that is was actually the fear of gaining weight that was stopping me all along. If we deny our fear then we are in fact giving it more power. Once you bring fear into the light and look at it for what it really is… it loses all its power over you, and you know what you gain? POWER!!

11. All that truly matters in the end is that you loved.

Love is pretty freaking awesome and you need it in your life. What I have learnt is that love won't be in your life if you don't give it out yourself. Love people, give into love, let yourself fall in love, be stupid in love, be clever in love, be head over heels in love. Your heart may get broken but this is all part of LOVE!!! Love thy neighbour, love thy cat, dog, mouse, whatever you can love, give it love. What you give out you receive back in oodles so don't be shy about it.

12. Love alone isn't enough.

As much as I wish it was enough, the reality is, that it is not. We must love, but it alone is not enough to survive. Relationships that live only on love will die after time. this actually hurts my heart to write but its true. Love can heal so much, but in the world we live in today there are just so many other factors that come into play. I had to break up with a guy that I was still in love with because our values no longer aligned, we were on two very different paths. I still to this day hold so much love for him but I know that we could have never gotten through life together with just the love we had for each other.

13. Take a deep breath.

When in doubt take a breath, it calms the mind. Meditate when and where you can. When you find yourself losing it, take a breath, when you just cant take anymore, take a breath. Breathing keeps us sane, helps us to focus and gain clarity. Simple, effective and free!!

14. If a relationship has to be a secret, you shouldn't be in it.

Nothing more to say, but you have to know this is SO TRUE! I have had to hide many a relationship and it was because I knew what people would say if they found out. If you love someone you should be able to shout it from the rooftops and you should be able to announce your love to everyone. Having to hide something means it shouldn't be.

15. Make peace with your past so it won't screw up the present.

I had a fucked up childhood, it made me a little bit crazy... but hey, it also made me who I am today and I am grateful for that. Let go of the past, it has no power over you, unless you let it. Whatever happened, happened. It doesn't matter anymore. What matters is the right now. Learn from the past and move forward, ALWAYS move forward. FACT – You cannot change the past, you can only deal with it. And how you deal with it will make you a stronger person.

16. Over prepare, then go with the flow.

I am all for a laid back approach to life but hey you can't plan anything without planning. And a life without anything is nothing. I like to be easy going but in the background I have made sure that I am covered for all and any curveballs.

17. No one is in charge of your happiness except you.

Yes, it is true. Not your partner, your mother, not your dad, brother, sister, no one else but you. And all those times you say to someone "you made me...." Are times that in fact you made yourself feel..... No one else can make you feel anything, only you can. Boy I am happy that I learnt this, as I was forever blaming others for making me sad.

18. Growing old is a beautiful thing.

And hey it beats the alternative of dying young..!! Embrace it, gracefully, and see how beautiful you can be. Someone who accepts age with grace is so much more beautiful than a Botox person whose face can show no emotion. The older you are, the wiser you are, or so they say.

19. Get outside every day. Miracles are waiting everywhere.

How often do you stop and look up at the sky? Have you ever wondered how far away a star is? When was the last time you took your shoes off and walked on some fresh cut grass? The beauty, the wonder, just stop, and take it all in.

20. Often those who are the hardest to love are the ones who need it the most.

People come into your life for a reason, and I believe that we choose our friends and family before we even come to this beautiful Earth. For the tough relationships, try to see what lesson that person is here to teach you. Put out compassion and love to them, even though you may want to kill them. It is kindness that will change the world, not hate. It is compassion that helps people change, not frustration. My mantra - "I will listen to those who want to be heard, help those who are in need, guide those who are lost and serve those who call for love."

21. Words have energy.

Try your own experiment. I placed some rice and some water into a small jar and labelled each jar, one with the word love, and the other with the word hate. I spoke to each jar with either loving or hateful words and after just 4 weeks there were astonishing results. The love jar had created the most beautiful pink circle of mould, whereas the hate jar had black and grey spikey mould. If words can do this to rice and water just imagine what they are doing inside of your mind.

22. Your thoughts create reality.

What you think about, you bring about. The law of attraction is true. Have you ever noticed that when you are in a bad mood that negative thoughts run freely through your mind, and when in a good mood or having a good time positive thoughts flow freely in your mind. Take note next time you feel sad. Its actually hard to feel sad when your happy and vice versa. You can train your brain to think mostly positive thoughts. I used to be a negative thinker, I used to bombard myself with stories and excuses as to why I could feel so sorry for myself. These days I spend more time focusing on the positive things in life and therefore train my brain to see the good in so much. Even when bad things happen I can now see what lesson it has taught me.

23. Obstacles are a space to grow.

For the tough times in your life, instead of throwing in the towel and walking away, which let's face it seems super tempting, try to see what lesson you need to learn from it. There is ALWAYS a lesson, sometimes you need to dig real deep to find it. Take my suicide attempt for example, I could have let this take over my life, I could have let it define me, I could have kept on trying until I succeeded but instead I chose to learn, change, to change and to grow. I made massive changes in my life that have ultimately saved my life. I have taken my suicide attempt as a lesson to look at the bright side, as a lesson that life is for living, as a lesson that life is what you make of it and you chose exactly what that is.

24. An attitude of gratitude will change your life.

Because when you stop and take a look around you will see that the life that you are living is pretty freaking fabulous! Even when it's not, it is! Gratitude creates solutions, it really does. Adopting an attitude of gratitude trains your brain to focus more on solutions than problems. It removes you from complaining mode and into a best-outcomes mindset. It is such an incredibly powerful exercise that absolutely anyone can start immediately! Get your friends and family involved and get them thinking about what they are grateful for to, share it with each other. Starting new habits is always easier when you have someone to start doing it with you.

25. People want validation, give it to them.

It doesn't cost you anything. That's why we hang with people who share our beliefs and similar values, because we also need to be validated. Give out to others what they need. But don't be cruel in the process.

26. Positive thinking has pros and cons.

I absolutely believe in seeing the best in everything and everyone. I believe that we should all have faith in the world and if someone takes your trust and throws it in the bin then throw them in the bin, not literally. Learn the lesson that was provided to you and move on. Don't bury your head in the sand, NO, NO! You cannot positively think your way out of a bad situation, BUT you can think that the situation has taught you something. We may be opening ourselves up to nasty people bursting our bubble every now and then, but these times are given to us for clarity. Positive thinking isn't about expecting the best to happen every time, but accepting that whatever happens is the best for that moment.

27. Being busy is actually a curse.

Yes, yes it is!!! Busy has become glorified and people are giving up friendships, relationships and more just so they can fill their lives with something to help them avoid life. That is what you are doing by being busy all of the time. You are avoiding the beautiful life that can be yours. By being so busy you are missing out on so much. Stop saying I'm busy, and replace with 'I have all the time I need.'

28. Breaking habits is actually easy when you want to.

All you have to do is choose. Make the choice and you will see just how easy breaking a habit can be. For years I thought I had to work 70,80, 90 hours a week to show that I was a hard worker, it became addictive. Just like smoking and drinking. Now I know I don't have to do anything I don't want to and if I want to stop working, smoking, drinking, all I have to do is decide. And I don't mean a half arse decision lie thinking it would be nice. I mean a full on decision, 110% commitment, and total belief that it will happen. Quit the excuses, and start getting down with the reasons that you CAN, because my dear, you truly CAN!!

29. Your health and happiness are linked.

Health is more important than most of us think. What we put into our bodies we get out. If you are filling yourself with junk food, alcohol, smoke or fatty foods then don't expect your body to give you much back! Equally if you are not giving your body the goodness it needs then your body and mind won't give you the goodness that you deserve. If you are feeling unhappy, stressed out or anxious it takes its toll on your body and health. It has even been proved that unhappiness/stress/anxiety can lead to premature aging. It's true! There are so many studies that prove to us that our happiness and health are linked, yet so many of us are unhappy. New scientific research has also identified that chronic stress can actually decrease our lifespan. Negative emotions can harm your body, where as positive emotions keep you healthy and happy.

30. Respond don't react.

If you manage to manage this then you are onto a winner!~ In any given circumstance if you respond you are doing so with emotion, you are thinking about yourself and you are diving on head first. When you react, you are going at it with your eyes wide open, calmly and with no emotion or judgement. We spend much of our lives in reaction, the problem with this is that reactions are not always the best way forward for us, and as a result, they can make others unhappy, or make things worse for us, even make the situation worse. We all do it, react, dive in head first without thinking, its in our blood, it's a our gut reaction, its programmed deep into our cells. It is often based on our fears and insecurities, and it's not necessarily the best way to act. Responding, on the other hand, is taking the situation in, and deciding the best course of action based on values such as reason, compassion, cooperation, etc. it's the cool, calm and collected method to stopping the madness from taking over. It takes practice, and can sometimes be super hard to do, but practice does help.

31. Don't judge.

"Today I will judge nothing that occurs." This should be you mantra every day. How would you feel if you heard what someone was saying about you while judging you? It is not a nice thing to hear so just try not to do it at all. After all, what do you gain from judging others? You have no idea what it is like to be in their shoes. By judging others we are implying to ourselves that we are superior to them, we are all the same, all of us are humans looking for love and trying to share love, some may do this is a very strange way to what you know but ultimately they are travelling the same road that you are. Next time you find yourself running your eyes up and down someone and thinking 'I would never wear that' quickly stop that though and insert 'we are all travelling the same journey and I wish this person well'.

32. Success is perspectival.

You are not your job and your job does not define you. Some people think success is having a six figure income and a fancy house and car, while others see success as being happy with whatever they have, even if it's very little. Define what success means to you because until you define exactly what it is for you, it will always be incredibly difficult to achieve. Success to me is my happiness. Now that I know what

33. Find your passion.

What do you LOVE to do? Really love? Now how can you make this your mission in life? Make more time to do what you love to do. If you had an appointment with the doctor you would go to it, right? Well book in some time to do what you love doing! I love to help others, I love to spread happiness, and I love to be honest and share my story in order to help others. It's what I love to do and what I will continue to do even if no one is listening. By I really hope that people do.

34. Be honest.

When was the last time you asked your friend how they were and really cared? I am very honest, sometimes to my detriment. But I will never change as I believe honesty is the best policy, and if you ask me how I am I will tell you! People these days tend to showcase their life through social media and only post the good stuff, no one shares what they are really feeling and you never see what lies behind that screen. Be honest with yourself first and foremost, then be honest with everyone else. And forget, when being honest, be kind.

35. Your story isn't over yet.

No matter what age you are, you are still here reading this, learning, growing, loving and living. It's never too late to do anything, EVER!

Choose Happy

If I could go back in time and explain this to my younger self I could have lived a much easier life. The joys of choosing happy are becoming more and more apparent, yet the world is becoming more unhappy. We are focusing on what we don't have, instead of celebrating what we do have.

We chase happiness, but we do not choose it. It's time we choose happy! We go around beating ourselves up, we judge others, we complain. We moan and whinge and we wonder why depression numbers are rising?

We give into negative thoughts; we even fuel them by succumbing to them.

We give up when things get too hard and let go without a fight. We choose to live in loneliness, in a world of a billion people. We build up walls to protect ourselves, and then use these walls as an excuse to be rude.

Be kind to others, be genuine, and be humble, because the great ripples you create by doing this will come back to you..... Think of the people you seek out to feel good– be one of them..... Share funny stories to make others laugh. Share acts of kindness, but don't tell anyone that you did. We all need kindness is our lives and the world has forgotten what it is. When was the last time you did something kind for someone expecting nothing in return?

Don't expect apples when you plant an orange tree. But do plant a tree, it's good for the environment, which we are destroying.

Don't spend hours on worry, and destroy precious moments. Worrying about what might of happened instead of living in the now, will only give you wrinkles. Worrying is simply using your imagination to attract what you do not want into your life.

By freaking out about the small things that really don't matter, we are training our minds to react unnecessarily. Maybe you don't like someone's choice of gift, but don't be sad about it. By freaking out you are wasting not only your energy, which is precious, but also your time, which is gold.

Make time to meditate, and learn to appreciate every single moment. For every breath that you take is a blessing, as soon, you could be taking your last. Breathe, in through your nose, and out through your mouth. My mother taught me this as a child. It is only now I can actually appreciate what it means.

Make fun a priority. We tend to avoid it, but life should be all about it. The responsibilities that we have when we are older, are all ones that we craved when we were younger.

See life through a child's eyes as much as you possibly can. Dance, even if it's only in the shower. Focus on what you have and be grateful for it. Many others have less than you and are happy for it. Build an attitude of gratitude, just do it and don't make excuses why you can't. Every day you have something to say thanks for, so go out there and find it, the harder you have to look initially, the better you're going to get eventually.

Don't focus on what others have compared to you, you have everything that you need. Trust that the universe has your back and is bringing you what you desire. Just don't forget to say thanks when it does!

Stop chasing a dream, you are already lucky enough to be living a dream. It may not be the dream you think that you want now, but it is the dream that you chose before coming to this beautiful earth.

Choose happy! To be happy you must make a choice, choose to be grateful, choose to be kind, choose to meditate, or simply breathe. Choose to have fun, choose to love life no matter what it throws at you. Choose love, be love and see the light that can shine from within you.

My Darling Choose Happy.

Authors Bio

I grew up in a broken home, that is, my parents split up when I was very young. Sadly, this is all too common these days. I was brought to live in Pakistan with my mother and two of my brothers when I was 12 years old. When I was 14, we then moved to Malaysia, before moving back home to Ireland at 16. I lived back home with my brothers and sisters, (no parents) until I was 18 and decided to go to university in London. I quit the university after one year and moved to New York. After six months in NY I came back home, and after another three months of being back home I wanted to get out of there again, so I moved to Australia for a year. There was a whole lot of moving around back then!

I am now 33. Needless to say I have a strange accent after living abroad for so many years in such different places. Most people never know that I was really Irish, but I am, and I am proud to be! All of this travelling around was completely normal to me and I enjoyed it immensely. It's only now that I realised that the past six years I have lived in Sydney were actually the longest I have been in one place since I was 12 years old. I have now made up for all of that moving around the world by not moving from my apartment for the past six years, which is unheard of in Sydney when renting.

Now that I was older and wiser I look back and realise that I was running from reality. I didn't want to be a grown up, even though I was one. The constant moving around helped me to continually live in never-never land, a land that I do love, but now only for visiting, not living! I was constantly chasing the 'dream' or trying to 'find myself' as they put it in the movies. I was looking, searching, running, moving just to try and figure out this crazy world and how I fit into it.

I suffered from some pretty bad cases of anxiety and depression and I recently hit rock bottom. But, the good thing is, I learned from it and no longer look at it as a mistake, but more a life lesson. I am proud to be where I am. I don't want you to go through what life threw at me and I want you to know the secret to being happy. Many people already know the secret, but many more still need to be told. I want you to be able to take a look around you and think, 'wow, I am so lucky!' I could now say this every day, yet not just because my life has changed dramatically. I didn't win the lottery or move into a big new house. I have simply learned what to takes to be and feel happy and I work on it EVERY DAY. I will never give up and I will continue to thank my lucky stars for all that I have.

Printed in the United States
By Bookmasters